Money, trade and payments

Money, trade and payments

Essays in honour of D. J. Coppock

edited by David Cobham,
Richard Harrington and George Zis

Manchester University Press

Manchester and New York

Distributed exclusively in the USA and Canada by St Martin's Press

Copyright © Manchester University Press 1989

Whilst copyright in the volume as a whole is vested in Manchester University Press, copyright in individual chapters belongs to their respective authors, and no chapter may be reproduced wholly or in part without express permission in writing of both author and publisher.

Published by Manchester University Press
Oxford Road, Manchester M13 9PL, UK
and Room 400, 175 Fifth Avenue,
New York, NY 10010, USA

Distributed exclusively in the USA and Canada
by St Martin's Press, Inc.,
175 Fifth Avenue, New York, NY 10010, USA

British Library cataloguing in publication data
Money, trade and payments
  1. Economics
  I. Harrington, Richard, *1942–*
  II. Cobham, David   III. Zis, George
  IV. Coppock, D. J. (Dennis John), *1921–*

Library of Congress cataloging in publication data applied for

ISBN 0 7190 2949 X *hardback*

Printed in Great Britain
by Billings and Son Ltd, Worcester

Contents

Contributors

Michael Artis, Professor of Economics, University of Manchester
Sir James Ball, Professor of Economics and former Principal, London
  Business School
David Cobham, Lecturer in Economics, University of St Andrews
Richard Harrington, Lecturer in Economics, University of Manchester
David Laidler, Professor of Economics, University of Western Ontario
J. Stanley Metcalfe, Professor of Economics, University of Manchester
Robert Millward, Professor of Economics, University of Salford
Lynden Moore, Lecturer in Economics, University of Manchester
Michael Parkin, Professor of Economics, University of Western Ontario
Ian Steedman, Professor of Economics, University of Manchester
Michael Sumner, Professor of Economics, University of Sussex
George Zis, Head of Department of Economics and Economic History,
  Manchester Polytechnic

Introduction

Since Dennis Coppock retired in 1981 after a long career as lecturer and then professor in the Department of Economics of the University of Manchester, many of his former students and colleagues have felt that a volume of essays should be produced in his honour. It has fallen to us to produce such a volume, and we are proud to have had the opportunity.

Dennis Coppock has always made a deep impression on people. Perhaps the main reason for this is the integrity which is his most distinctive characteristic. He set high standards for himself, and he judged everyone else by the same standards. Naturally he was often critical of his students, colleagues and friends, but his criticisms did not evoke resentment for they were recognised as honest exhortation and encouragement. Dennis has never been motivated by narrow self-interest, and he has always drawn satisfaction from the successes of his students and colleagues.

His integrity manifested itself in his teaching in a variety of ways, from his regular rewriting of lecture notes to his detailed comments on students' essays. He was also ready to devote any amount of his time to helping his students overcome difficulties in understanding specific points or articles. And he was equally generous with his time when students turned to him for advice or help with personal problems.

When supervising doctoral theses Dennis was never interested in just assisting his students to obtain their PhDs. He was more concerned to inculcate in them the essential values of scholarship, and he inspired them not only through his academic advice and encouragement but also through his own commitment to their work.

His help was also invaluable to the research efforts of his colleagues. He always made time to comment extensively on their papers, and while some felt that he was often asking the impossible he was the first person they would ask for comments. If Dennis did not dismiss their work as 'interesting' they knew it must be of reasonable quality.

He was equally painstaking and demanding in his own research. Every paper he wrote was revised again and again, more often than not as a result of his own desire to improve it rather than in response to comments by colleagues. In fact many of his papers were never submitted for publication because he himself did not feel satisfied with the final version even though other economists had been highly impressed. Professor Harry Johnson remarked in the early 1970s that if his own articles had been refereed by Dennis only five per cent would have been accepted for publication.

In his research Dennis Coppock combined analytical rigour with clarity of exposition. He was a highly accomplished mathematician but he never let the algebra dictate the economics, and he had little time for economic theories that rested only on mathematical manipulation and lacked intuitive economic interpretation. Many of his colleagues came to learn that they were on weak ground when Dennis declared that he understood the mathematics but had difficulties with the economics of some proposition they were advancing. Furthermore his empirical studies are classic examples of how much can be gained from the careful marshalling of well-understood economic data, without recourse to econometrics.

At the same time Dennis had remarkably wide research interests, extending from the history of economic thought to monetary economics, from problems of macro and monetary policy to theoretical and empirical issues in international economics, and his contributions to the literature on business cycles have been much appreciated by economic historians as well as economists. Indeed his command of economic history contributed to the enrichment of both his writings and his lectures.

Dennis's academic career is a story of devotion and commitment to the University of Manchester. He studied there after the war and was appointed assistant lecturer in 1950. He spent a year at MIT but returned to devote his energies to the Department of Economics for over three decades: he was lecturer from 1953, senior lecturer from 1961, professor from 1966 and Stanley Jevons Professor of Political Economy from 1979. He suffered for this loyalty in so far as he never received the recognition he deserved. But he never felt that he was paying a price for his devotion to the University of Manchester. He regarded it simply as a matter of basic self-respect. His attitude was typified by his immediate reaction to the offer of a personal chair during the mid-1960s, which was to question his own ability to assume the responsibilities involved.

The appointment made no difference to his commitment to the department or the university. But it enabled him to contribute in a different way: as a result of the deep and universal respect in which he was held he was able to provide a sense of continuity and a steadying influence without which the difficulties that the department experienced in the 1970s would have been more damaging.

Of course Dennis is more than a scholar of economics devoted to Manchester University. Among his wider interests are rocks, of which he has built up an impressive collection. He is an avid reader of science fiction (which, tongue in cheek, he always alleged helped him to coexist with and understand non-British members of staff in his department). Classical music and photography have always been sources of great pleasure. In more recent years he has been absorbed by the history of mathematics, while his fascination with astronomy remains as intense as ever.

His friends are all well aware of how devoted he is to his wife, Hilda, without whose support he claims he would not have accomplished what he has and would not be able to enjoy all his interests. There can be little doubt that those who have benefited from their relationship with Dennis owe a debt to her also.

Finally it should be said that behind the severe exterior which he so mischievously cultivates there is a warmth and humanity that make Dennis a very special person and, for so many of his colleagues, above all a friend.

In the initial stages of producing this book we decided that, in order to give the volume some thematic coherence and to reflect the work of its inspirer, we should seek papers in the three areas of money, trade and payments: these are the areas in which Dennis both made important contributions to the research literature himself and had his most fruitful interactions with his colleagues. In the event we were offered twelve papers, whose authors are all people who worked closely with Dennis at one time or another.

Part I consists of six papers in the area of monetary economics and monetary systems. Richard Harrington provides a reconsideration of the classical quantity theory of money, arguing that the British classical writers had a more sophisticated and less mechanical idea of the relationships involved than the popular textbook version of their ideas which has more in common with the genuinely mechanical exposition of Irving Fisher.

David Laidler examines the views on monetary theory and policy held by both the Radcliffe Committee and the 'quantity theorists' who gave evidence to it, in the light of later monetarist and rational expectations thinking: he shows that the quantity theorists were in important respects un-monetarist, while the committee itself had at least some ideas in common with monetarism.

David Cobham provides an analysis of the particular quantitative ranges involved in UK monetary targets, arguing that the selection of the target ranges was not conducive to the efficient use of monetary targeting as an instrument of macro policy.

George Zis argues the case for an international monetary *system* in the light of the experience of exchange rate flexibility since the collapse of

Bretton Woods, and analyses the prospects for the emergence of a new system.

Michael Artis surveys the achievements and prospects of the European Monetary System and the debate on UK participation in its exchange rate mechanism.

Michael Parkin proposes ways of discriminating between 'real', 'equilibrium monetary' and 'New Keynesian' theories of the business cycle; his empirical results, on Japanese data for 1965–85, decisively reject the first and third of these, but not the second.

Part II consists of six papers on industry, trade and investment. Sir James Ball contributes a critique of the 1985 House of Lords report on manufacturing and the balance of payments, rejecting the whole concept of a 'balance of payments constraint' on economic growth in favour of an emphasis on supply-side competitiveness.

Lynden Moore looks at the long-run transformation of UK trade since 1950 in terms of relative price changes and productivity growth, using the offer curve analytical apparatus.

Michael Sumner analyses inventory investment in the UK in the light of Dennis Coppock's early work and more recent work by Alan Blinder, using data from the CBI industrial trends survey to distinguish between planned and unplanned changes in inventories.

Robert Millward discusses the current proposals for privatisation of the UK water industry, drawing for a historical perspective on the experience of the industry under private ownership in the nineteenth century.

Stan Metcalfe explores the relationships between trade patterns and technological change by drawing on the recent literature on evolutionary technological change in order to formulate a dynamic analogue of the traditional static concept of comparative advantage.

Ian Steedman examines the importance of transport costs (where transport requires the use of produced inputs) for comparative advantage and the pattern of trade, within a Sraffian perspective.

These papers connect in different ways with the work and approach of Dennis Coppock. Most relate to monetary or international economics in one way or another, others to the business cycle literature or economic history. Some are concerned with the history of economic thought, some are exercises in pure theory, some are directed to current policy issues; many involve more than one of these elements. They are diverse, like Dennis's own work, but their authors are united in believing that their contributions to economics, both here and more generally, are the richer for their contact with him.

We hope that this volume has succeeded in reflecting something of Dennis's interests in and approaches to economics. It is perhaps inevitable that the editors of (and contributors to) a Festschrift volume should feel that they have not done full justice to the scholar to which it is dedicated; however, we also know that Dennis is a modest man and he will accept this volume for what it is: an expression of sentiments of gratitude and affection which are shared by many others.

David Cobham
Richard Harrington
George Zis

Part I

Monetary economics and monetary systems

1

The classical quantity theory

Richard Harrington

1 Introduction

The classical quantity theory is generally portrayed as being a mechanical relationship between money and prices with the latter changing proportionally with changes in the former and doing so due to a direct (i.e. real-balance) mechanism. Velocity is fixed by institutional factors whilst output is determined by real forces and usually assumed to be at full employment. The economy is dichotomised into real and monetary sectors with real forces determining real things and monetary forces determining monetary things.

I shall argue that this view, which appears to stem from the work of Irving Fisher, is a quite inappropriate characterisation of the quantity theory as put forward by earlier, predominantly British, classical economists. The argument is organised as follows. In Section 2, there is a brief look at the work of John Law, as he may be plausibly considered to have had an influence on much of subsequent classical writing on money. I then make a distinction between the long-term and the short-term quantity theory of money and the former is discussed in Section 3 and the latter in Section 4. Sections 5 and 6 consider classical views on the transmission mechanism and the costs of inflation respectively, and there is then a short conclusion.

The major omission in all this is any discussion of the balance of payments even though this was an important part of classical monetary theory. It is omitted both for reasons of space and because it raises less controversy. Hume's price–specie-flow mechanism is well known and it has been discussed in a number of works dealing with the modern monetary approach to the balance of payments.

In a short chapter such as this, I cannot hope to do justice to my subject, nor can I expect to convince the critical reader. But if I can raise enough doubts in the minds of those interested in those issues, such that they will themselves read or re-read what the classical economists actually said about money, that will be sufficient.

2   John Law and his influence

John Law, having tried and failed in 1705 to interest the Scottish Parliament
in establishing a new bank, had more success eleven years later when the
Duke of Orleans, acting as Regent for Louis XV, allowed him to set up a
bank in Paris. The bank issued paper money – the *assignats* – and made
loans to the Regent. The bank became the Banque Royale and Law became
Controller General of Finance for France. The bank increased its loans
and, for a time, this had a beneficial effect on trade, and the country saw
a period of prosperity. But it was not to last: the bank multiplied its notes
in absurd fashion – in 1719 alone, notes outstanding went from about £4
million to about £44 million – and in 1720, it could no longer maintain
convertibility, and went bankrupt.

Law is generally viewed as a confidence trickster and one who operated
on a large scale, but for contemporaries he was more than that. He was
a theorist who had, in several publications, argued that increasing the
quantity of money in an economy was a means to economic development.
His original proposal to the Scottish Parliament was accompanied by a
book *Money and Trade Considered with a Proposal for Supplying the
Nation with Money* (1705). He was later to write various memoranda and
letters about banking and about the new financial system as he called it,
when his bank was still operating. His last work was a self-justifying mem-
orandum, some years after the crash.

Law's writings had two notable ingredients: first, he argued that each of
the precious metals provided a poor standard of value due to unpredictable
changes both in supply and in non-monetary demands; secondly, he argued
that money was a stimulant to economic activity. At times, this was argued
by association: rich countries were observed to have more money than
poor ones; at times it was argued by an early version of the multiplier
theory: one person spends the new money and this buys the produce of
another, he then spends the money, . . . , and so on.

Law's arguments were well known and it seems not unreasonable to
attribute to him an influence on subsequent writings as suggested by Charles
Rist in his *Histoire des Doctrines Monétaires* (1938); especially is this so,
given his Scottish origins. When classical writers assert so strongly the
irrelevance of the absolute quantity of money within a nation, it is plausible
that it is the ideas of Law, as much as anything else, that they are attacking.

3   The long-term quantity theory of money and the stability of velocity

The evidence is that most classical writers regarded the long-term proportionality between money and prices as no more than approximation: in the
short term, no proportionality was argued; money affected output as well

as prices. There was neither short-term nor long-term neutrality of money.

If we start with Hume, we find in the essay 'Of Money' (1752a) that he does state a long-term proportionality between money and prices. But one should not read too much into this: it is only a short essay where the main objective is clearly to rebut the ideas of Law. Thus the key statement at the beginning of the essay: 'If we consider any one nation by itself, it is evident that the greater or less plenty of money is of no consequence, since the prices of commodities are always proportioned to the plenty of money.' Other statements follow in the same vein. Clearly, Hume is arguing a quantity theory approach but, from this short and general essay, it would be wrong to infer that Hume believed the theory was or was not more than an approximation to reality. And, as we shall see below, Hume was only too well aware of the effects of money on output and employment.

With Adam Smith (1776), things are not much clearer. He frequently asserts or implies that more money (or more metals) will raise prices, but he never asserts any rigid proportionality. There is considerable discussion, in general terms, of currency debasement and discussion in particular of the effect of the inflow of silver from South America on the value of silver, but few statements of an explicitly quantity-theory nature. It must be said that Smith's treatment of money is remarkably weak: O'Brien (1975) describes it as a puzzle and adds that 'the strange thing is that although Adam Smith undoubtedly understood the quantity theory, and although it is clear from his lectures that he understood the price-specie-flow mechanism, he nevertheless confined himself in his great *magnum opus* to vague generalisations about the "channels of circulation overflowing" if the money supply was too great'.

Thus, all we can conclude is that Smith held the view that an increase in the quantity of money would raise prices to the extent that it did not flow abroad but, no more than in the case of Hume can we claim that he adhered to any view as to an exact proportionality between money and prices.

When we come to Thornton we are on firmer ground and it is in his book *An Inquiry into the Nature and Effects of the Paper Credit of Great Britain* (1802) that we find the first detailed statement of the quantity theory. Chapter 8 discusses the effects of an excessive issue of bank notes and we are told that this will raise prices: on one occasion we are told it 'is scarcely necessary to be proved' that this should be so. In the following chapter, Thornton sets out the assumptions implicit in the view that the value of money (Bank of England notes) depends upon its quantity. The assumptions he makes are as follows:

(1) Bank of England notes are the only notes to circulate in and around London and they circulate nowhere else;

(2) Bank of England paper remains the same;
(3) Payments within the district are the same;
(4) 'The general circumstances are such as to render the same quantity
    of circulating medium just as sufficient as before to effect the same
    payments.'

This is clearly the quantity theory. Assumption (1) is to deal with the
fact of the number of different banknotes then in circulation in the kingdom, Assumption 3 is of constant volume of transactions, Assumption 4 is
of constant velocity such that with a given quantity of money (Assumption
2) we cannot but get price stability.

Having made explicit the assumptions involved in arguing that prices
move in proportion to the quantity of money, Thornton goes on to examine
these assumptions. He points out that the demand for Bank of England
notes may vary: that, in practice, they are in competition with coins and
also with the notes of country banks. It should be understood that, at this
time, Bank of England notes circulated in London, whilst notes issued by
provincial banks circulated elsewhere, these latter being convertible into
Bank of England notes. In some areas there was an overlap. Normally,
there would be some roughly constant ratio between the two kinds of note,
but this would vary.

Another reason why the demand for banknotes (i.e. the demand for
money) will vary is that 'the talent for economizing bank notes is also a
continually improving one' and the 'private bankers in London, who are
the chief holders of Bank of England paper, by no means find it necessary
to enlarge their stock of it in full proportion to the increased number of
their pecuniary transactions'. Another reason was that there was a pro-
cyclical velocity of circulation: demand for money would be high in a
'period of alarm' and low when trade was good.

Throughout this chapter and others it is clear that Thornton is thinking
in terms of a demand for money as the following quotation illustrates. Here
Thornton is discussing the roughly constant ratio between Bank of England
notes and country-bank notes.

> By saying that the country paper is limited in an equal degree [to that of Bank of
> England paper], I always mean not that one uniform proportion is maintained
> between the quantity of the London paper and that of the country paper, but
> only that the quantity of the one, in comparison with the demand for that one, is
> the same, or nearly the same, as the quantity of the other in proportion to the
> call for the other.

Given that the demand for banknotes can vary, Thornton is insistent
that he is not putting forward any *simpliste* theory that money and prices
are always correlated. We have the statement:

> I believe... very little correspondence has subsisted between the fluctuations in the amount of Bank of England notes in circulation at different times, and the variations in the general price of articles at the same period.

And:

> Let it, therefore, be carefully remembered, that I by no means suppose a limitation of London paper to operate simply by causing an equal reduction in country paper, and then such a fall in the price of goods over the Kingdom as is exactly commensurate with the general diminution of paper; and finally, also such a variation in the exchange as is precisely proportionate to the reduction of paper, and to the fall in the price of goods. Counteracting circumstances of various kinds may prevent these proportions from being maintained: and the full effects may not follow their cause until after the lapse of some period of time.

Nevertheless in spite of these caveats it remains true that, in the end, the value of banknotes may be expected to depend, to a large extent, on their quantity. Limitation of the supply of Bank of England notes remains important.

Let us now turn to David Ricardo, one of the foremost advocates of the quantity theory in the nineteenth century. He participated actively in the bullionist debates during the Napoleonic Wars, and argued consistently that the depreciation of the pound sterling was the direct result of an excessive issue of Bank of England notes and that the remedy lay in an appropriate reduction in these notes. Later on, when concerned with postwar monetary policy, he actively campaigned for rules versus discretion. Ricardo is the most monetarist of the classical writers.

Yet, as Sayers (1953) points out, 'Ricardo was often careful to explain that the demand for money could vary so that it was dangerous to expect the price level to move exactly in step with the quantity of money'. Thus we find Ricardo, in *The High Price of Bullion* (1809), replying to the argument that the quantity of Bank of England notes had only increased in proportion to the growth of trade, by saying that were this true, which he did not believe, it would be irrelevant; and this because 'the daily improvements which we are making in the art of encouraging the use of circulating medium, by improved methods of banking, would render the same amount of notes excessive now, which were necessary for the same state of commerce at a former period'. He also refers to the possibility that the use of Bank of England notes outside London may have varied. Further on, in the same pamphlet, he makes the general point:

> The value of the circulating medium of every country bears some proportion to the value of commodities which it circulates. In some countries this proportion is much greater than in others, and varies on some occasions, in the same country.

It depends upon the rapidity of circulation, upon the degree of confidence and credit existing between traders, and above all on the judicious operations of banking. In England so many means of encouraging the use of circulating medium have been adopted.

Ricardo does not then believe in any constancy of velocity in the short or in the long run. Nor does John Stuart Mill, notwithstanding the fact that, in his *Principles of Political Economy* (1873), the chapters on money and credit (eleven in all) commence with an admirably succinct statement of the quantity theory:

> If we assume the quantity of goods on sale, and the number of times those goods are resold, to be fixed quantities, the value of money will depend upon its quantity, together with the average number of times that each piece changes hands in the process.

Yet in the same chapter in which he outlines the theory, he goes on to say that it only applies in the simplest case. It is a legitimate starting point and a scientific truth but it would only hold if a lot of other things were equal. Notably it only applies 'to a state of things in which money, that is gold or silver, is the exclusive instrument of exchange, and actually passes from hand to hand at every purchase, credit in any of its shapes being unknown'.

Given the complexities of money it is necessary to start with the simplest case. But:

> In any state of things, however, except the simple and primitive one which we have supposed, the proposition is only true other things being the same...the doctrine [of the quantity theory] though a scientific truth, has of late years been the foundation of a greater mass of false theory and erroneous interpretation of facts, than any other proposition relating to interchange.

> It is habitually assumed that whenever there is a greater amount of money in the country, or in existence, a rise of prices must necessarily follow. But this is by no means an inevitable consequence...money hoarded does not act on prices. Money kept in reserve by individuals to meet contingencies which do not occur, does not act on prices.

Mill's rejection of any naive version of the quantity theory should not make us forget that he remains a believer in the need to limit the quantity of paper money and to keep it convertible into gold. Only this can maintain its value. In the long term, and approximately, it is still the quantity of money which determines prices, or at least it can be made to do so.

Two other things about Mill's work are worth noting here. First, when talking about the rapidity of circulation of money (as he calls it) he describes a pro-cyclical velocity of circulation. This was mentioned by Thornton, it reappears in Fisher (1911) and is subsequently stressed by Friedman (1959). Secondly, Mill considers different motives for holding money and in one passage breaks down the total quantity of money into the following three categories:

(1) money 'which goes into the market of commodities, and is there actually exchanged against goods';
(2) 'money hoarded';
(3) money 'kept in reserve by individuals to meet contingencies'.

Marshall's views can best be summed up by the following quotation taken from his written evidence to the Royal Commission on the Values of Gold and Silver (1887).

> Whilst accepting the doctrine that, 'other things being equal, prices rise or fall proportionately to every increase or diminution in the metal or metals which are used as the standard of value', I consider the conditioning clause 'other things being equal' is of overwhelming importance and requires careful attention.

Like Mill, Marshall was not going to adhere to any rigid link between money and prices but, like Mill, he continued to regard the quantity of money as of great importance and to regard convertibility as necessary to effectively limit its supply

When we come to Irving Fisher, things are different. His book *The Purchasing Power to Money* (1911) is, in effect, a treatise written round the equation $MV=PT$. Velocity is determined, in a mechanical way, by such things as habits, systems of payments, density of population and means of transport. In the long run, it can be taken as exogenous, as can the number of transactions, hence there is a strict proportionality between money and prices. Much of the argument is by analogy and the analogies are invariably drawn from the world of mechanics. The theory presented by Fisher is the archetypal mechanical quantity theory.

This judgement remains, notwithstanding the attempt of Boris Pesek (1976) to rescue Fisher from criticism such as this. Pesek points out that Fisher explicitly accepted that the determinants of velocity would change over time and hence so would velocity. This is correct, but such changes are presented as akin to technological changes: there is no dependence on volitional behaviour or choice. What is more, Fisher presents the quantity theory as being like a system of weights in balance and gives diagrams in which the four variables of the quantity-theory equation are represented by two weights and two distances from a fulcrum. If you do do such things, no one can be surprised if critics see your theory as mechanical.

4 The short-run quantity theory and the problem of deflation

The foregoing is intended to support the idea that the classical quantity theory, even on its own ground – that is, as a theory of long-term equilibrium

– is, Fisher apart, far less mechanistic than has generally been believed. The present section turns to what classical writers had to say about the short-term effects of monetary changes.

David Hume (1952) is often quoted for his remarks on the effects of a monetary increase in stimulating output. He argues that the initial effect of an increase in the quantity of money is on output, but that this effect only lasts for a short while until prices have risen and the real money stock is as before: 'it is only in this interval or intermediate situation, between the acquisition of money and rise of prices, that the increasing quantity of gold or silver is favourable to industry'. There is a similar deflationary effect:

> this interval [between changes in money and changes in prices] is as pernicious to industry, when gold and silver are diminishing, as it is advantageous when these metals are increasing. The workman has not the same employment from the manufacturer and merchant; though he pays the same price for everything in the market. The former cannot dispose of his corn and cattle, though he must pay the same rent to his landlord. The poverty and beggary, and sloth, which must ensue, are easily foreseen.

The last sentence shows how it is regarded as obvious that prices are not instantaneously flexible downwards. The implication, that nations should avoid sudden reductions in the quantity of money, is a view common to virtually all classical writers.

Thornton, throughout his '*Paper Credit*', continues to preach the evils of deflation and to affirm that it should never be other than gradual and that it should not be resorted to unless necessary. It is impossible, in the space available, to do justice to Thornton: his arguments are detailed and surprisingly modern. He argues that a drop in the quantity of money will lead to a drop in purchases which will lead more to a fall in output than in prices. Even if it does result in some prices falling this will still lead to reduced output and workers being laid off because 'the rate of wages, we know, is not so variable as the price of goods'. He argues that this reduction in output will not stimulate exports, nor will it be likely to substantially check imports since these will be composed mainly of food and raw materials.

Ricardo also is well aware that prices are not quickly flexible downwards. Thus we find him in *The High Price of Bullion* advocating a gradual decrease of banknotes until they reach par with the coins they represent. He confirms the importance of this happening over a period of time:

> I am well aware that the total failure of paper credit would be attended with the most disastrous consequences to the trade and commerce of the country, and even its sudden limitation would occasion so much ruin and distress that it would be highly inexpedient to have recourse to it as a means of restoring our currency to a just and equitable value.

Subsequently, in a letter to James Mill, Ricardo (1816) acknowledges that prices do not fall easily and talks of:

> the resistance which is offered – the unwillingness that every man feels to sell his goods at a reduced price, induces him to borrow at a high interest and to have recourse to other shifts to postpone the necessity of selling.

The return to the gold standard after the end of the Napoleonic Wars involved Ricardo in arguments over price deflation. He proposed that there should be no reintroduction of gold coinage but that banknotes should only be convertible into bullion in large amounts. This would have meant that the domestic money would have consisted solely of paper, whereas the link with gold would have been maintained via the foreign exchanges. Several reasons were advanced for this proposal: one of them was precisely that it would economise gold and obviate the need for the Bank of England to build up a large stock of gold thereby raising its price, that is, deflating commodity prices.

In the event, Ricardo's plan was not implemented. When Britain went back to gold, in 1819, the pound was still some 4% below par, thus that amount of price deflation was required. Ricardo advocated gradual deflation, by which he meant, over a period of a year, or two years at the outside. The operation was, however, mismanaged; the Bank of England did seek to build up its gold stock and in the process pushed up the value of gold. The fall in prices amounted to something over 10% and provoked considerable distress. Ricardo spent much of the rest of his life protesting that this was not his fault and that he had not advocated more than a relatively small deflation.

The resumption of specie payments in the UK is instanced by Say (1841) as an example of the cost of deflation. He points out that this was a redistribution to creditors; all debts and pensions, and notably the national debt being raised in value. Say referred with approval to a proposal which had been made to return to gold at a lower value in order to avoid the many evils of deflation.

John Stuart Mill has little to say explicitly about the short-term effects of money; but it follows from what has already been said, he did not generally expect a close correlation between short-term changes in the quantity of money and short-term changes in prices. He does talk about what he calls commercial crises and says that these will be situations in which everyone is a seller and no one a buyer.

Marshall shares the general concern about sudden changes in the quantity of money and states that sudden falls will lead to reductions in output. He stresses that violent fluctuations are a greater evil than gradually falling prices. In fact, Marshall likes the redistributive aspect of falling prices since he believes prices are always more flexible than wages. Thus, Marshall also had no belief in the so-called neutrality of money.

Irving Fisher accepts that a sudden increase in the quantity of money will have the initial effect of raising output but he tends to belittle the importance of this. However, monetary changes by causing price changes and thus altering the real rate of interest are, in his view, the main source of the trade cycle.

5 The transmission mechanism: money and the rate of interest

The classical theory of the rate of interest is usually seen as a real-forces theory and is contrasted with the Keynesian monetary determination of the rate of interest. This view is incomplete, however: the full classical view was that the equilibrium or long-term rate of interest was determined by saving and investment (and ultimately by productivity and thrift) but that, in the short term, the rate of interest would be influenced by changes in the supply of money. Furthermore, in differing degrees, several writers stress this monetary effect on the rate of interest as being a link in the transmission mechanism from money to prices.

First, consider the effects of money on the rate of interest. Ricardo consistently states that increases in the quantity of money will lower the rate of interest but that this will only be temporary: in the long run, when the extra money has raised all prices, the rate of interest will return to its equilibrium level. The following quotation from *The High Price of Bullion* is typical of many:

> I do not dispute, that if the Bank were to bring a large additional sum of notes into the market, and offer them on loan, but that they would for a time affect the rate of interest. The same effects would follow from the discovery of a hidden treasure of gold or silver coin.... It is only during the interval of the issues of the Bank, and their effect on prices, that we should be sensible of an abundance of money; interest would, during that interval, be under its natural level.

Hume had made the same point in his essay 'Of Interest' (1752b) and had referred to how the influx of Spanish silver had, for a time, depressed interest rates in Spain and elsewhere in Europe.

Mill (1873) takes this theme further. He argues that the rate of interest is, in the long run, determined by real forces, or at least it is for the most part. He is not so sure that monetary influences, as well as having temporary influences, may not occasionally have permanent effects as well. Thus in his chapter on the rate of interest, after a section in which there is an embryonic version of liquidity preference, we are told:

> there is a real relation which it is indispensable to recognise, between loans and money...we should naturally expect that among the causes which affect more

or less the rate of interest, would be found not only causes which act through capital, but some causes which act, directly at least only through money.

It is worth noting that whereas an increase in money will lead to a fall in interest, for Mill, this effect has to compete with subsequent pressure towards a rise in rates of interest due to expected inflation.

It is also worth noting that Mill is explicit where earlier writers were implicit that an increase in the quantity of money comes into the economy through the money market and that this is how it makes its effect felt. Thus he writes:

> In England, and in most other commercial countries, the paper currency in common use, being a currency provided by bankers, is all issued in the way of loans, except the part employed in the purchase of gold and silver. The same operation, therefore, which adds to the currency also adds to the loans... considered as an addition to loans it tends to lower interest.

And in the same paragraph talking about an influx of gold Mill says: 'The newly-arrived gold can only get itself invested, in any given, state of business, by lowering the rate of interest.' With Mill, as with Ricardo, there are times when one thinks he is about to complete the picture and make the distinction between market and natural rate of interest which was later to be made by Wicksell. Neither of them quite achieve this, although they both – Mill explicitly and Ricardo implicitly – do have a money-market transmission mechanism. But both Thornton and Marshall offer the Wicksellian mechanism as a transmission mechanism between money and prices.

Thornton (1802), having made the point that an increasing money supply will lower interest rates whereas a purely higher money supply will not, goes on to discuss the operation of the usury laws which, in those days, limited the Bank of England to charging 5% on loans. The incentive to borrow, says Thornton, depends on the difference between the mercantile rate of profit and the loan rate and if the former is above 5%, then if the Bank does not decide to limit its lending it will find itself faced with un-ending demands for loans and this will lead to a continuing rise in prices.

Marshall also makes the distinction between the rate of interest charged by banks and the mercantile rate of profit. He also is very clear that this is the transmission mechanism to the extent of explicitly repudiating the so-called direct mechanism by saying that if there were more gold in cir-culation than people wanted 'they would simply send it to the banks' and this would lead to an 'inflation of credit' 'enabling people to borrow who could not borrow before, raising prices'. During his cross-examination by the Royal Commission on the Value of Gold and Silver, Marshall (1887) was questioned repeatedly on *how* an increase in money affected the economy and he reiterated every time that it would have its effect by lowering interest and increasing loans.

All this is a far cry from the conventional view of the classical direct mechanism. To find a clear statement of the latter we have to go to Irving Fisher. In his *Purchasing Power of Money* we are told that if there is excessive money, people will try to get rid of it 'by buying goods'. 'Everybody will want to exchange this relatively useless extra money for goods...there cannot be surplus money and deposits without a desire to spend it.'

6   The costs of inflation and price expectations

In general, there was a clear understanding of the costs of inflation. Most classical writers, from Adam Smith on, make the point that inflation redistributes income from creditors (including the holders of money) to debtors. Adam Smith distinguishes corn rents from money rents as do Say, Jevons and Marshall. John Stuart Mill talks about a tax being levied on the holders of money. Both Thornton and Marshall suggest that inflation redistributes income away from wage earners.

Thornton, Mill and Marshall refer to expectations of price rises being self-fulfilling and both Mill and Marshall point out that nominal rates of interest will rise because of expected inflation.

Marshall (1887) has more to say on expectations. In answer to a question on the speed of the effect on prices of a change in mining of gold and silver he says that the older economists said the effect would only work slowly as the stock of the precious metals increased. But, says Marshall, nowadays a change 'is canvassed far and wide and exerts an almost immediate influence on hoarding by governments, by banks and by private persons' and hence it has a quick effect on prices.

Various writers go further and point out that, as well as the arbitrary redistribution of income, inflation introduces an extra uncertainty which can only have harmful effects on the economy. Thus Say (1841) after having discussed income redistribution adds: 'But it [inflation] has other grave consequences. It causes the prices of different commodities to be altered in different ways according to particular circumstances and this upsets even the most useful and the best planned speculations. It destroys all confidence in borrowing and lending.' He is echoed by Jevons (1908): 'The whole incitement to industry and commerce and the accumulation of capital depends upon the expectation of enjoyment thence arising and every variation of the currency tends in some degree to frustrate such expectation and to lessen the motives for exertion.' Mill (1873) also discusses the uncertainty caused by inflation and adds that such variations in the value of the circulating medium are far worse when they are engineered deliberately by a government which stands to gain thereby.

7 Conclusion

The classical quantity theory as it was shaped and understood by eighteenth- and nineteenth-century British writers was nothing more than a long-run approximation. Prices were not seen as instantaneously flexible, nor even quickly flexible: in the short run the impact of monetary changes was on output not price. There was neither short-run nor long-run neutrality of money. Changes in prices did have redistributive effects as well as having other effects on the economy. Had it not been so, the classical economists would not have been so passionately concerned about inflation. The emphasis given to the long-run unimportance of the quantity of money can be plausibly seen as an attempt to refute the inflationist fallacy of such as John Law.

The transmission mechanism through which money affected the real economy was through the money market and rates of interest. The rate of interest was a monetary phenomenon in the short term although not in the long. There was a belief in the need to maintain convertibility and to impose rules on the money supply process. This arose not from any naive belief in some mystical virtues of gold but from a strongly and consistently held view that a monetary standard left in the unfettered hands of government would inevitably lead to inflation.

In sum, the standard view of the classical quantity theory seems a sorry misrepresentation of the truth and could be consigned to the scrap heap were it not for one writer: Irving Fisher. Fisher's book *The Purchasing Power of Money* is fully in line with the traditional mechanical quantity theory, so much so that one imagines most accounts of the classical quantity theory must be derived from it.

But Fisher can in no way be seen as representative of the much older British tradition. The preface to his book refers to economics being, or being about to become, an exact science on a par with the physical sciences. One can only surmise that it was this view which led him to be impatient with the scholarly but verbose British writers and to put forward the quantity theory in the mechanical way that he did. If so, one can only say that he threw out the baby with the bath water and turned a tradition of rich and fertile thought into a sterile one. Monetary theory would be much better served by a wider realisation that Fisher's work on the quantity theory was quite out of line from, and not in any way the culmination of, the older and more subtle tradition of British classical economics.

References

Fisher, I. (1911). *The Purchasing Power of Money* (New York: Macmillan).

Friedman, M. (1959). 'The demand for money – some theoretical and empirical results', *Journal of Political Economy*, vol. 67.

Hume, D. (1752a). 'Of money'; in *Essays, Moral Political and Literary*, Edinburgh; reprinted (Oxford: Oxford University Press, 1963).

Hume, D. (1752b). 'Of interest'; in *Essays, Moral Political and Literary*, op. cit.

Jevons, W. S. (1908). *Money and the Mechanism of Exchange*, 19th edn (London: Kegan Paul).

Law, J. (1705). *Money and Trade Considered with a View to Supplying the Nation with Money* (Glasgow).

Marshall, A. (1887). Evidence to the Royal Commission on the Values of Gold and Silver, published in J. M. Keynes (ed.), *Official Papers of Alfred Marshall* (London: Royal Economic Society, 1926).

Mill, J. S. (1873). *Principles of Political Economy*, 7th ed (London: Longman).

O'Brien, D. P. (1975). *The Classical Economists* (Oxford: Oxford University Press).

Pesek, B. P. (1976). 'Monetary theory in the post-Robertsonian "Alice in Wonderland" era', *Journal of Economic Literature*, vol. 14.

Ricardo, D. (1809). *The High Price of Bullion*, reprinted in P. Sraffa (ed.), *The Works and Correspondence of David Ricardo* (Cambridge: Cambridge University Press, 1951–73).

Ricardo, D. (1816). Letter to James Mill, reprinted in P. Sraffa (ed.), *The Works and Correspondence of David Ricardo* (Cambridge: Cambridge University Press, 1951–73), vol. 7, p. 67.

Rist, C. (1938). *Histoire des Doctrines Monétaires*. (English translation: *History of Monetary and Credit Theory: from John Law to the Present Day*, 1940, London: Allen & Unwin.)

Say, J. B. (1841). *Traité d' Economie Politique*, 6th ed (Paris: Guillaumin).

Sayers, R. S. (1953). 'Ricardo's views on monetary questions', in T. S. Ashton and R. S. Sayers (eds), *Papers in English Monetary History* (Oxford: Oxford University Press).

Smith, A. (1776). *An Enquiry into the Nature and Causes of the Wealth of Nations*, reprinted 1976 with Introduction by R. M. Campbell, A. S. Skinner and W. B. Todd (Oxford: Oxford University Press).

Thornton, H. (1802). *An Enquiry into the Nature and Effects of the Paper Credit of Great Britain* (London: J. Hatchard), reprinted 1939 with Introduction by F. A. von Hayek (London: Allen & Unwin).

2

Radcliffe, the quantity theory, and monetarism

David Laidler

I   Introduction

The publication of the Radcliffe Report in 1959 represented the high tide of Keynesian influence on monetary theory and policy in Britain. Though the Radcliffe Committee took much evidence from witnesses who might reasonably be classified as advocates of the quantity theory of money, that evidence had no discernible influence on their findings, and the report seemed at the time to represent the final defeat of quantity theory ideas in British monetary debates. However, the supremacy of Radcliffe thinking was short-lived. What Kaldor (1970) was later to call 'The New Monetarism' was already being developed in the 1950s by Milton Friedman and his associates, and by the early 1970s, what is often referred to as a new version of the quantity theory of money had been established as an important piece of economic doctrine, in Britain nearly as much as in the United States.

A question naturally arises as to what is the relationship between the old quantity theory which the Radcliffe Committee rejected, and the 'new monetarism'. Was the latter really a restatement of the old quantity theory, or was it rather, as Patinkin (1969) claimed, an alternative development of Keynesian thought? This debate still continues.[1] However, the evidence cited in it has been largely American, and it is my purpose in this chapter to address some of the issues involved using as evidence material generated by the Radcliffe Committee. First, I shall set out the position on monetary theory and policy which the Radcliffe Committee expounded in its report, and then I shall describe the quantity theory approach to these same issues as put to the committee by some of its witnesses. In the course of my account, I shall point up the differences and similarities between the views under debate in 1958–9 and the monetarism of the 1970s and 1980s. As we shall see, though they have important common elements, the latter doctrine is far from being a simple replica of the quantity theory which Radcliffe rejected. Before I begin my narrative though, a few definitions and caveats are in order.

First, I discussed 'monetarism' in considerable detail in Laidler (1981), and argued there that monetarism is appropriately defined in terms of the following beliefs: that there exists a stable aggregate demand-for-money function; that variations in the quantity of money are the main cause of variations in the price level; that there is no important long-run trade-off between inflation and unemployment; that the monetary approach to balance of payments and exchange rate analysis is valid; and that the quantity of money should be used as a built-in stabiliser, rather than as an instrument of activist stabilisation policy.

Second, in what follows I shall use the phrase 'quantity theory', as does Patinkin (1969), to refer to a body of doctrine in which the quantity of money is seen as an important determinant of the general price level. Such a definition makes an immediate connection between the old quantity theory and monetarism. However, the former doctrine left room for in-dependent fluctuations in the velocity of circulation to affect prices too. In any event, adherence to this viewpoint is my criterion for identifying the quantity theoriests among the Radcliffe Committee's witnesses; and this viewpoint lends a certain coherence to their views on policy issues. All of them regarded control of the price level as the central aim of monetary policy, and all of them regarded control of the money supply as the key instrument of monetary policy. Even so, their evidence displays a consider-able variety of opinion about other matters, as we shall see.

Third, what follows is largely based on the text of the Radcliffe Report, and on the Memoranda and Minutes of Evidence published along with it.[2] The main burden of writing the report fell on Professor Richard Sayers and Sir (then Professor) Alec Cairncross, who held academic appointments at the London School of Economics and the University of Glasgow respec-tively at the time the report was under preparation. Many of the witnesses with whom they dealt were long-standing friends and colleagues, whose views were already well developed and widely known before the com-mittee began its work, as indeed were those of Sayers and Cairncross themselves. In particular, Sayers's widely read *Modern Banking* had reached its fourth edition in 1958, and propounded many ideas which also appeared in the report. In the light of these facts it would be a great mis-take to regard the Radcliffe Report as being the outcome of anything approaching a dispassionate consideration by its authors of views and facts of which they had been previously unaware. Furthermore, the Memoranda and Minutes upon which I shall draw are in no sense research papers like those prepared at about the same time for the United States Commission on Money and Credit. Rather they are summaries of views based upon previous research and debate. In short, the report and its supporting documents provide a series of snapshots, taken at a particular time, of an ongoing debate, and that is how I shall treat them in this chapter.

Finally, let it be clear that this essay deals with the Radcliffe Committee's views on monetary theory and monetary policy, and not with its entire report. The committee's terms of reference required it to report on 'the Working of the Monetary System' and it paid much attention to such matters as the structure of the British financial system at the end of the 1950s, the relationship between the Treasury and the Bank of England in the conduct of policy, the role of sterling as an international currency, and the need for systematic and comprehensive monetary statistics. The committee's views about monetary theory and policy can, I believe, sensibly be discussed in relative isolation from the particular historical and institutional background against which they evolved, and I shall attempt to do so in the following pages.

II   The Radcliffe view

The *Radcliffe Report* lists five goals for policy:

> (1) a high and stable level of employment. (2) Reasonable stability of the internal purchasing power of money. (3) Steady economic growth and improvement in the standard of living. (4) Some contribution, implying a margin in the balance of payments, to the economic development of the outside world. (5) A strengthening of London's international reserves, implying a further margin in the balance of payments.
>
> (R69, p. 22)

and 'acknowledge[s] that there are serious possibilities of conflict between them'. (R70, p. 23) These goals are explicitly referred to as 'objects in pursuit of which monetary measures may be used' (R69, p. 22) rather than as objects particularly amenable to attainment by monetary means. The Radcliffe Report's discussion of monetary policy, here as elsewhere, must therefore be read with the idea firmly in mind that other policy instruments – various fiscal measures and direct controls – are always available. The report does not have much to say about these other measures because its authors regarded any such discussion as beyond their terms of reference (cf. R515, p. 183), not because they thought monetary policy to be the most important tool available for the pursuit of any of the above-mentioned objectives.

The committee thought of monetary policy as normally playing a supporting role, particularly to fiscal policy, in macroeconomic management, even that aimed at the general price level. Only in some rather unlikely emergency, involving a 'threat of headlong inflation' (R529, p. 180), might monetary policy have a special claim to effectiveness, though here the relevant monetary measures were 'controls of capital issues, bank advances and consumer credit' (R524, p. 187), that is, direct controls on credit markets, rather than more traditional devices. The Radcliffe Report's lack of emphasis on the link between monetary policy and inflation marks an important difference with the quantity theory tradition (and with modern monetarism). From at least the beginning of the nineteenth century, the quantity theory tradition gave price-level stability pride of place among the goals of monetary policy, and monetary policy pride of place among the tools available for the attainment of price-level stability. Quantity theorists had always regarded inflation as very much (though usually not exclusively) a monetary phenomenon, and the Radcliffe Committee did not, though its report is remarkably unforthcoming about just what its authors thought the causes of inflation to be.

Their reticence here is perhaps understandable in the light of their views on how monetary policy affected the economy and their general reluctance, already noted, to interpret their terms of reference too broadly. It is an important theme of the Radcliffe Report that 'it is on the total pressure of demand that monetary measures should in the first place be expected to work' (R383, p. 130) and the report discusses the causes of inflation only to the extent that its authors believed these to involve the pressure of aggregate demand. It is worth quoting the report at some length on the aggregate demand–inflation relationship.

> It is sometimes argued that the rate of rise of wage rates is very closely related with changes in the percentage of unemployment. But it has also been argued to us with no less authority and force that over a significant range of variations in the demand for labour there is a 'band of indeterminacy' within which the precise rate at which wage rates and prices rise depends upon institutional factors which, although variable from year to year, have little or no connection with the pressure of demand in that or the preceding year. All that can be asserted as agreed opinion is that, as the fullness of full employment rises, the risk of accentuating a rise of prices increases. How great that risk is at any time, whether it would be responsive to other measures, and whether it is a risk to be taken in preference to jeopardising employment or technical progress, are all questions of political judgement that are not resolvable by any rules of monetary manipulation.
>
> (R64, p. 21)

If aggregate demand was but one potential influence on the inflation rate, and monetary policy was but one potential influence on aggregate demand, a detailed discussion of the causes of inflation and the role of monetary policy in combatting it might have seemed to be of no special relevance to the committee's task.

The committee's cursory treatment of the influence of monetary policy on inflation is but one aspect of a general tendency to downgrade the importance of such tools. As the report itself puts it: 'When all has been said on the possibility of monetary action and of its likely efficacy, our conclusion is that monetary measures cannot alone be relied upon to keep in nice balance an economy subject to major strains from both without and within. Monetary measures can help, but that is all' (R514, p. 183). This passage, and others like it in the report, can be read as an explicit rejection of an important aspect of the evidence given by 'quantity theorists' to the committee. However, note that it is the efficacy of monetary policy as an instrument for keeping an economy in 'nice balance', as a tool of what we would now call 'fine tuning', that the report here and elsewhere denies. It does so because its authors believed that 'Monetary measures...are incapable by themselves of having an effect sufficiently prompt and far reaching for their purpose, unless applied with a vigour that itself creates a major emergency' (R980, p. 337), and that, as a consequence, monetary policy should not be used 'as a major short-term stabiliser of demand'. Rather, in conducting monetary policy, 'The authorities...should take a view as to what the long-term economic situation demands and be prepared by all the means in their power to influence markets in the required direction' (R498, p. 177).

To downgrade monetary policy as a short-term stabilisation device by invoking the existence of time lags, and to urge that it be deployed to the achievement of longer-term goals, however it may look in the light of the traditional quantity theory, nevertheless appears to be very much a step towards 'monetarism'. Indeed, as long ago as 1963, Harry Johnson pointed out the strong similarity between the views, on this very issue, of Milton Friedman on the one hand and the Radcliffe Committee on the other.[3] But, as Johnson also stressed, there is a major difference here as well. The Radcliffe Committee put rates of interest, rather than some monetary aggregate at the centre of policy. It used phrases like 'monetary measures' and 'interest rate policy' almost interchangeably in its discussions of the issues involved, as the reader who cares to fill in the 'dots' in the above quotations will soon discover.

My attribution of prime (but not sole) importance to interest rates in the committee's thinking, despite the stress that it also laid on 'liquidity' when discussing the means whereby monetary policy impinges upon aggregate demand, may be defended by referring to its own comments on the issue. Thus, having pointed out that the authorities 'can theoretically influence the total level of demand in two ways...by bringing about a change in interest rates' and by 'bring(ing) about a change in the liquidity condition' of economic agents, the committee immediately went on as follows: 'The contrast...is incomplete, for movements in the rate of interest have a central part to play in bringing about changes in liquidity' (R385, p. 130). Though it certainly regarded the interaction of interest rates with 'liquidity' as a two-way affair, the committee itself here explicitly asserted the primary importance of interest rates. Moreover, citing the evidence of Richard Kahn, the committee insisted upon 'the structure of interest rates rather than some notion of the "supply of money" as the centre-piece of monetary action' (R395, p. 134).

This point is worth some elaboration, because the Radcliffe Committee's notion of 'liquidity' is ill-defined, and has sometimes been interpreted, for example by Johnson (1962), as denoting a broad spectrum of assets which includes, but goes far beyond, the 'money supply'; and if it is, the committee's views on monetary theory and policy may be presented as similar to, but less rigorous than, those developed at about the same time in the United States by James Tobin and his associates. I do not find this interpretation of the committee's 'liquidity' concept satisfactory, even though the Radcliffe Committee explicitly argued that the 'money supply' included too narrow a spectrum of assets to be of much significance; even though the committee (taking a position that is now well known to the point of notoriety) declared itself unable 'to find any reason for supposing, or any experience in monetary history indicating, that there is any limit to the velocity of circulation' (R391, p. 133); and even though it finds support in statements such as the following, of which there are a number in the report: 'Though we do not regard the supply of money as an unimportant quantity...our interest in the supply of money is due to its significance in the whole liquidity picture' (R389, p. 132). Such reasoning *could have led* the committee to do no more than argue that some aggregate of the short-term liabilities of the financial system, broader than 'the money supply' as conventionally defined, ought to be regarded as the strategic variable for monetary policy.[4] However, it went far beyond this.

The Radcliffe Report emphasised the *asset*, rather than *liability* position of the financial sector, and concentrated on credit market conditions in general and interest rates in particular, rather than any money supply concept, however broadly defined, when discussing monetary policy. In setting out its views upon the role of the banks in 'the liquidity structure', the committee stressed that any special concern 'ought to be aimed at the banks as key lenders in the system and not at the banks as "creators of money"'. It asserted, in the same context, that the 'behaviour of bank deposits is of interest only because it has some bearing...on the behaviour of other lenders' (R395, p. 134). The interpretation of the 'liquidity' concept most consistent with the main thrust of the Radcliffe Report as exemplified in statements like these, is as some index of the cost and availability of credit, rather than as anything resembling a broad monetary aggregate; and if this interpretation is accepted, the central importance of interest rates in the committee's view of monetary policy is surely established. So is the claim that the Radcliffe Committee's rejection of the quantity theory involved much more than an opinion that some traditional definition of money needed broadening.

Now the committee did not simply assert the central importance of interest rates for monetary policy. It went into considerable detail about the ways in which they did (and did not) influence the level of demand, placing the major emphasis here on long rates. Though it conceded 'a considerable external significance' (R441, p. 153) (i.e. for the balance of payments) to bank rate, the committee did not regard fluctuations in short-term interest rates as being of any direct importance for domestic aggregate demand. As we shall see, in taking this position, the committee contradicted the views of such quantity theorists as Gregory and Hawtrey, while White (1961) later argued that it had in fact seriously misinterpreted the survey evidence, on the influence of short rates on inventory investment, available to it. Even so, it conceded at least potential importance to long rates of interest, but, because it accepted an essentially Hicksian view of the role of expectations in determining the term structure of interest rates, the committee frequently talked of the influence of the 'structure' of interest rates on aggregate demand rather than that of long rates *per se* (cf. R447, p. 155).

The Radcliffe conception of the connection between the level of interest rates and the level of aggregate demand cannot be summarised in a smooth functional relationship. Rather the committee adopted 'a "three gears" view of the level of interest rates. At any given time people consider the current level as "high", "low", or "middle" (normal), and how they behave seems to be governed not so much by the precise percentage but whether that percentage fits into the high, low or normal bracket' (R442, p. 153). The committee gave quantitative content to these notions. Citing the evidence of Sir John (then Professor) Hicks, it placed the historical normal value for the interest rate on long-term government debt at about 3%, noting that this value had been 'an anchor to the whole rate structure (though the anchor could be dragged upon occasion)' (R444, p. 153).[5] Two factors in particular could thus 'drag the anchor', namely a high level of government borrowing, (cf. R571, p. 211) and 'the continuing expectation of inflation...[which] has been a real force in the course of security markets in the post-war period' (R572, p. 211).

The committee illustrated the potential influence of inflation by suggesting that an expected inflation rate of 2% would raise the 'normal' interest rate level from 3% to 5%, but it stopped short of suggesting that this numerical example in fact described the situation in Britain at the end of the 1950s. The illustration is interesting though, because the 'Fisher effect' is usually thought of as being a component of the quantity theory tradition in monetary economics, and not of Keynesian economics, some of whose most distinguished adherents (including Keynes, 1936, himself, pp. 141–3) explicitly denied it.[6] Indeed the 'Fisher effect' is probably the only matter on which the Radcliffe Committee agreed with the quantity theorists among its witnesses, and the only matter on which monetarist readers might later agree with the committee.

Some comment on the Radcliffe Committee's discussion of the exchange rate is needed to round out this account of its views. It expressed itself 'strongly in favour of a fixed parity for Sterling rather than a system of fluctuating rates' (R722, p. 260), a fixed parity that could be changed from time to time, to be sure, but only in exceptional circumstances, such as might arise when 'the failure of exports to make headway is plainly restricting the level of domestic activity and other countries are not experiencing the level of domestic activity and other countries are not experiencing similar difficulties' (R716, p. 259). As a general matter, the committee argued that 'it would be quite wrong to base policy on the expectation of a recurring need to devalue'. Such an expectation would make it 'more difficult . . . to keep domestic costs in line with costs abroad, and the need to devalue might result from the very ease with which the external value of the currency could be adjusted' (R721, p. 260).

Now what we might nowadays call an 'open-economy monetarist' would, as did the Radcliffe Committee, stress the stabilising influence on inflation expectations of a government's stated determination to maintain a fixed parity against a currency of rather stable purchasing power, which the United States dollar certainly was in the 1950s; and an open-economy monetarist would also argue the impossibility of controlling the domestic money supply under such an exchange rate regime. However, to forge a link between monetarism and the Radcliffe Report on this basis would be misleading. The Radcliffe Committee based its rejection of the importance of the quantity of money first of all, and mainly, on the view that velocity was malleable at best and unstable at worst, and secondarily, on a denial that the authorities could control the volume of bank deposits in contemporary Britain.[7] These arguments were advanced without reference to the exchange rate regime, as were the committee's views on the long-term stability of interest rates, though modern monetarist analysis of such stability naturally connects it to stability of expectations associated with a fixed exchange rate. With benefit of hindsight, it might be possible to erect an 'open-economy monetarist' defence of certain propositions to be found in the Radcliffe Report, but there is no evidence that the committee itself considered such a defence, let alone subscribed to any element of it.

In supporting a fixed exchange rate regime, or rather an exchange rate peg that was movable only with difficulty, while still according some domestic significance to monetary policy, the Radcliffe Committee reflected the views of the majority of its witnesses, not least of the quantity theorist Lord (then Professor Lionel) Robbins (cf. M57, p. 216). Only two witnesses took a different view, namely James Meade and Sir Ralph Hawtrey, but with the exception of the latter's statement that 'in view of the economic preponderance of the United States in the world, and the concentration of gold in American reserves, a fixed dollar parity means a complete subordination of British monetary conditions to American' (M73, p. 122), there is no more trace of 'open-economy monetarism' in the evidence that the committee took, at least from British economists, than there is in its report.[8] More generally, however, the Radcliffe Committee did consider a 'quantity theory' approach to the issues with which it was confronted, and received much evidence based upon that approach. As we have seen, though, the committee self-consciously and comprehensively rejected that approach. I shall now turn to a more detailed account of the particular version of the quantity theory whose validity the committee so explicitly denied. As will become apparent, that version has little to do with monetarist doctrine, beyond a common claim that the quantity of money is the crucial variable determining price-level behaviour.

III The quantity theory position

Among its witnesses, Mr W. Manning Dacey, Sir Theodore Gregory, Sir Ralph Hawtrey, Professor Frank Paish and Professor Lionel Robbins, are readily identifiable as the main protagonists of the alternative 'quantity theory' viewpoint to which the Radcliffe Committee so often referred and so decisively rejected in its report. The evidence of these witnesses, though far from homogeneous, does state certain important common themes. In particular, all of them put control of inflation at the centre of things when discussing the aims of monetary policy. Dacey focused 'attention upon inflation as the main danger' (M3, p. 65); Gregory thought that 'the fundamental objective of monetary policy should be the maintenance of confidence in the unit of account' (M4, p. 106) and identified 'a measurable stability of value' as a necessary condition for the maintenance of such confidence; for Robbins 'the first objective...[of monetary policy]...is the objective of stable money' (M6, p. 211); while for Paish 'the main function of monetary policy is to help to maintain internal price stability' (M4, p. 183); and so on.

We have already seen that the Radcliffe Committee attached no special significance to monetary policy in the control of inflation because it regarded aggregate demand as only one, perhaps not very important, influence upon the behaviour of money wages and prices. The committee's disagreement here with the quantity theorists was above all an empirical matter rather than a theoretical one. Although the committee was acutely sceptical of the *quantitative importance* of the influence of demand on wages and prices, and of monetary policy on demand, it never denied *the theoretical possibility* of the existence of some such influence. On the other hand, the question of monetary policy having a direct effect on inflation by an expectations mechanism was not considered by the committee, though it was raised in Lionel Robbins's evidence, as we shall see in a moment.

Whatever one may think nowadays of its position on these issues, a dispassionate reading of the evidence available at the time at which it produced its report makes it hard indeed to be unequivocally critical of the Radcliffe Committee for reaching the conclusion that it did. A. W. Phillips's celebrated (1958) article on the influence of unemployment on wage inflation only appeared while the committee was at work, though its members were certainly aware of this contribution.[9] However, Professor A. J. Brown, who had examined much the same evidence as Phillips in considerably more detail in his book *The Great Inflation* (1955) only a few years earlier, had explicitly warned the committee that 'It is extremely difficult to reach firm conclusions about the extent to which wage increases are sensitive to...changes in the level of unemployment' (M11, p. 49).

As to the capacity of monetary policy to cope with inflation, Brown had argued that 'monetary policy alone cannot stop inflation of the kind which we have experienced since the war without a relatively high level of unemployment' (M12, p. 49). When asked to elaborate on this in his oral evidence, Brown suggested that an unemployment rate in the 4–5% range might be necessary to keep wage inflation down to the rate of growth of productivity (as opposed to 10–12% unemployment in the 1930s) (cf. MN9174, p. 591). Such an unemployment rate was quite unthinkable in 1959. Moreover, much of Sir Robert Hall's evidence, on behalf of the Treasury, dealt with the tenuousness of the link between the pressure of demand and the inflation rate in the range of unemployment within which the British economy had operated in the 1950s, and this evidence drew on empirical work which had been carried on within the Treasury. Though the work in question does not seem to have been made available to the committee, Hall's evidence nevertheless carried great weight with it.[10] The Radcliffe Committee's downgrading of the role of monetary policy in dealing with inflation, and hence of the very linchpin of the quantity theory approach to monetary policy, seemed therefore to be consistent with the best quantitative evidence available to it.

The quantity theorists examined by the committee took a very different view of the relationship between inflation and unemployment, a view which, with the benefit of hindsight, seems well supported by evidence, but which at the time was based mainly on *a priori* argument and empiricism which was casual even by the standards of 1959. First, they suggested that the unemployement experience of the 1950s was unusual and unsustainable in the long run. Robbins argued that 'recent talk about the dangers of underemployment, with an unemployment percentage of under 2.5% seems...very unrealistic' (M28, p. 213); while Hawtrey asserted that 'British industry exhibits all the symptoms of over-employment' as a result of an undervaluation of sterling caused by the excessive (in his view) devaluation of 1949 (cf. M69, p. 121). Second, and more important, they suggested that the apparent propensity of British labour market institutions to generate inflationary wage pressure, which underlay such pessimistic estimates as Brown's, was not independent of the pursuit of 'full employment' in general, and of the conduct of monetary policy in particular.

Robbins stated the latter view most fully. To his own rhetorical question: 'Is it true that we must inevitably assume a disposition of the trade unions...to confront financial policy with the alternative of unemployment or inflation?' he answered as follows:

> Personally I see no such necessity. Of course, if it is accepted as a fixed maxim of policy that full employment is to be sought whatever the movement of incomes, then such a development is highly probable...but I see no inevitability about it. I see no reason to believe that the representatives of the trade unions will necessarily wish to create unemployment.
>
> (M31–32, p. 214)

Robbins therefore concluded that 'there is nothing fundamentally incompatible between such an aim [price stability]...[and that of providing] high levels of employment' (M37, p. 214). This evidence has something in common with the 'rational expectations' approach to the analysis of economic policy, stressing as it does the endogenous response of behaviour patterns and institutions to the conduct of policy; but although Robbins might now appear to have been ahead of his time in 1958–9, then he appeared to be behind it, because such views were inherent in the Austrian economics which he had expounded in the 1930s and which by the 1950s appeared to have been superseded by a combination of Keynesian economics and econometrics whose basic premise was the independence of the structure of the economy to the conduct of policy. The Radcliffe Committee might have been unwise to reject Robbins's views on this matter, but in doing so it simply placed itself in the mainstream of contemporary British macroeconomic thought.

Now there are (at least) three links in the causative chain that runs
between the quantity of money and prices, and so far I have commented on
the quantity theorists' views on only two of them, that connecting aggregate demand to the price level and that connecting the conduct of monetary
policy to inflation expectations. On these matters, the quantity theory
approach, which Radcliffe rejected, and modern 'monetarism' have a good
deal in common. However, the same cannot be said about the remaining
link, namely that connecting the quantity of money to aggregate demand.
Monetarism (rightly or wrongly is not an issue here) places an empirically
stable demand for money (or velocity) function at the very centre of things,
and, with the *possible* exception of the evidence of Paish, this hypothesis is
conspicuous by its absence from the quantity theory approach as it was put
to the Radcliffe Committee by its proponents.[11]

Amont the quantity theorists, Hawtrey took the most extreme position
on this matter: 'The only test of whether the supply of money is above or
below requirements or just right, is the occurrence of an excess or deficiency
of spending (M42, p. 119)...the proportion of the quantity of money to
the flow [of expenditure] cannot be relied on as a guide to monetary policy'
(M52, p. 120). For him, fluctuations in velocity were manifestations of
what, in another context, he referred to as 'the inherent instability of
credit' (M80, p. 122). Though Hawtrey's fellow quantity theorists did not
go quite that far, they left questions about the determination and stability
of velocity surprisingly open in their evidence, both written and oral. Thus
Dacey, in replying to a question from Caincross about how 'one could
judge whether the quantity of money had been reduced sufficiently' replied
'By the state of the economy' (MN10060, p. 661); while Robbins was
careful to note that his evidence did 'not imply that variations in the supply
of money are the *only* influence, either on prices or the level of activity';
and J. L. Carr, whose evidence on this issue falls in the quantity theory
camp, was willing to go no further than asserting 'The argument that
limiting the stock of money has no effect on the flow of money is fallacious'
(M24 (iv), p. 54).

Now, none of this is to argue that the quantity theorists took the same
view about the instability of velocity as did the Radcliffe Committee itself.
Among the witnesses who appeared before the committee, it was Nicholas
Kaldor – 'the velocity of circulation...is not determined by factors that are
independent either of the supply of money or the volume of money payments; it simply reflects the relationship between these two magnitudes'
(M2, p. 146) – and Richard Kahn – 'The velocity of circulation...is an
entirely bogus concept.... It is an effect and not a cause [of variations in
the level of activity and prices]' (M61, pp. 144–5) – who set out the position
closest to, indeed perhaps more consistently extreme than, that which the

committee itself embraced. In doing so they were simply reiterating views that they had propounded in the 1930s (see Tavlas, 1981, pp. 326–8), a period when, incidentally, both Sayers and Cairncross has been closely associated with the circle of younger 'Keynesians' at Cambridge. For the quantity theorists, velocity, though it varied for largely unspecified reasons, was nevertheless independently important in determining the behaviour of the system. It was not a 'purely passive factor', as it was for Kahn (cf. M61, p. 145) and as it frequently seemed to be for the committee.

Inherent in the quantity theory view put to the Radcliffee Committee was the proposition that monetary policy was an important instrument of short-run stabilisation policy, for keeping the economy in 'nice balance' as the committee itself put it. Indeed, this position was explicitly defended by the quantity theorists, notably Hawtrey and Gregory. The former argued that 'Bank rate can be altered to any extent at short intervals, can be used as a weapon in a very short period, and can stop the initial stages of any undesirable tendency towards inflation or deflation. Fiscal policy cannot do that' (MN9356, p. 599). Thus he directly contradicted the views of Professor James Meade and Messrs. Little, Neild and Ross for whom just such flexibility was the most desirable characteristic of fiscal policy.[12] Gregory, discussing the effect of interest rate changes, conceded that 'as regards commercial borrowers. . . the effect tends to be delayed', but he then went on to assert that

'in certain parts of the monetary field. . . the effects are much more immediate and the psychological consequences much more marked than current thinking. . . has been prepared to admit'.

(MN10786, p. 726)

Some quantity theorists were less enthusiastic about the scope for monetary fine-tuning, but Dacey saw no great problem about 'determining the volume of bank deposits. . . by reference to the monetary situation' (M12, p. 97) while Robbins, for whom lags in the effects of monetary policy were not to be ignored, nevertheless concluded that 'I do not think we go far wrong if. . . we liken the task of the monetary authorities to that of the driver of some wheeled vehicle. Now we all know that, in such matters, a small turn of the wheel, made quickly, is likely to be much more effective than a large turn, if action has been slow' (M84, p. 218). I have already remarked above (pp. 20–1) that the Radcliffe Committee, in assigning to monetary policy the role of contributing to the longer-run stability of the economy, came, in some respects, rather close to modern monetarist ideas. It is now apparent that, on this same matter, the quantity theorists who gave evidence to the committee were a long way from their monetarist successors.

The two most confident advocates of monetary fine-tuning, Hawtrey and Gregory, laid particular stress on the importance of short interest rates for monetary policy, while the committee itself saw short rates as important mainly to the extent that variations in them brought about changes in long-term rates. On this particular issue, not all the quantity theorists agreed with Hawtrey and Gregory.[13] Paish devoted much of his evidence to demonstrating statistically the influence of the quantity of money on long rates because, as he put it

> It is doubtful whether any but the widest fluctuations in short term rates have much direct effect upon the willingness to borrow for investment, unless the new rates are expected to last for a long time, though they may well...have a substantial psychological effect. A change in long term rates is, however, likely to be effective.
>
> (M4, p. 183)

However, Robbins, though warning that it was 'unwise...to assume that movements of short term rates have no further function to perform' nevertheless conceded that 'The recent emphasis on long term rates...serves to correct errors of perspective which may lead to important omissions of policy' (M81, p. 218). In this respect, their views were only a little removed from those ultimately expressed by the Radcliffe Committee in its report.

The quantity theory case as put to the committee seemed vulnerable here. If, as the committee concluded on the basis of much survey evidence (though not necessarily correctly as White, 1961, argued), monetary policy mainly works through long rates of interest, and if they affect expenditure only with a long and unpredictable lag, how can monetary policy be used for fine tuning? And if interest rates, the key factors in transmitting the effects of changes in the money supply, can themselves be manipulated directly, why is it nevertheless important, as the quantity theorists asserted, to control the stock of money? Their position thus stated is easy to ridicule, and Richard Sayers and Richard Kahn did not miss the opportunity to do so:

> Professor Sayers: I wonder if we might have your comments on another view which has been put to us, for which mystique is not perhaps quite the appropriate word: that though it is through rates of interest and availability of credit and so on that monetary policy works on the level of economic activity, the appropriate way for the monetary authorities to work is not to make up their minds that such and such rates of interest and such and such availabilities of credit are appropriate in particular directions, but to operate in some way on the situation as a whole by increasing the quantity of money when demand needs to be stimulated, and decreasing the quantity of money in other circumstances, leaving it to the market to produce the effects on the particular interest rates?

[Richard Kahn] Am I being asked not to apply the word 'mystique' to that view? [Richard Sayers] I think that answers my question.

(MN10983, p. 742)

There is of course a readily available response here, and its main ingredient was clearly stated by Robbins in his written evidence:

In popular discussion there exists a habit of speaking as if the absolute height of rates of interest were the main criterion by which they should be judged... If the incentive to invest is very high, then rates of interest which are high but not high enough to prevent inflationary borrowing, may be too low. If it is very low, then rates which are low but not low enough to arrest a decline in borrowing may be too high... It is just not true that there is any simple correlation between the absolute height of interest rates and prosperity and depression, growth and stagnation.

(M83, p. 218)

Unfortunately, Sayers was not present when Robbins gave oral evidence to the committee, so their difference of opinion on this crucial issue was not explored as it might have been.

Views such as Robbins expresses in the above quotation, and the Fisher effect, which Robbins also discussed, when taken in combination with the existence of time lags, form much of the basis for the monetarist case for treating money growth as a built-in stabiliser.[14] However, even Robbins treated monetary policy as a device of active stabilisation policy, though less uncritically than did some of his fellow quantity theorists. Moreover, in taking their 'three gear' view of the role of interest rates, the Radcliffe Committee in effect declared that the absolute height of interest rates *was* a reasonable criterion whereby to judge their significance. *Given this view*, which I certainly do not wish to defend, the committee's position on the desirability of linking the conduct of monetary policy directly to interest rates, rather than operating indirectly through control of the quantity of money, was logically coherent.

Moreover this position could have been supported by reference to the evidence of Frank Paish, who showed, with a time series chart in his written evidence, and a scatter diagram presented with his oral evidence, that there was a clearly discernible inverse correlation between the ratio of the money supply to national income and the level of long interest rates in British data. He presented these data in support of his view that long interest rates, which were for him, as for the committee, the important direct monetary influence on aggregate demand, could be controlled by manipulating the quantity of money (cf. M6, p. 183). In fact, the committee did not cite Paish's evidence and indeed would have found it difficult to do so: whatever else he may have argued, Paish's statistical evidence on the

relationship between velocity (or rather its inverse) and interest rates flatly
contradicted the committee's own inclination to follow Kahn and Kaldor in
attaching no significance whatsoever to the concept.

It is tempting to read Paish's statistical evidence as demonstrating a vital
link, in the form of the hypothesis of an empirically stable demand-for-
money function, between the version of the quantity theory of money rejected by the Radcliffe Committee and modern monetarism, but to do so
would be a mistake. He presented his data as reflecting what would not call
a 'reduced form' relationship between a policy variable, the quantity of
money, and the interest rate, and did not discuss the possibility that a
stable demand-for-money function might be an important component of
the structure underlying that reduced form. A point of view very like
Paish's, and supported with similar statistical analysis including a scatter
diagram, *was* presented to the committee in evidence by another witness
who *did* put matters explicitly in terms of the supply and demand for
money, and who presented the following 'reinstatement' (M58, p. 84) of
the quantity theory based on that analysis.

> It could be argued that a reduction in interest rates (brought about by an increase
> in the volume of money) would increase investment and that the consequent
> increase in demand would cause prices to rise. This in turn would increase the
> money value of the cash balance people want to hold...and gradually force
> security prices to [their] old level.... If nothing else...changed...the price rise
> would be proportionsal to the increase in the volume of money.
>
> (M58, p. 84)

These however are the words of the Keynesian, Christopher Dow, not
of any quantity theorist among the witnesses, and he immediately concluded that this piece of analysis 'seems valid but not...of great practical
importance' (M58, p. 84). Nevertheless, it is interesting that the notion of
an empirically stable aggregate demand for money function appears only in
Dow's evidence rather than anywhere else. This fact is consistent with
Patinkin's (1969) view that this aspect of modern monetarism is more closely
related to Keynesian economics than to the traditional quantity theory.[15]

Finally, it should be explicitly noted that, in the light of Dow's evidence
(and that of Paish), the Radcliffe Committee's notions about the velocity
of circulation cannot be excused on the grounds that relevant evidence
concerning its determination was unavailable. The committee's position on
the uncertain influence of aggregate demand on inflation reflected the best
available quantitative evidence on the issue; its view on the instability of
velocity, on the other hand, reflected an inexplicable neglect of evidence
of similar quality which was actually placed before it by witnesses, and
involved the committee in taking a position far more extreme than was

necessary to defend its case for putting interest rates and credit conditions at the centre of monetary policy.

IV Concluding comments

It is uncontroversial that monetarism, in emphasising the link between the quantity of money and the general price level, shares important common ground with the old quantity theory approach to monetary theory and policy which the Radcliffee Committee rejected. Moreover, as we have seen, for example in Robbins's comments on the responsiveness of behaviour and institutions to the policy regime, there are other links between the older doctrine and the new one. However, as we have also seen, there are major differences as well. The quantity theorists who gave evidence to the Radcliffe Committee all advocated activist monetary policies, though Robbins did so less enthusiastically than the others. It was the committee which, noting that monetary measures were subject to long and variable lags in their operation, proposed that monetary policy be assigned to longer-run goals.[16] In this instance the contrast between traditional quantity theory views and monetarism is sharp.

This is not to say that the Radcliffe Committee was, after all, an early proponent of monetarism: its emphasis on interest rates and credit conditions as the key variables in monetary policy stands in too sharp a contrast to the monetarist emphasis on the quantity of money for it to be possible to sustain such an argument. Nor is there any trace in the Radcliffe Report of an attempt, such as an open-economy monetarist might make, to justify the proposition that the quantity of money is irrelevant as a policy variable because of the existence of a fixed exchange rate. Instead the committee made its case for the irrelevance of money with two arguments: first that, since changes in the quantity of money work through interest rates anyway, it is better to operate directly on the latter variables; and second that the velocity of circulation is a statistical artefact of no economic significance.

Though Robbins's views on the variability of interest rates have much in common with monetarist ideas, the quantity theorists' position on velocity bears little relationship to monetarism. For all of them, the velocity of circulation of money was a variable capable of significant autonomous shifts, and only Paish presented evidence to suggest that some of the variations in velocity might systematically be related to interest rate movements. Even Paish, however, did not express his views in terms of that *sine qua non* of monetarism, a stable demand-for-money function. It was Christopher Dow who did that, and he was no early monetarist. However, the presence of the concept of a stable demand-for-money function in

Dow's evidence and its absence from the evidence of the quantity theorists, points, as I have already noted, to a Keynesian (or at least a Cambridge) origin for this all-important aspect of monetarist doctrine. Monetarism, then, is by no means the same doctrine as the traditional quantity theory of money.

Notes

I am grateful to Sir Alec Cairncross, Ann Carlos, Tom Courchene, Kevin Dowd, Joel Fried, Richard Harrington, Peter Howitt, Michael Parkin, Lionel Robbins, Richard Sayers and William White, for comments on earlier drafts of this essay, one of which was circulated in 1982 as University of Western Ontario Research Report #8207. I am grateful to the Social Science and Humanities Research Council of Canada for the financial support that made it possible to prepare this extensively revised version.

1 See for example the recent exchange between Parkin and Patinkin in the February 1986 issue of the *Journal of Money Credit and Banking*.
2 In this paper I quote extensively from these three sources. Quotations from the report are identified by R followed by a paragraph number and a page number. Quotations from Volume 3 of the Memoranda are prefixed with M and are similarly identified. Quotations from Minutes are identified with the letters MN. All the passages from the report quoted in this paper except those dealing with international matters on pp. 12–13 were probably written by Sayers. Cairncross probably wrote the passages dealing with international matters (private communications from Professor Sayers and Sir Alec Cairncross 1982.)
3 At the 1969 Money Study Group Conference held to mark the 10th anniversary of the Radcliffe Report there was some discussion of this very point; as an inspection of Croome and Johnson (1970, pp. 34–6) would indicate. If my memory serves me right, it was Richard Sayers himself who introduced this particular topic and made very much the same point as did Harry Johnson.
4 Note that among the witnesses to the committee, Victor Morgan used the word 'liquidity' to refer to a broader spectrum of assets than merely the money supply, see M10, p. 178. Paish also discussed the influence of 'near money' on the demand for money, see MN10436, p. 694. Robbins (1960) reprinted as Ch. 4 of Robbins (1971) criticises the committee for concentrating its analysis of the effects of 'liquidity' on lending, as opposed to spending, activities. See Robbins, 1971, pp. 108–9.
5 The committee could also have cited the evidence of Mr (later Sir) Roy Harrod on this matter. Section V of his evidence was headed 'Normal long-term interest rate in Britain should be 3%'. He based this proposition on the same historical evidence that Hicks cited, but Hicks, of course, did not draw the policy conclusion that the rate should be held at 3% in the way that Harrod did. Harrod, the reader will recall, is one of those disciples of Keynes who always denied the relevance of the 'Fisher effect'. See Harrod (1971).
6 Note that Dacey, in his written evidence, recommended the issue of indexed government bonds. He based his case on an analysis of the Fisher effect, see M15, p. 67. The Radcliffe Committee explicitly rejected this suggestion on the grounds that a commitment to the issue of indexed bonds might itself create an expectation of inflation, see R573, p. 211.
7 Here the existence of a large outstanding stock of short-term government debt interacting with a 'deliberate policy on the treasury bill rate' prevented 'any statutory or other restraint on the supply of cash' (R376, p. 127) and hence on what the report refers to as the 'credit base' of the banks. This large stock of outstanding treasury bills was an important factor in

the British financial system in the 1950s. It was the empirical basis for the proposition that the liquid assets ratio, rather than the cash ratio, was the effective constraint upon the creation of money. The quantity theorists who gave evidence to the Radcliffe Committee were all, therefore, proponents of funding the debt in order to bring the money supply back under control.

8 Hawtrey's approach to monetary policy was, in other respects, far removed from modern monetarism, and in any event, the committee does not appear to have taken much notice of his evidence. If it had, it is hard to see how it could have stated that 'Professor Meade was the only one of our witnesses who entertained the idea [of a fluctuating rate of exchange]' (R719, p. 259), when Hawtrey also explicitly had advocated an, albeit heavily managed, floating rate. Even so, the reader might note that there are strong overtones of a monetary approach to balance of payments analysis in the evidence submitted to the Radcliffe Committee by the President of the Netherlands Bank, M. W. Holtrop. Holtrop's evidence, of course, reflects a long-standing tradition in Dutch monetary economics, one to which Harry Johnson referred in his (1972) De Vries Lectures. For Holtrop's evidence see *Memoranda of Evidence*, vol. 1, pp. 260–8, and *Minutes of Evidence*, pp. 805–19.

9 Phillips's paper had been widely circulated and discussed at the London School of Economics long before its publication and Richard Sayers as Editor of *Economica* had read it and drew his colleagues' attention to it (Private Communication from Professor Sayers 1982). Perhaps the reference to the close relationship between wage changes and unemployment in the quotation on p. 20 above is an oblique reference to Phillips's paper.

10 For Hall's evidence, see in particular MN1386–1404, pp. 98–100. See also Treasury Paper No. 6, *Memoranda of Evidence*, vol. 1, pp. 92–9. This evidence was particularly influential according to Sir Alec Cairncross (Private Communication, 1982).

11 But see below, pp. 31–2.

12 The evidence of Messrs Little, Neild and Ross is to be found in *Memoranda of Evidence*, vol. 3, pp. 159–68. These proponents of fiscal policy apparently did not give oral evidence to the committee. On the other hand, James Meade's evidence was presented to the committee in the form of his inaugural lecture at the University of Cambridge, entitled 'The Control of Inflation' and is therefore not included in the *Memoranda of Evidence*. Meade, however, did give oral evidence. See *Minutes of Evidence*, pp. 565–660.

13 Of course, in their evidence on the importance of short interest rates, Hawtrey and Gregory were simply reiterating views that they had propounded in the debates of the 1920s and 1930s. A realisation of the importance of long rates of interest for fixed investment was in some measure a product of the Keynesian revolution. The fact that Paish and, in particular, Robbins among the quantity theorists, put such emphasis on long rates of interest in their evidence to the committee, shows how strong was the Keynesian influence on the whole of British monetary economics by the 1950s.

14 Robbins is here stating a position which is to be found in the works of Wicksell (1898 and, in particular, 1907).

15 Patinkin (1969) reached this conclusion when considering the relationship between Friedman's work and the Chicago quantity theory tradition. Modern monetarism, that is to say, is more closely affiliated with the old quantity theory tradition in its emphasis on the role of the quantity of money in the conduct of economic policy than it is in its emphasis on the demand-for-money function as a foundation of a stable (but not constant) velocity of circulation. This is not, of course, to say that older quantity theorists never discussed the notion of velocity as reflecting behaviour which could be modelled in terms of a demand-for-money function. That is after all the essence of the cash-balance version of the theory which is used explicitly by, for example, Robbins (1971, Ch. 4). It is the hypothesis of *empirical stability* of the demand-for-money function which is the distinguishing charac-

teristic of the monetarist contribution, while the grounding of this hypothesis in a capital-theoretic approach to the analysis of the demand for money represents the Keynesian element in monetarism. Even here, though, as I have argued elsewhere, Keynesian liquidity preference theory is a little more closely related to the analysis of Marshall and Pigou than Patinkin allows. See Laidler (1986).

16 Though it ought to be noted that one witness, Professor Thomas Wilson, whose views do not really warrant the label 'quantity theorist', nevertheless advocated in his written evidence the adoption of a rule to govern the rate of growth of the note issue.

References

Brown, A. J. (1955). *The Great Inflation* (London: Oxford University Press).

Committee on the Working of the Monetary System (The Radcliffe Committee) (1959). *Report* (London: HMSO).

Committee on the Working of the Monetary System (The Radcliffe Committee) (1960). *Principal Memoranda of Evidence*, 3 vols (London: HMSO).

Committee on the Working of the Monetary System (The Radcliffe Committee) (1960). *Minutes of Evidence* (London: HMSO).

Croome, D. R., and Johnson, H. G. (eds) (1970). *Money in Britain 1959–1969* (London: Oxford University Press).

Harrod, R. F. (1971). 'Discussion Paper', in G. Clayton, J. C. Gilbert and R. Sedgwick (eds) *Monetary Theory and Monetary Policy in the 1970s* (London: Oxford University Press).

Johnson, H. G. (1962). 'Monetary theory and policy', *American Economic Review*, vol. 52 (June), pp. 335–84.

Johnson, H. G. (1963). 'Alternative guiding principles for the use of monetary policy in Canada', *Princeton Essays in International Finance*, no. 44.

Johnson, H. G. (1972). *Inflation and the Monetarist Controversy* (The 1971 de Vries Lectures), Amsterdam.

Kaldor, N. (1970). 'The new monetarism', *Lloyd's Bank Review*, July, pp. 1–18.

Keynes, J. M. (1936). *The General Theory of Employment Interest and Money* (London: Macmillan).

Laidler, D. (1976). *Essays on Money and Inflation* (Manchester: Manchester University Press).

Laidler, D. (1981). 'Monetarism: an interpretation and an assessment', *Economic Journal*, vol. 91, March.

Laidler, D. (1986). 'What was new about liquidity preference theory?' University of Western Ontario (mimeo).

Parkin, J. M. (1986). '*Essays on and in The Chicago Tradition*, by Don Patinkin, a review essay', *Journal of Money, Credit, and Banking*, vol. 18 (February), pp. 104–15.

Patinkin, D. (1969). 'The Chicago tradition, the quantity theory, and Friedman', *Journal of Money, Credit and Banking*, vol. 1 (February), pp. 46–70.

Patinkin, D. (1986). 'A reply', *Journal of Money, Credit, and Banking*, vol. 19 (February), pp. 11–12.

Phillips, A. W. (1958). 'The relation between unemployment and the rate of change of money wage rates in the United Kingdom', *Economica*, N.S., vol. 25 (November), pp. 283–99.

Robbins, L. (1960). 'Monetary theory and the Radcliffe Report', paper delivered at University of Rome in 1960, reprinted in Robbins (1971).

Robbins, L. (1971). *Money, Trade and International Relations* (London: Macmillan).

Sayers, R. S. (1958). *Modern Banking* (4th ed.) (Oxford: The Clarendon Press).

Tavlas, G. S. (1981). 'Keynesian and monetarist theories of the transmission process: doctrinal aspects', *Journal of Monetary Economics*, vol. 7 (May), pp. 317–37.

White, W. H. (1961). 'Inventory investment and the rate of interest', *Banca Nazionale del Lavoro Quarterly Review*, vol. 57 (June), pp. 141–83.

Wicksell, K. (1898). *Interest and Prices* (tr. R. F. Kahn for the Royal Economic Society, London, 1936).

Wicksell, K. (1907). 'The influence of the rate of interest on prices', *Economic Journal*, vol. 17 (June), pp. 213–20.

3

UK monetary targets 1977–86: picking the numbers

David Cobham

One of the remarkable features of monetary targeting in the UK has been the almost complete lack of official explanation for the numbers selected for the target ranges,[1] a lack which is paralleled by the paucity of comment on the subject in non-official discussions of the experience of monetary targets in the UK. This chapter is designed to fill some part at least of the latter gap. It concentrates throughout on £M3, on the grounds that this was the most important targeted monetary aggregate and the only one for which the authorities had a genuine policy of controlling the supply. No attempt is made to distinguish between the different components of 'the monetary authorities' – the Treasury and the Bank of England – although it is known that there have been important differences of emphasis between and within these two institutions at different times.

We start by comparing the target ranges with the official forecasts (so far as they can be obtained) for the growth of money GDP over comparable periods, and with the previous period growth (as known when the targets were set) of money GDP and £M3. Section II attempts to reconstruct, on the basis of the information available, the forecasts for the various counterparts of £M3 which the authorities presumably made alongside the (published) monetary targets. Section III discusses the target and out-turn for £M3 in each year of the period in turn. Section IV then argues a number of propositions regarding the way in which the monetary authorities publish the numbers for the target ranges. Section V sets out some conclusions.

I

On *a priori* grounds, or on the basis of practice in other countries,[2] it might be expected that the numbers chosen for the target ranges for £M3 would be systematically related to the official forecasts for the growth of money GDP, and/or to the recent growth of money GDP and of £M3 itself. Table 3.1 provides a selection of relevant data. Column (3) gives the implicit forecast for the growth of money GDP over the target period derived from the published official forecasts for real GDP and retail price inflation in columns (1) and (2). Column (4) gives the explicit forecast for the growth of money GDP between financial years given in the Financial Statement and Budget Report (FSBR) for the second half of the period. Columns (5), (6) and (7) give the latest figures for the growth of money GDP, retail prices and £M3 as known at the time of the various budgets. Column (8) gives the £M3 target range, and columns (9) to (12) compare the midpoint of the target range with, respectively, the implicit and explicit forecasts for money GDP, the previous period growth of money GDP and the previous period growth of £M3.

It is convenient to take first the comparison of the target with the previous out-turns. Column (11) shows the considerable variation in the relationship between the target and previous money GDP growth, while column (12) shows some large fluctuations in the gap between the target and previous £M3 growth. Some of these variations can be attributed to one-off effects such as the June 1979 rise in VAT and the post-corset distortion to £M3: in so far as the former was thought to have given a once-for-all boost to prices and hence money GDP in 1979/80 an unchanged stance of monetary policy would have involved a larger gap between the target and previous money GDP growth for 1980/81; and in so far as the post-corset distortion to £M3 was not expected to be repeated an unchanged monetary stance would have involved a larger gap between the target and previous £M3 growth for 1981/2. A further part of the variation in column (11) may be due to a change in the authorities' expectations regarding the velocity of £M3: we have no precise knowledge of these expectations on a year-by-year basis, but it seems that in the late 1970s and very early 1980s the authorities reckoned on a trend rise in velocity of 1–2% a year, and then from 1982 or so they began to assume a trend fall in velocity of around 2% a year, and this change would account for part of the reduction in the gap between the target and previous money GDP growth as between the first four or five years and the last five years of the period. A similar effect may have occurred with the upward revision of the target ranges in 1982 which affects the figures in column (12). However, it is highly unlikely that effects of these kinds could account for all the variations in columns (11) and (12) – what remains is presumably in some sense the variation in the intended severity of policy.

Columns (9) and (10) compare the target with the money GDP forecasts. Again the figures suggest considerable variations from year to year. In this case one-off effects of the kind discussed in the previous paragraph

Table 3.1 £M3 targets and other indicators (%)

Year	Forecasts				Previous period out-turns			£M3 target	Money GDP forecasts £M3 target minus			
	Real GDP (1)	Retail prices (2)	Money GDP (implicit) (3)	Money GDP (explicit) (4)	Money GDP (5)	Retail prices (6)	£M3 (7)	(8)	implicit (9)	explicit (10)	Money GDP previous (11)	£M3 previous (12)
1977/8	1½	11¼	12¾	n.a.	14.6	16.2	9	9–13	−1¾	n.a.	−3.6	2
1978/9	3	7½	10½	n.a.	12.9	9.5	12	8–12	−½	n.a.	−2.9	−2
1979/80	−1	14¾	13¾	n.a.	10.3	10.3	11½	7–11	−4¾	n.a.	−1.3	−2½
1980/81	−1½	15	13½	n.a.	16.6	19.1	12	7–11	−4½	n.a.	−7.6	−3
1981/2	1	9	10	n.a.	13.4	12.5	20	6–10	−2	n.a.	−5.4	−12
1982/3	2	8¼	10¼	9.8	10.2	11.0	14½	8–12	−1¼	0.2	−0.2	−4½
1983/4	2½	6	8½	7.6	9.7	5.3	10	7–11	½	1.4	−0.7	−1
1984/5	2½	4¼	6¾	7.9	8.3	5.1	9¾	6–10	1¼	0.1	−0.3	−1¾
1985/6	2½	4¾	7¼	8.3	6.6	5.4	9½	5–9	−¼	−1.3	0.4	−2½
1986/7	2½	3½	6	6.7	11.0	5.1	14¾	11–15	7	6.3	2.0	−1¾

(1) Growth of GDP at factor cost between first halves of calendar year of budget and following calendar year, as given in FSBR.
(2) Average of two estimates which span financial year, as given in FSBR.
(3) = (1) + (2)
(4) Growth in GDP current market prices between forthcoming and previous financial years, calculated from financial year totals in FSBR.
(5) Growth in GDP at current market prices, expenditure based, s.a., for latest four quarters available, as given in *Economic Trends*, July 1979 and April of all other years.
(6) Growth of RPI over latest 12 months available, as given in *Economic Trends*, June 1979 and March of all other years.
(7) For 1977/8 growth over latest 12 months, January 1976 to January 1977, as given in BEQB 1977a; for other years growth at annual rate over previous target period as given in FSBR: April 1977 to February 1978; April 1978 to April 1979; June 1979 to February 1980; February 1980 to February 1981 and similarly for remaining years.
(8) Targets (at annual rates) for April 1977 to April 1978; April 1978 to April 1979; June 1979 to April 1980; February 1980 to April 1981 and similarly for remaining years.
(9) to (12) = (8) minus, respectively, (3), (4), (5) and (7).

are not relevant since the monetary authorities would have taken account of them in their money GDP forecasts. Changes in the intended severity of policy are not relevant either, because changes in policy would also have been taken into account in the money GDP forecasts. Thus the figures in these columns amount (with their signs reversed) to the change in velocity which would have occurred if the money GDP forecasts had been correct and if £M3 had grown in the middle of the target range. They can therefore be compared with the authorities' explicit beliefs about velocity – as indicated above we have no detailed information on these beliefs but, while they probably moved from an expected trend rise to an expected trend fall as between the first and second halves of the period in a way that is consistent with part of the variation in column (9), it seems highly unlikely that they could have varied on a year-by-year basis by anywhere near as much as is implied by the figures in the table.

What comes out of Table 3.1, then, is that the numbers picked for the monetary targets do not appear to have been related at all closely either to the official forecasts for money GDP or to the previous period growth of money GDP or £M3. Instead, the closest relationship in the table is that between the target range in each year and that for the previous year: with the exception of the 'standstill' in 1979/80 and the increases of 1982/3 and 1986/7 (both of the latter also representing upward revisions to the monetary targets for those years presented in earlier versions of the Medium Term Financial Strategy), there is a consistent 'n-1' relationship between the monetary targets in succeeding years.

II

It is clear that the UK monetary authorities approached the question of monetary control during this period in terms of the counterparts of £M3. However, complete sets of their forecasts for the counterparts consistent with the monetary targets are not available (they are covered by the Thirty Year Rule and the Official Secrets Act). Table 3.2 represents in the odd-numbered rows those forecasts that are available and a tentative reconstruction of those that are not, while the even-numbered rows give the outturn figures. The point of this reconstruction is to shed light on the internal consistency of policy: given the instruments of monetary control at the disposal of the authorities and their way of approaching issues of control, would the targets have appeared realisable? The reconstruction is necessarily speculative and broad-brush, but as will be seen it enables some interesting points to be made. It also provides a framework for an analysis of monetary growth as such, but it will not be used for that purpose here.

Row (1) gives the target growth of £M3, obtained by multiplying the stock outstanding at the end of the previous financial year by the midpoint

Table 3.2 *£M3 and counterparts, forecasts and out-turns (£bn)*

Row	Item		1977/8	1978/9	1979/80	1980/81	1981/2	1982/3	1983/4	1984/5	1985/6	1986/7
(1)	ΔfM3	target	4.4	4.6	4.6	5.2	5.5	8.6	8.7	8.2	8.0	17.4
(2)		out-turn	6.2	5.3	6.4	10.7	9.8	10.1	7.9	11.8	19.1	25.4
(3)	PSBR	forecast	8.5	8.5	8.3	8.5	10.6	9.5	8.2	7.2	7.1	7.1
(4)		out-turn	5.6	9.2	9.9	13.2	8.8	9.2	10.0	10.2	5.8	3.3
(5)	Public sector debt sales to private sector (−)	forecast	−5.5	−7.0	−7.5	−8.0	−10.5	−9.5	−8.2	−7.2	−7.1	−4.6
(6)	Gilt-edged securities (−)	out-turn	−6.7	−8.5	−9.2	−10.8	−11.3	−8.4	−12.5	−12.6	−3.5	−1.2
(7)		forecast	(−3.9)	(−5.8)	(−6.4)	(−5.4)	(−7.2)	n.a.	n.a.	n.a.	n.a.	n.a.
(8)	National savings (−)	out-turn	(−4.9)	(−6.2)	(−8.3)	(−8.9)	(−7.1)	(−4.6)	(−9.8)	(−9.3)	(−2.8)	(−1.5)
(9)		target			–	(−2.0)	(−3.0)	(−3.0)	(−3.0)	(−3.0)	(−3.0)	n.a.
(10)		out-turn	(−1.1)	(−1.6)	(−1.4)	(−4.2)	(−3.6)	(−3.0)	(−3.4)	(−3.1)	(−2.1)	(−3.4)
(11)	Sterling lending to private sector	forecast	3.0	4.0	6.0	8.0	8.0	13.0	14.0	14.0	18.0	21.0
(12)	External and foreign currency counterparts	out-turn	3.7	6.3	9.3	9.2	14.9	14.4	15.2	18.6	21.4	30.3
(13)		forecast	−0.5	0	−1.0	−2.0	−1.0	−1.0	−2.5	−1.5	−2.0	−2.5
(14)	Net non-deposit liabilities	out-turn	+4.0	−0.6	−2.4	+0.6	−0.8	−2.6	−0.2	−1.7	−2.5	−2.4
(15)		forecast	−0.8	−0.8	−1.0	−1.2	−1.5	−1.8	−2.4	−3.5	−2.5	−2.5
(16)	Residual	out-turn	−0.4	−1.0	−1.2	−1.5	−1.7	−2.4	−4.7	−2.7	−2.0	−4.6
(17)		forecast	−0.3	−0.1	−0.2	−0.1	−0.1	−1.6	−0.4	−0.8	−5.5	−1.1
		(%£M3)	(−0.8)	(−0.2)	(−0.4)	(−0.2)	(−0.1)	(−1.9)	(−0.4)	(−0.8)	(−4.8)	(−0.8)

Notes to Table 3.2

(1) Target growth of £M3 obtained by applying midpoint of target range to outstanding stock at end of previous financial year.

(3) PSBR forecast from FSBR.

(5) Estimated forecast (see text for details).

(7) Forecast for sales of gilts to non-bank private sector given in Coleby, 1983.

(9) Target for sales of National Savings debt given in BEQB and/or Budget Statements: BEQB, 1982c. p. 350; House of Commons Report – Hansard (HC), vol. 1000, col. 764; vol. 19, col. 735; vol. 39, col. 140; vol. 56, col. 290; vol. 75, col. 786.

(11), (13) and (15) Estimated forecasts (see text).

Relationships between rows: (1) = (3) + (5) + (11) + (13) + (15) + (17);
(2) = (4) + (6) + (12) + (14) + (16).

Out-turn figures in even columns from BEQB, *Financial Statistics*, various issues; adjusted to consistency with definitions used in forecasts.

of the target annual growth range (the monetary targets applied to slightly different time periods but the other published forecasts applied to financial years and that period is therefore used here). Row (3) gives the PSBR forecasts published in FSBR. Row (7) gives the forecasts for sales of gilt-edged securities to the non-bank private sector from Coleby (1983), the only published source of such forecasts. Row (9) gives the National Savings (NS) debt sales targets from the *Bank of England Quarterly Bulletin* (BEQB) and the 1981–5 Budget Statements. Row (5) gives an estimate of the authorities' forecast for total public sector (PS) debt sales based partly on (7) and (9). Rows (11), (13) and (15) give estimates of the authorities' forecasts for sterling lending to the private sector, the external and foreign currency counterparts, and net non-deposit liabilities respectively, based on a variety of considerations specific to the financial year concerned. Finally, row (17) shows the difference between the target growth of £M3 in row (1) and the sum of the counterpart forecasts, rows (3) + (5) + (11) + (13) + (15). The specific assumptions made in constructing each year's estimates will now be discussed in turn.

For 1977/8 the PSBR forecast was a little lower than the 1976/7 out-turn and much lower than the out-turn for the two previous years. The official forecast for gilt-edged sales from Coleby (1983) is at £3.9bn nearly £2bn below the 1976/7 out-turn. No NS debt target is available but NS debt sales had been rising in recent years, from £0.1bn in 1974/5 to £1.0bn in 1976/7. Other public sector debt sales had averaged £0.9bn but varied widely over the last three years. These considerations suggest a forecast for total debt sales in row (5) of £5.5bn, roughly the average of the three previous years (when the PSBR had been slightly higher on average) and implying a public sector contribution to monetary growth (i.e. PSBR minus PS debt sales) of £3bn, above that for 1976/7 but below the average for 1974/5 to 1976/7. Sterling lending to the private sector had risen to £3.4bn in 1976/7 after the exceptionally low levels of late 1974 and 1975/6; however, this was thought to have been at least partly due to the prolonged sterling crisis of 1976, and the corset had been reintroduced in November 1976. The authorities are therefore likely to have expected a somewhat lower level in 1977/8, such as the £3bn figure in row (11). The estimated forecast for external and foreign currency counterparts in row (13) is less negative than the out-turn for recent years, because the current account was expected finally to move into surplus in the first half of 1978.[3] The estimated forecast for net non-deposit liabilities in row (13) is in line with the recent trend. These forecasts sum to £4.7bn, £0.3bn (0.75% of £M3) above the growth of £M3 implied by the midpoint of the 9–13% target range; such a residual is probably within the margin of error that needs to be attached to this sort of exercise and can be disregarded.

For 1978/9 the PSBR forecast was the same as the forecast for the previous year (which had been undershot) while the gilt-edged sales target was much higher. The estimated forecast in row (5) for total PS debt sales is between the out-turns for 1976/7 and 1977/8; it implies both a lower PS contribution to monetary growth than that forecast for 1977/8 and a narrowing of the gap between the gilts target and the total debt sales forecast to take account of the crowding out of sales of other forms of PS debt by sales of gilts. The forecast of £4bn for sterling lending to the private sector is a little above the out-turn for 1977/8 on the grounds that the economy was expected to expand more rapidly and the corset had been suspended in August 1977 (it was reimposed in June 1978 when bank lending turned out higher than expected[4]). The externals forecast in row (13) is put at zero in response to the unprecedented positive out-turn for 1977/8 (associated with the attempt to hold the exchange rate down in the face of large capital inflows in the late summer and autumn of 1977). The net non-deposit liabilities forecast in row (15) is in line with the trend. These forecasts sum to £4.7bn, just £0.1bn above the growth of £M3 implied by the midpoint of the target range.

For 1979/80 the PSBR forecast was again little changed on recent forecasts. The gilts sales forecast was higher than the 1978/9 out-turn and much higher than the 1978/9 forecast. No NS debt sales target is available, but sales had risen further in recent years to £1.6bn in 1978/9. Other PS debt sales on the other hand had been very low. These considerations point to a forecast for total PS debt sales in row (5) of around £7.5bn, which implies a PS contribution to monetary growth of £0.8bn, roughly equal to the out-turn for 1978/9. Sterling lending to the private sector had been £6.3bn in 1978/9 with some upward trend through the year; it seems likely that the authorities would have expected it to continue at something like the same level since the corset remained in operation and had been neither tightened nor relaxed, but minimum lending rate (MLR) was raised by 2% in the June 1979 Budget 'primarily to moderate bank lending':[5] hence the estimated forecast of £6bn. The estimate in row (13) for the external counterparts is in the centre of the recent range for this item, whereas that in row (15) for net non-deposit liabilities allows for some trend growth. These forecasts sum to £4.8bn, giving a residual of −£0.2bn, which is again within the margin of error and can be disregarded.

For 1980/81 both a gilts sales forecast and an NS debt sales target are available; the total debt sales figure in row (5) allows for a small amount of other debt sales, and with the PSBR forecast little changed implies a slightly lower PS contribution to monetary growth. Sterling lending to the private sector had turned out much higher in 1979/80 than forecast; the figure in row (11) for 1980/81 moves some of the way towards the 1979/80

out-turn, but not all the way since the authorities expected the industrial
demand for bank credit to 'be reduced in the course of the recession'[6] and
the out-turn of £9.2bn was later described as 'much more than expected'.[7]
The figure for the external counterparts in row (13) is set (absolutely)
higher than the 1979/80 forecast in the light of the 1979/80 out-turn and the
current account deficit which was forecast for 1980/81.[8] The net non-
deposit liabilities estimate in row (15) is in line with recent trends. These
forecasts yield a negligible residual in row (17) of −£0.1bn.

For 1981/2 the PSBR forecast was significantly higher than that for
previous years, following the large overshoot of 1980/81; the gilts sales
forecast and the NS debt sales target were also much higher. The estimated
total PS debt sales forecast in row (5) allows for a smaller amount of other
debt sales than the estimated forecast in 1980/81, since other PS debt sales
had been negative in 1980/81 and the authorities are unlikely to have aimed
to overfund. The estimated sterling lending forecast in row (11) is the same
as that for 1980/81 − the latter had been exceeded but the authorities
thought the demand for credit was 'moderating'[9] and no repeat of the re-
intermediation that had affected the 1980/81 out-turn was expected; moreover the 1981/2 out-turn was later described as 'substantially larger than
expected'.[10] The externals estimate in row (13) represents a reversion to
trend; the 1980/81 out-turn had been positive rather than negative and a
small current account surplus was forecast for 1981/2,[11] but the authorities
were emphasising that a current account surplus does not necessarily
produce a positive external influence on £M3,[12] and that capital outflows
were running at a high rate,[13] presumably partly in response to the
abolition of exchange controls. The figure for net non-deposit liabilities in
row (15) again follows the trend, and the total of the counterpart forecasts
yields a negligible residual of −£0.1bn.

For 1982/3 no gilts sales forecast is available. In 1981/2 the authorities
had overfunded but it is unlikely that they intended to do this again; on the
other hand they now clearly recognised the strength of the demand for
bank lending.[14] The estimated forecast for total PS debt sales in row (5)
therefore assumes the intention of full funding of the PSBR. The 1981/2
sterling lending forecast had been greatly exceeded by the out-turn of
£14.9bn, with lending to companies lower in the first half and higher in the
second half of the year partly as a result of the delay in tax payments
caused by the civil service dispute. For 1982/3 the authorities thought that
lending to persons might ease to some extent, but 'this may be less likely
for lending to business'.[15] This suggests their forecast must have been at
least the £13bn of row (11). The estimated externals forecast in row (13) is
the same as that for the previous year, which had been relatively accurate:
a current account surplus was expected[16] but 1981/2 had seen a consider-

able surplus associated with a negative external counterpart and the capital outflow remained high.[17] The net non-deposit liabilities figure in row (15) is again in line with the trend. In this case, however, the total of the counterpart forecasts exceeds the £M3 target by £1.6bn (indeed the total is only £0.1bn less than the £M3 growth implied by the upper bound of the target range).

Such a divergence immediately prompts a reconsideration of the counterpart forecasts, but it is difficult to see how these could be made any less: it is not plausible that the authorities *intended* from the beginning of the year to overfund (they had been under criticism for some time for the growth of the bill mountain associated with the overfunding of 1981/2); after years of underpredicting sterling lending they were trying to take full account of its likely course (this was the main reason why the £M3 target had been revised upwards this year) and might well have expected an even higher level; and the expected contractionary impact of the other two counterparts together was larger than the out-turn in most recent years. It therefore seems likely that the authorities' forecasts for the counterparts added up to a figure near the top rather than the middle of the target range, even though the latter was revised upwards, from the 5–9% specified in the 1980 and 1981 versions of the MTFS to 8–12%.

For 1983/4 again no gilts sales forecast is available and the figure in row (5) assumes the intention of full funding (there had been slightly less than full funding in 1982/3). The authorities appear to have expected bank lending to remain high, though perhaps a little lower than in 1982/3,[18] hence the figure of £14bn in row (11) as against the 1982/3 out-turn of £14.4bn. The externals forecast in row (13) is set much higher in the light of the 1982/3 out-turn and the smaller current account surplus expected in 1983/4.[19] The net non-deposit liabilities figure in row (15) reflects the sharp rise in the 1982/3 out-turn. This leaves a small residual of −£0.4bn.

For 1984/5 it is again assumed that the authorities intended full (narrow) funding of the PSBR, despite the substantial overfunding which had occurred in 1983/4. The estimated forecast for sterling lending is the same as the forecast but lower than the out-turn for 1983/4 (and the two previous years' out-turns); the authorities expressed the hope that the Budget might encourage companies to fund their overdrafts.[20] Moreover they later described the acceleration of bank lending in the last two quarters of the financial year as 'puzzling'.[21] The externals and net non-deposit liabilities forecasts in rows (13) and (15) each show a reversion to trend levels after the unusual out-turn of 1983/4, but their total is roughly equal to the out-turn for both 1982/3 and 1983/4. This leaves a residual of −£0.8bn.

For 1985/6 the intention of full funding is again assumed. The forecast for sterling lending to the private sector is significantly higher than recent forecasts, but slightly below the out-turn for 1984/5; there is no indication that the authorities expected sterling lending to fall back sharply from the previous level, but they had found the latter 'puzzling' and the March 1985 BEQB mentioned the possibility that the 'approval of short-term capital market borrowing' and the 'fuller capital gains tax indexation' introduced in the Budget might encourage companies to borrow more from the capital markets and less from the banks.[22] The externals and net non-deposit liabilities forecasts each show a further reversion to trend levels, with the total in line with the 1984/5 out-turn. These forecasts exceed the midpoint of the £M3 target range by £5.5bn, much the largest residual in the table, and its upper bound by £3.2bn.

It is possible that the authorities were a little more optimistic on sterling lending, and that they expected a slightly larger negative impact from the externals and net non-deposit liabilities. It is conceivable that they planned on overfunding the PSBR to a limited extent. But it is not plausible that differences such as these from the estimated forecasts in the table could amount to £5bn or even £3bn – in other words the authorities must have known at the beginning of the year that the £M3 target which they were announcing was not realisable.

Finally for 1986/7 the intention of full *wide* funding is assumed: the Chancellor's Mansion House speech of October 1985 had announced the abandonment of overfunding in favour of a policy of full *wide* funding, that is, covering the PSBR out of the sum of external and foreign currency financing of the public sector and sales of debt to the domestic non-bank private sector.[23] The sterling lending forecast is in line with the out-turn for 1985/6; it is clear that the higher out-turn in 1986/7 was above official expectations.[24] The estimated forecast for net non-deposit liabilities is in line with recent levels. These figures leave a small residual of −£1.1bn (0.8% of £M3) relative to the midpoint of the new, upward-revised, target range of 11–15%.

What comes out of Table 3.2, then, is that although most of the target ranges were consistent with how the authorities appear to have expected the counterparts to £M3 to develop, there was one year – 1985/6 – when the authorities cannot have believed the target range was realisable, and another year – 1982/3 – when they must have expected monetary growth to be at the top rather than the middle of the target range.

III

It will now be useful to go through the ten years of monetary targets in turn, noting whether the particular target chosen was *reasonable* in the light of the analysis of Section I, that is, consistent with the authorities' economic and velocity forecasts; and whether it was *feasible* in the light of the analysis of Section II, that is, consistent with their (estimated) counterpart forecasts. The discussion also indicates other factors which may have influenced the authorities' choice of target, and considers whether the (*a priori*) reasonableness and/or feasibility of the targets might contribute to the explanation of any deviation of the out-turn of monetary growth from the target.

For 1977/8 the target was clearly reasonable in relation to the money GDP forecast and the authorities' likely expectations about velocity; and it was feasible in terms of their expectations for the counterparts. The 9–13% range was above the previous period out-turn of 9%, but that had been depressed by the extraordinary gilt-edged sales of 1977:1. Strictly the 9–13% range was not originally a *target*, but what the authorities expected to be consistent with the formal target for domestic credit expansion (DCE) agreed with the IMF in December 1976; the same range had also been given then as consistent with the (higher) DCE target for 1976/7.[25] However, the estimates in Table 3.2 imply that the authorities' own objectives for DCE in both 1977/8 and 1978/9 were well below the DCE targets agreed with the IMF. And in any case, the 9–13% range rapidly assumed the status of a target as the balance of payments improved and attention was shifted away from DCE on to the money supply. As it turned out (see Table 3.3) the 1977/8 target was significantly overshot, but this was due essentially to the conflict between monetary and exchange rate targets that developed in the autumn of 1977, which is reflected in Table 3.2 in the record positive entry for the external counterparts, only partly offset by (unplanned) overfunding.

For 1978/9 the target range of 8–12% was rather high in relation to the money GDP forecast, which was more than 2% lower than that for the previous year; it was clearly feasible in terms of the authorities' counterpart forecasts. The 1978 Budget was a moderately expansionary one; it included the introduction of rolling monetary targets with the suggestion that a lower target might be set in the autumn (in the event it was not), while the 8–12% range was said to give 'ample room' for the expected increase in bank lending.[26] In fact, £M3 grew within but towards the top of the target range.

For 1979/80 the target range set by the new government in its first Budget in June 1979 was again 1% lower than that for the previous year, but money GDP was expected to grow some 3% faster (largely because of the VAT increase) and the implied velocity change is not compatible with what the authorities probably believed at the time: thus the authorities, or at least the ultimate decision-makers, must either have not believed the official inflation and GDP forecasts, or have chosen to disregard the incon-

Table 3.3   £M3 targets and out-turns

Target period	Target range	Out-turn over target period	Out-turn over financial year
April 1977 to April 1978	9–13%	16.0%	15.6%
April 1978 to April 1979	8–12	10.5	11.4
June 1979 to April 1980	7–11	9.6	12.5
February 1980 to April 1981	7–11	19.1	18.5
February 1981 to April 1982	6–10	13.7	14.3
February 1982 to April 1983	8–12	11.1	11.7
February 1983 to April 1984	7–11	9.5	8.2
February 1984 to April 1985	6–10	11.9	11.5
1985/6 (average of 12-month growth rates)[a]	5–9	13.8	16.7
1986/7 (average of 12-month growth rates)[b]	11–15	18.3	19.0

[a] Target suspended in October 1985; out-turn for target period is average of 12-month growth rates from May 1985 (when this method was introduced) to April 1986.
[b] Out-turn for target period is average of 12-month growth rates from March 1986 to April 1987.

Out-turn figures from BEQB, *Financial Statistics*, various issues.

sistency.[27] On the other hand, the target did look feasible in terms of the counterpart forecasts. The out-turn was within the range for the target period, partly thanks to the disintermediation associated with the corset, but above it for the financial year which included the acceleration of monetary growth in April and May 1979.

The year 1980/81 saw the introduction of the MTFS. The target range was kept at 7–11% while the money GDP forecast was also little changed from the previous year, so that the target remained incompatible with the authorities' expectations about monetary growth and velocity. On the other hand, the target again appeared feasible in terms of the counterpart forecasts in Table 3.2. A curious feature of this year is that the Chancellor envisaged in his Budget Statement some upward pressure on £M3 in the summer of 1980 from post-corset re-intermediation which 'cannot be precisely measured or predicted' but which he hoped could be accommodated within the target range;[28] however, the BEQB made no mention of this phenomenon until after it had occurred. In the event, £M3 grew well above the target range, partly because of this re-intermediation, but largely because of a deliberate decision by the authorities to allow it to do so, on the grounds that monetary conditions were already tight enough, if not too tight.[29]

For 1981/2 the inflation and money GDP forecasts were much lower so that the lower target range of 6–10%, as set out in the 1980 version of the MTFS, was a much more reasonable one. In terms of the authorities' view of the likely development of the counterparts it was also a feasible target. However there was another large overshoot, again essentially allowed by the authorities, who were by now becoming convinced of the importance of structural changes in the financial system tending to raise the demand for money and reduce the velocity of circulation.

It was presumably these convictions as much as the recorded overshoots of 1980/81 and 1981/2 that led the authorities to revise upwards the 1982/3 target range from the 5–9% set out in the 1980 and 1981 versions of the MTFS to 8–12%. However, with an explicit money GDP forecast (published for the first time) of 9.8%, the new range was still not consistent with the trend fall of about 2% a year in the velocity of circulation which the authorities probably now expected. Moreover the authorities' likely forecasts of the counterparts suggested a growth of £M3 towards the top of the target range. However, the 8–12% could at least be presented as significantly lower than the 1981/2 out-turn;[30] and it was no higher than the last target range of the previous government. In the event £M3 grew towards the top of but within the target range, partly due to a movement out of bank time deposits into term shares with building societies.[31]

For 1983/4 the further fall in the inflation and money GDP forecasts (particularly the explicit money GDP forecast) made the 7–11% range envisaged in the 1982 version of the MTFS look more reasonable; it also looked feasible in terms of the likely growth of the counterparts. In fact, £M3 grew near the centre of the range, again assisted by a shift into building society term shares.

The following year, 1984/5, the implicit and explicit money GDP forecasts point in different directions, but the 6–10% range set out in the 1982 and 1983 versions of the MTFS did not look too unreasonable; and the authorities probably believed it to be feasible. However, £M3 turned out to grow above the target range, mainly because of a surge in sterling lending to the private sector towards the end of the target period.

The 1985/6 Budget was delivered under the shadow of the most serious sterling crisis since 1976. With money GDP expected to accelerate slightly the 5–9% target range previously envisaged would have looked unreasonable even if the authorities had expected velocity to remain constant, but by now they clearly expected it to rise. This expectation also underpinned their likely forecast for sterling lending to the private sector, which was largely responsible for the major inconsistency between the probable development of the counterparts and a 5–9% target range for £M3. Moreover in a lecture in October 1984 the Governor of the Bank of England had emphasised the need for pragmatism and discretion rather than mechanistic rules in operating monetary policy.[32] Nevertheless the 5–9% target was confirmed in the Budget. Instead of slowing down, however, £M3 accelerated and the target was formally suspended in October 1985.

The 1986 Budget reintroduced a £M3 target at the much higher range of 11–15%. This made a generous allowance for a large fall in velocity, and looked feasible in terms of the counterparts. But in the event it was greatly exceeded as sterling lending expanded even more rapidly and the authorities could no longer offset it by overfunding, which had been abandoned in October 1985.

IV

The three preceding sections enable a number of propositions about the way in which the UK monetary authorities 'picked the numbers' for the target ranges to be put forward.

Proposition 1: The severity of the targets, that is, the restrictiveness of monetary policy, varied considerably from year to year.

This proposition follows simply from the analysis of Section I: it is clear that the targets were not systematically related to previous money GDP growth or to previous £M3 growth, and that they were not closely related to the money GDP forecast for the target period either, even if changes in the authorities' expectations about the trend of velocity are taken into account. The targets were particularly severe in 1979/80, 1980/81 and 1985/6, and relatively lax in 1978/9.

Proposition 2: Some of the targets promulgated were inconsistent with the authorities' inflation and money GDP forecasts and/or with their beliefs about velocity.

This again follows from Table 3.1; it refers particularly to 1979/80, 1980/81 and 1985/6.

Proposition 3: Some of the targets promulgated cannot have been regarded as attainable by the authorities themselves.

This proposition follows from Section II which showed that although most of the targets were roughly consistent with what the authorities expected in terms of the counterparts, that for 1982/3 was consistent only with monetary growth at the top of the target range and that for 1985/6 only with monetary growth well above the target range.

Proposition 4: In choosing the target ranges the authorities were not trying primarily to influence inflation expectations or to provide a precise 'guarantee of stability'.

Conventional expositions of the role of monetary targets suggest that they can (a) help to stabilise the economy by helping the private sector to make more accurate and more certain economic forecasts; (b) exert an independent influence on inflation expectations; and (c) improve the credibility of the authorities' policies and the financial markets' confidence in them. The key Bank of England statement on the role of monetary targets – the 1978 Mais lecture – emphasises above all their role as an alternative guarantee of stability to that provided in earlier periods by 'fixed exchange rates or Gladstonian budgetary principles'.[33] However, from the analysis of Sections I and III – and from a comparison of the official inflation forecasts and the target ranges in Table 3.1 – it seems highly unlikely that the authorities had any serious intention of affecting inflation expectations, while the lack of relationship between the money GDP forecasts and the targets implies that the targets were a potential source of instability rather than stability. The only sense in which they can be said to have provided a guarantee of stability is the general and minimal sense of refusal to reflate in response to recession – indeed the Bank of England has throughout the period tended to play down the significance of the target numbers either in themselves or relative to the out-turn.[34]

Proposition 5: The dominant consideration in the choice of target ranges was an attachment to the '*n*-1' principle.

The '*n*-1' idea was first introduced with the 1978/9 target but it was followed in 1979/80 and became firmly embodied in each version of the MTFS: the authorities were primarily concerned to show a continuous tightening of policy, primarily with respect to the previous year's target but also on occasions with respect to the previous year's out-turn.[35] Thus the choice of 7–11% in 1979/80 – a range which was thoroughly unreasonable in the light of official expectations at the time – must be ascribed essentially to this concern; similarly the even more inappropriate choice of 5–9% for 1985/6. It should be noted that the '*n*-1' principle is essentially arbitrary and does not provide a sound discipline for monetary policy over the medium term: it did not preclude the expansion of 1978/9, for example, and in the absence of the fall in velocity would not have precluded periods of greater expansion in the 1980s, for example in 1983.

Proposition 6: The setting of targets on this basis contributed to some of the overshoots of the targets.

As has been argued above, the targets for 1979/80 and 1980/81 were unreasonably tight; there can be little doubt that the severe pressures (closely associated with sterling appreciation) which developed in the economy during 1980 and led to the authorities' decision to permit a substantial overshoot of the 1980/81 target were partly due to the tightness of the targets promulgated and the attempt to observe them. If a higher target range – more reasonable and more feasible – had been set in 1982/3 the out-turn would have been nearer the centre rather than the upper bound of the target range. And if a more reasonable and more feasible target had been set for 1985/6 it would not have been necessary to suspend the target halfway through the year.

V

The propositions set out in Section IV amount to the argument that the way in which the numbers for the UK monetary targets were chosen could not have been expected to make monetary targeting perform as useful a role as it might have done. The authorities seem to have been influenced most of all by very short-term considerations of the announcement effects of the numbers, in a manner that is consistent with their traditional pre-occupation with the short-term state of confidence in financial markets,[36] but this militated against other possible beneficial effects. Thus explanations of the demise of monetary targeting which attribute it purely to financial innovation[37] are seriously incomplete: the way in which the UK monetary authorities operated the targeting system also made an important contribution to its demise.

Moreover there *was* an alternative: the authorities could have set the targets on a more systematic basis, ensuring that they were both reasonable and feasible in the senses used above, but avoided any possible harmful short-term effects on confidence due to more variable, non-'n-1', targets by providing much more information on the reasons for their choices, including their expectations about the likely development of money GDP, velocity and so on; they could also have set much narrower target ranges. If they had followed this sort of procedure the authorities' credibility would have been higher and more sustainable over the long term, monetary targets would have made a greater contribution to stability and they might even have had a useful effect on inflation expectations. Discretionary decisions to allow monetary growth outside the target ranges could have been explained more easily in terms of the divergences from the (known) forecast of variables such as the exchange rate. And it would have been unnecessary (and more difficult) for the authorities to abandon targeting altogether as they did in 1987.

Notes

Much of the work on which this chapter is based was undertaken while the author was a Houblon-Norman Fellow at the Bank of England, but neither the Houblon-Norman Trustees nor the Bank are in any way responsible for its contents.

1 The *Financial Statement and Budget Report* typically refers to the Chancellor's Budget Statement in the House of Commons as the source of the decision, but the Budget Statements contain little explanation of the numbers chosen and no analysis of alternative target numbers. The Treasury and Civil Service Committee (1979–80) tried in July 1980 to get the Chancellor to justify his choice of 7–11% for 1980/81 but without significant result.
2 See, for example, Courakis, 1981, on the USA and West Germany; Cobham and Serre, 1987, on France.
3 FSBR 1977–8, p. 12.
4 BEQB, 1978b, p. 169; 1978c, p. 344.
5 BEQB, 1979c, p. 261.
6 BEQB, 1980b, p. 140. On the other hand the Budget Statement expected some upward effect on bank lending from re-intermediation following the abolition of the corset (HC, vol. 981, col. 1445).
7 BEQB, 1981b, p. 164.
8 FSBR 1980–81, p. 27.
9 BEQB, 1980d, p. 389; see also 1981a, p. 21.
10 BEQB, 1982b, p. 180.
11 FSBR 1981–2, p. 28.
12 BEQB, 1981a, p. 5.
13 BEQB, 1981a, p. 17; see also 1981b, p. 162.
14 See, for example, BEQB, 1982a, p. 6; 1982b, pp. 179–80.
15 BEQB, 1982a, p. 6.
16 FSBR 1982–3, p. 24.
17 Including the balancing item. See BEQB, 1982a, p. 18, where it is also suggested that the current account surplus for 1982 would be considerably smaller than the estimated outturn of £8bn for 1981.
18 BEQB, 1983a, p. 7.
19 FSBR 1983–4, p. 20.
20 BEQB, 1984a, p. 7.
21 BEQB, 1984d, p. 453; see also 1985a, p. 6.
22 BEQB, 1985a, p. 7.
23 BEQB, 1985d, p. 518.
24 BEQB, 1986b, pp. 185, 187; 1986d, p. 476; 1987a, p. 28.
25 See, for example, BEQB, 1977a, p. 16; 1977b, pp. 148–9.
26 Budget Statement, HC, vol. 947, cols 1191–2.
27 There is some evidence in favour of the former possibility in the 1979 Budget Statement, HC, vol. 981, cols 243, 263, quoted in Atkinson and Hall, 1983, pp. 162–3.
28 HC, vol. 981, col. 1444.
29 See Fforde, 1983.

30 The following passage from Bruce-Gardyne, 1986, pp. 186–7, suggests that this kind of consideration was indeed important:

> The last update of the MTFS, at the time of the previous Budget, might have pencilled in, for the year confronting us, a range of 6–10 per cent growth in our £M3 lodestar... And that might, come February of the following year, look too ambitious for our comfort. But if we could by then assert – and we usually could – that in the financial year drawing to its close £M3 looked like growing by 13 per cent, instead of the 7–11 range set for it...then we could make a virtue of our iniquities. Brushing aside our past intentions, we would boldly repeat the previous year's 7–11 per cent range for £M3...and emphasise the progress this would constitute not against the previous year's intentions (which would be assigned to the memory hole) but against our latest expectations of the previous year's performance.

31 BEQB, 1987b, p. 216.
32 BEQB, 1984d, pp. 474–81.
33 BEQB, 1978a, p. 34.
34 See, for example, BEQB, 1977b, p. 151; and Fforde, 1983, p. 207.
35 See the quotation from Bruce-Gardyne, 1986, in note 30 above.
36 See, for example, Cobham, 1982, on the authorities' response to the 1976 sterling crisis (which included the introduction of monetary targets).
37 This is the main thrust of the Loughborough lecture (BEQB, 1986d, pp. 499–507).

References

Atkinson, F. and Hall, S. (1983). *Oil and the British Economy* (London: Croom Helm).
Bank of England Quarterly Bulletin (BEQB); issues 1, 2, 3 and 4 of each year are designated by the suffixes a, b, c and d attached to the year.
Bruce-Gardyne, J. (1986). *Ministers and Mandarins* (London: Sidgwick & Jackson).
Cobham, D. (1982). 'Domestic credit expansion, confidence and the foreign exchange market: sterling in 1976', *Kredit und Kapital*, vol. 15, pp. 434–56.
Cobham, D. and Serre, J-M. (1987). 'The variability of monetary growth in France and the UK, 1970–84', in C. Goodhart, D. Currie and D. Llewellyn (eds), *The Operation and Regulation of Financial Markets* (London: Macmillan).
Coleby, A. L. (1983). 'The Bank's operational procedures for meeting monetary objectives', *BEQB*, vol. 23, pp. 209–15.
Courakis, A. S. (1981). 'Monetary targets: conceptual antecedents and recent policies in the US, UK and West Germany', in A. S. Courakis (ed.), *Inflation, Depression and Economic Policy in the West* (Oxford: Mansell).
Fforde, J. S. (1983). 'Setting monetary objectives', *BEQB*, vol. 23, pp. 200–8.
Treasury and Civil Service Committee (1979–80), *Monetary Policy: Minutes of Evidence*, House of Commons paper HC 679-vi (London: HMSO).

4

The case for an international monetary system

George Zis

Introduction

Triffin (1982) disputed whether the international monetary practices prevailing since 1973 amounted to a system. Instead, he suggested that the 'World Monetary Scandal' would be a more accurate characterisation. Similarly, Williamson (1983a) has labelled the post-1973 world monetary arrangements as a 'non-system'. These economists' indictment of exchange rate flexibility, though it commands wide support, is not universally accepted. There continues to exist a significant body of opinion in favour of flexible exchange rates. Proponents of freely determined exchange rates maintain that the experience since 1973 does not justify the advocacy of establishing an international monetary system of essentially fixed exchange rates.

In what follows, the arguments supporting the judgement that flexible exchange rates have failed are outlined and the defence of exchange rate flexibility is discussed. The next section is devoted to an assessment of the arguments for flexible exchange rates. Finally, an evaluation of proposals relating to the reform of international monetary relations is presented.

Exchange rate volatility

Proponents of flexible exchange rates in the 1950s and 1960s argued that market-determined exchange rate changes would be small, continuous and predictable.[1] Exchange rate behaviour since 1973 has revealed the expectations of advocates of exchange rate flexibility to have been ill-founded. Changes in nominal exchange rates have been large and unpredictable. These changes have not systematically offset differentials in countries' inflation rates. Therefore real exchange rates have been volatile and unpredictable. Forward exchange rates have proved to be poor predictors of future spot rates. Critics have maintained that exchange rate volatility and unpredictability would tend to discourage international trade and investment. Further, it has been suggested that exchange rate uncertainty would induce a shift of resources from the traded goods sector to the non-traded goods sector which, other things equal, would lead to an increase in countries' natural rates of unemployment.

De Grauwe (1988) has presented empirical evidence indicating that the volatility of real exchange rates is a significant factor in explaining the sharp decline in the rate of growth of international trade since 1973. De Grauwe's findings are consistent with those of Cushman (1983) who also concluded that exchange rate volatility had adversely affected international trade.[2]

IMF (1984) in assessing the effects of exchange rate behaviour since 1973 presents empirical evidence which suggests 'that exchange rate variability has been accompanied by greater shifts of resources into and out of the foreign sector' (p. 23). It follows, therefore, that exchange rate uncertainty can partly explain the increase in countries' levels of unemployment. The same study also presents findings which indicate that the share of manufacturing output in the advanced industrial countries has declined more rapidly since 1973.

Proponents of exchange rate flexibility, however, argue that judgements resting solely on exchange rate volatility are misplaced. They maintain that what is pertinent is whether the observed exchange rate variability since 1973 has been 'excessive'. This line of argument is based on the perception of the exchange rate as the relative price of two durable assets (moneys). Frenkel (1983), for example, has argued that 'The central insight of the modern approach to the analysis of exchange rates is the notion that the exchange rate, being the relative price of two durable assets [moneys], can best be analysed within a framework that is appropriate for the analysis of asset prices' (p. 8). The treatment of the exchange rate as an asset price necessarily implies that it will be highly sensitive to changes in expectations regarding future events and policies. Therefore, volatile expectations will result in volatile exchange rates. Now, if the foreign exchange market is efficient and exchange rate expectations are continuously revised in response to new information, then inevitably exchange rate changes will be highly unpredictable.

The perception of the exchange rate as an asset price distinguishes it from wages and goods' prices. The exchange rate will be highly responsive to changes in expectations about the future while wages and goods' prices tend to be more sticky in the short run as they predominantly reflect contractual obligations made in the past. Consequently, in periods of highly volatile expectations we should expect to observe sharp deviations from purchasing power parity. That is, the treatment of the exchange rate as an asset price implies that real exchange rates will be volatile and unpredictable.

Frenkel (1983) argued that exchange rate behaviour since 1973 is consistent with 'the hypotheses that in recent years the foreign exchange market behaved as an efficient asset market and that much of the volatility of exchange rates reflected frequent and large changes in expectations concerning the future' (p. 12). If exchange rates have behaved as asset prices since 1973, then it is not appropriate to compare exchange rate volatility with the volatility of inflation rates. That the latter is significantly lower is to be expected. Exchange rate volatility must be compared with the volatility of other asset prices. Frenkel and Goldstein (1986) note that exchange rate variability has been smaller than, for example, the volatility of stock market prices, short-term interest rates, or commodity prices. Therefore, it is possible to argue that the observed exchange rate volatility since 1973 has not been 'excessive'.

Supporters of flexible exchange rates accept that it is conceivable that exchange rate uncertainty could discourage international trade. However, they argue that there is no reason why this should necessarily happen. The forward exchange market and options markets allow economic agents to safeguard against exchange risk. This argument is less than convincing. First, many countries simply do not have forward exchange markets. Second, the forward exchange market, even when highly developed, does not offer cover opportunities over the longer run. Third, the economic agent can employ the forward market over individual transactions. However, as Lanyi (1969) noted this is not the same as cover for engaging in international trade as an economic activity. Fourth, the costs of exchange risk management can be more easily absorbed by large companies than by small businesses. To this extent, then, it is arguable that exchange rate flexibility discourages competition.

It is also maintained that had it not been for exchange rate flexibility countries would have resorted to the erection of new trade barriers and the imposition of stringent controls on capital movements since 1973. That is, without exchange rate flexibility the rate of growth of international trade would have declined even more sharply. This is a rather difficult proposition to support. Acceptance of it implies that belief in the benefits of exchange rate flexibility becomes a matter of faith.

Exchange rate misalignment

Critics of the post-1973 exchange rate regime argue that the world economy has suffered not only because of eschange rate volatility but also because of persistent exchange rate misalignments. Williamson (1983b) defines misalignment as a 'persistent departure of the exchange rate from its long-run equilibrium level' (p. 10). Sterling exchange rates during 1979–81 and dollar exchange rates during 1981–5 are examples of grossly misaligned exchange rates. Critics of exchange rate flexibility maintain that exchange rate misalignments impose costs on economies by inducing misallocation of resources, increases in unemployment and distortions in capital formation, and by encouraging protectionist forces.

Supporters of exchange rate flexibility argue that the effects of misalignments are often exaggerated. What may appear as grossly misaligned exchange rates may in fact be the outcome of changes in the equilibrium relative price of countries' national outputs. Second, it is noted that misalignments of exchange rates were also a feature of the Bretton Woods system. Third, it is observed that the magnitude of a particular misalignment crucially depends on what is judged to be the 'equilibrium' exchange rate. Given that there is no consensus on how the latter can be estimated at any moment in time, it follows that estimates of misalignments are somewhat arbitrary.

Supporters of flexible exchange rates are quite right when arguing exchange rate misalignments cannot be estimated with a high degree of accuracy. However, this is less than persuasive when defending the post-1973 exchange rate regime. The sterling exchange rates during 1979–81 were grossly misaligned. The precise magnitude of the misalignment is not of particular importance. What can be said with confidence is that had the UK authorities intervened and prevented sterling from appreciating as sharply as it did, the country's manufacturing sector would not have contracted as dramatically and manufacturing output would have reached its 1979 level before 1987. It is perfectly true that under the Bretton Woods system misalignments did occur. But critics of exchange rate flexibility do not argue for the restoration of that system. The Bretton Woods model is not the only alternative to the current 'non-system'.

Finally, the proposition that what appear as exchange rate misalignments may in fact be equilibrating changes will be discussed later as it is one of the arguments in favour of exchange rate flexibility.

Divergent economic policies

Exchange rate volatility and misalignments are largely symptoms of countries' pursuing divergent and variable economic policies. With the collapse of the Bretton Woods system in 1973 countries ceased to be constrained by any exchange rate obligations. Thus economic policies and particularly monetary policies became increasingly divergent even though the major industrial countries all adopted the control of inflation as their principal policy priority after the mid-1970s.

Policy autonomy was claimed to be the main advantage of flexible exchange rates. Under such a system, its advocates in the 1950s and 1960s argued that countries would have the ability to determine their money supply growth rates and, therefore, their rates of inflation. Exchange rate flexibility would insulate the individual economy from external monetary disturbances while, if it acted 'irresponsibly', the rest of the world would not have to import inflation. For example, Laidler (1982) argued that 'only a flexible exchange rate regime permits each country to choose its own degree of monetary discipline independently of the choices made by others' (p. 166). Exchange rate flexibility, however, did not prove to be particularly effective in enabling countries to control inflation. It was largely the recognition that inflation cannot be controlled by countries acting unilaterally that prompted EEC member countries to establish the European Monetary System (EMS) in March 1979. The objective of the system was to create a 'zone of monetary stability' through the 'monetary cooperation' of member countries. The conditions that inspired the creation of the system were described as follows by the Commission (European Communities, 1984):

> During the 1970s it became apparent that Community monitoring and cooperation was in some ways a failure. That failure was, indeed, one of the main reasons why the first attempts to introduce a stable exchange rate system in the Community [the 'Snake'] did not work out very well. Faced with a seriously disturbed international environment where fixed exchange relations had been abandoned and oil prices were soaring, the member countries sometimes opted for economic policy choices which were fundamentally different; no one being really prepared to submit to an exchange rate constraint if that entailed sacrificing a domestic aim. (p. 2)

Similarly Bilson (1979) interpreted the establishment of the EMS as 'the first step back from the rugged individualism and national self-interest that lay behind the formal acceptance of flexible exchange rates at the Jamaica meetings of the International Monetary Fund in January 1976' (p. 154). Ludlow (1982) in discussing the politico-economic background to the creation of the EMS explained that France's enthusiasm for the system was largely motivated by the judgement that it would facilitate the acceptance and success of the anti-inflation policies of the government of the day. In this respect the Commission (EC, 1984) noted that 'Attitudes converged on recognising that the main thrust of national economic policies should be directed towards achieving price stabilisation, and that the level to be desired was that of the most successful performer on this front' (p. 3). As is well documented, the EMS has been highly successful in reducing exchange rate volatility and inflation rates in member countries.[3]

Defenders of exchange rate flexibility dispute the proposition that the post-1973 regime has resulted in countries not being subject to any policy discipline. Laidler (1982) observed that in 'a world whose political organisation is such that the individual nation state is the highest level at which effective and responsible government exists' it follows that 'it is at the level of the individual nation state that the policies determining inflation rates are going to be debated and implemented' (p. 165). Laidler's argument implies that external constraints cannot be imposed on a country's government. Only the electorate can impose policy discipline on a government. It may, therefore, be said that exchange rate flexibility was not an obstacle to the USA and the UK adopting policies which were successful in reducing inflation during the 1980s. The impetus for the adoption of these policies was generated by internal pressures.

It is beyond dispute that governments primarily respond to domestic pressures. However, it is not entirely clear that these pressures on a government are not partly determined by the prevailing exchange rate regime. Second, it is doubtful whether the effectiveness of policies adopted in response to domestic pressures is not significantly determined by the country's exchange rate policy. The examples of the UK and US experiences are not entirely convincing as a response to the argument that under the current exchange rate regime countries are not subject to an effective policy discipline and, therefore, by acting in an uncoordinated fashion increase the costs of achieving their policy objectives. The UK would not have been less successful in reducing its inflation rate if it were a member of the EMS. But if it were a member, the costs of reducing inflation in terms of increases in unemployment would certainly have been less severe. Further, it is arguable that the success of the UK was largely due to the fact that EMS member countries, collectively, and the United States introduced anti-inflation policies at the same time, rather than to the unilaterally determined policies of the British government. On the other hand, the USA, because of its size, does enjoy a high degree of policy autonomy which is largely independent of the nature of the prevailing exchange rate regime.

Exchange rate expectations

Exchange rate volatility also reflects the absence under the current regime of an 'anchor' for exchange rate expectations. Thus new information leads to large and unpredictable exchange rate changes. But just as important, the absence of such an anchor may result in new information or market rumours generating bandwagon effects and speculative 'bubbles' with the exchange rate becoming increasingly divorced from its fundamental determinants.

Defenders of exchange rate flexibility argue, as already noted, that observed exchange rate changes hve not been 'excessive' and that they are primarily equilibrating in character. Furthermore they dismiss speculative 'bubbles' on empirical grounds.

The empirical evidence appears to favour the critics of exchange rate flexibility. Gros (1987) employed the monetary and portfolio balance models of exchange rate determination in testing the hypothesis that the variability of exchange rates is determined by the variability of the fundamental determinants of exchange rates. His principal finding is that the variability of the fundamentals does explain the variability of the intra-EMS exchange rates. However, in the cases of the German mark/dollar, German mark/yen and German mark/Swiss franc exchange rates, the variability of the fundamentals is much smaller than the variability of these exchange rates. Gros concludes that his results imply that 'the EMS has created an environment in which the variability of the exchange rates has been reduced to the minimum that can be achieved given the variability in the fundamentals' (p. 10). Therefore, even if exchange rate misalignments and volatility cannot adequately be explained in terms of speculative 'bubbles' the absence of an expectations anchor under the current regime does appear to result in exchange rates changing in directions inconsistent with the evolution of their fundamental determinants. The further implication is that changes in the non-EMS exchange rates have been 'excessive'.

The case for exchange rate flexibility

The defence of the current regime does not rest solely on the responses made to the criticisms advanced by the opponents of exchange rate flexibility. Proponents of flexible exchange rates maintain that there is a positive case that can be made and that the post-1973 regime has had beneficial effects for the world economy. The arguments for exchange rate flexibility will now be considered.

Flexibility of relative prices

Supporters of exchange rate flexibility note that real economic conditions which necessitate adjustments in the relative prices of national outputs are continuously changing. If exchange rates are fixed, then relative price changes will occur gradually via changes in national price levels. But under flexible exchange rates these relative price adjustments are effected much more rapidly through exchange rate changes. Frenkel and Goldstein (1986) in elaborating this argument note that 'there is no general presumption that slow adjustment of relative prices is preferable to rapid adjustment' (p. 644), while Frenkel and Mussa (1980) suggest that 'Given the apparent stickiness of national price levels, the flexibility of relative prices of national outputs (that is, real exchange rates) provided by floating exchange rates may contribute to the efficient functioning of the economic system' (p. 379). This proposition assumes that the rapid adjustment of relative prices of national outputs will necessarily be accompanied by rapid reallocation of resources. However, there is no reason why this should necessarily be the case. McKinnon (1981) has suggested that exchange rate unpredictability may result in a tendency among economic agents to delay changes in existing patterns of resource allocations until they are convinced that a particular trend in exchange rates will not be reversed. In this case the implication is that the price mechanism becomes less efficient in transmitting information. Therefore, even if it is true that what appear to be misaligned exchange rates are in fact exchange rates which reflect new equilibrium values of the relative prices of national outputs, this in itself does not necessarily indicate a more efficient functioning of the economic system. It is equally plausible, and perhaps more probable, that real exchange rate unpredictability will result in the price mechanism becoming less efficient.

Adjustments to shocks

Frenkel (1983), among others, maintains that flexible exchange rates have not been a failure. Foreign exchange markets have efficiently absorbed the shocks and disturbances experienced since 1973. Frenkel (1983) suggests that since goods' prices tend to be sticky 'it may be desirable to allow for "excessive" adjustment in some other prices' such as the exchange rate. Reliance on the foreign exchange market as an absorber of disturbances may be preferable to allowing these disturbances to affect other markets, 'such as labor markets, where they cannot be dealt with in as efficient a manner' (p. 18).

   This argument rests on the assumption that the foreign exchange market plays a useful role as a shock absorber allowing the economy time to effect the adjustments required by particular disturbances and shocks. However, if we were to consider the case of the UK during 1979–81 the relative advantages of the foreign exchange market in absorbing shocks could not be judged to provide an adequate basis for presevering with flexible exchange rates. As already noted the sharp appreciation of sterling resulted in the dramatic contraction of the manufacturing sector. It is difficult to accept that the efficiency of the foreign exchange market during that period yielded benefits exceeding the costs of allowing sterling to appreciate as sharply as it did. Nor is it clear that the UK has enjoyed a superior economic performance in comparison to the EMS.

Monetary autonomy

Supporters of exchange rate flexibility continue to argue that it allows countries to enjoy the ability to control their own money supply growth rates and, therefore, determine their long-run rates of inflation. They do accept that the insulation properties of exchange rate flexibility have not proved to be as effective as was anticipated in the 1950s and 1960s and that exchange rate changes are a means via which even monetary disturbances can be transmitted across countries in the short-to-medium term. However, it is maintained, exchange rate flexibility does allow each country to choose its long-run rate of inflation.

Critics respond by observing that governments have not found the control of the money supply growth rate a particularly easy task. This has been specially true in the case of the UK where the government has effectively abandoned its attempts to control the money supply since the autumn of 1985. It follows, then, that if the money supply growth rate cannot be controlled, exchange rate flexibility is not necessary for the control of inflation.

A more important argument, however, against the proposition that under flexible exchange rates countries can choose their inflation rates rests on the implications of the currency substitution literature. If economic agents hold diversified currency portfolios, then exchange rate flexibility cannot ensure a country's autonomy and ability to determine its own long-run rate of inflation. Each country's inflation rate will be partly determined by foreign money supply growth rates. McKinnon (1982) presented empirical evidence indicating that countries' rates of inflation have been affected by the *world* money supply growth rate even in the period after 1973. However sceptical one may be regarding the quantitative importance of currency substitution, it is the case that in the presence of diversified currency portfolios which systematically respond to changes in particular variables the control of the money supply growth rate is not sufficient for a country to determine its rate of inflation.

Foreign exchange market efficiency

Important in the defence of the record of exchange rate flexibility is the assertion that foreign exchange markets have behaved since 1973 as efficient asset markets. The relevance of this assertion is assessing the case for flexible exchange rates crucially depends on the empirical findings of the various studies of foreign exchange market behaviour.[4] As already noted, exchange rates since 1973 have exhibited characteristics very similar to those associated with asset prices. However, there is no theory of the equilibrium exchange rate that is generally accepted.[5] But testing foreign exchange market efficiency does require such a theory. If we do not know what is the equilibrium exchange rate then it is difficult to assess whether the market-determined rate is in fact the equilibrium rate. The observation, for example, that the forward exchange rate premium/discount accounts for a very small part of the actual exchange rate with the forecast errors not containing any systematic information is not sufficient to establish the efficiency of the foreign exchange market. Levich (1985), for example, has commented: 'In the absence of agreement on a hypothesis about the equilibrium exchange rate, it is not possible either to prove or disprove the efficiency hypothesis in the foreign exchange market' (p. 1025).

A summary assessment

Critics of exchange rate flexibility have argued that the post-1973 exchange rate regime has been a failure. Proponents of flexible exchange rates accept that a number of the criticisms are not without foundation. However, they do maintain that the weaknesses of the current regime are often exaggerated while its strengths do not receive sufficient praise. Further, they suggest that these weaknesses are not more severe than those of the Bretton Woods system.[6] Such a contrast in the assessment of the performance of the post-1973 regime can be identified when comparing the conclusions and recommendations of the reports on the international monetary system prepared by the Group of Ten and the Group of Twenty-Four.[7] The former states:

> The Deputies have concluded that the basic structure of the present system, as reflected in the Articles of Agreement of the IMF, has provided the essential flexibility for individual nations and the international community as a whole to respond constructively to a period of major adjustment to global change. *They agree that the fundamental approach of the Articles remains valid and that the key elements of the current international monetary system require no major institutional change.*
>
> (paragraph 97, p. 56, italics added)

In contrast, the Group of Twenty-Four report concludes that 'the experience with the present exchange rate system has not been satisfactory' (paragraph 2, p. 60) and goes on to argue that:

> Exchange rate stability should be an important objective of policy, instead of being a residual of other policy actions of individual countries, as is the case at present. *It is necessary to devise an exchange rate system to overcome the*

recognised rigidities of the par value system and the destabilising uncertainties of floating rates.

(paragraph 4, p. 60, italics added)

Thus it is suggested that:

Adoption of target zones for the exchange rates of major currencies could help achieve the objective of exchange rate stability and sustainable levels of payments balances.

(paragraph 5, p. 60)[8]

On the other hand, the Group of Ten consistently with its judgement that the current regime requires 'no major institutional change' indicates that there is a need to improve its functioning

in order to foster greater stability by promoting convergence of economic performances through the adoption of sound and compatible policies in IMF member countries. The conclusions of the Deputies are based on this approach and call for enhanced cooperation and a stronger role for the IMF.

(paragraph 98, p. 56).

It is evident, then, that though there is a consensus on the desirability of greater exchange rate stability there are sharp differences on how this could be achieved.

Improving the current regime

The Group of Ten suggests that the performance of the current regime could be improved by countries adopting 'sound and compatible policies'. It is claimed that compatibility of policies can be achieved if each country when determining its policies does take into account the effects of its decisions on the rest of the world. If policies are thus determined, inevitably greater exchange rate stability will emerge. The pursuit of policy compatibility will foster greater policy co-ordination. Such co-ordination will be greatly facilitated by countries maintaining 'close and continuing co-operation and a strengthening of international surveillance' (paragraph 33, p. 48).

One may justifiably view this line of argument for the improvement of the current regime with extreme scepticism. It is beyond dispute that if countries were to co-operate in co-ordinating their policies so that their compatibility was ensured, exchange rates would be much less volatile than they have been since 1973. But acceptance of the principle that policy co-ordination is desirable is not sufficient to persuade countries to co-ordinate their policies in practice. Second, if countries were to behave in such a fashion, without being under any obligation to do so, then a system of fixed exchange rates would be as viable and durable as a system of flexible exchange rates. The basic question is how the exchange rate system can induce countries to engage in policy co-ordination. The current regime has failed in promoting convergent national economic policies because it has no mechanism encouraging policy co-ordination. In this context the experience of the EMS member countries is instructive. Prior to the establishment of the system they were pursuing divergent economic policies. After 1979 this was significantly changed. The Commission (EC, 1984) in its evaluation of the performance of the system concluded that 'The most striking achievement recorded is surely the progress that has been made towards economic policy convergence; there is no doubt that this, recent, progress was made possible by the EMS, which provided the necessary framework' (p. 18). The important contribution that a formal mechanism can play in preventing countries from giving in to the temptation of adopting policies regardless of their external implications was demonstrated in the case, among others, of France in the early 1980s which abandoned policies because of their incompatibility with continued membership of the EMS.

The Group of Ten advocates the strengthening of international surveillance which, it believes, can be achieved within the present institutional setting. The report states that 'The Deputies emphasize that strengthened surveillance requires enhanced dialogue and persuasion through peer pressure, rather than mechanically imposed external constraints' (paragraph 38, p. 48). It is agreed that surveillance involves highly sensitive issues and the report stresses that countries must be treated symmetrically. Further, it is argued that surveillance must encompass not only macroeconomic policies but also microeconomic policies if it is to lead to the improvement of the functioning of the current exchange rate regime.

This proposal of the Group of Ten is of doubtful usefulness. The Group of Ten fails to explain why surveillance during the period of floating exchange rates 'has not been as effective as desirable in influencing national policies and in promoting underlying economic and financial conditions conducive to exchange rate stability' (paragraph 36, p. 48). It may well be that this failure is due to the absence of 'mechanically imposed external constraints'. However, as the Group of Ten notes, surveillance does involve sensitive issues. It is the political unacceptability of surveillance that deprives it of any effectiveness. Surely 'mechanically imposed external constraints' are less politically unacceptable. It is easier for an EMS country to formulate its policies so as to be consistent with its membership of the system than to revise its policies to accord with the views expressed by some international institution, be it the IMF, OECD, or GATT.

Similarly it is difficult to see how 'enhanced dialogue and persuasion through peer pressure' on their own could be effective in persuading countries to adopt policies likely to lead to greater exchange rate stability. Peer pressures have not been particularly successful in convincing the United States of the desirability of reducing its budget deficit.

The Group of Ten also suggests the liberalisation of capital markets and declares itself against capital controls. Such an objective is desirable for the advanced industrial countries. However, it cannot be a principal feature of an international monetary system. By definition such a system must cater for the interests of all countries. It follows, then, that the Third World countries cannot be ignored. To expect them to abandon capital controls and protectionism would reveal lack of political understanding of these countries' special circumstances.

Exchange rate flexibility has failed to live up to the expectations of its advocates because it provides no inducement to countries to pursue the policies that would ensure its success. The proposals to reform the current regime without major institutional changes could not alter its unsatisfactory nature. Its supporters have failed to demonstrate that formal external constraints are not a necessary feature of a smoothly functioning and viable international monetary system. In assessing the need for such constraints the experience of the Bretton Woods system is irrelevant. The Bretton Woods system failed, as Triffin has been arguing for decades, because of the role played by the dollar. The lesson from this failure is not that a system of fixed exchange rate is not viable but that a system which rests on a national currency which is also an international currency is inherently unstable and lacking in durability. The EMS has performed successfully and even Sir Alan Walters would not predict that its demise is imminent.

Target zones for exchange rates

Target zones for exchange rates were first proposed by Williamson (1983b) as the basis for a new international monetary system. As already noted the Group of Twenty-Four suggested that the adoption of such target zones 'could help achieve the objective of exchange rate stability and a sustainable pattern of payments balances'. As Frenkel and Goldstein (1986) in their excellent survey of the arguments for and against the adoption of target zones observe, a variety of arrangements are consistent with the principal features of the scheme first suggested by Williamson.

A system of target zones would involve countries' establishing target zones for the exchange rates and being expected to conduct their monetary policies so as to ensure that actual exchange rates remain within the target zones. However, such a system would not necessarily require countries to commit themselves to intervene in the foreign exchange market to maintain exchange rates within the target zones. Further, target zones are not envisaged to be fixed. Indeed, proposals for their adoption stress the need for the target zones to be reviewed periodically and altered if thought necessary. Williamson (1983b) explained that 'a system of target zones is a *form of floating*, rather than a form of pegging. Target zones have "soft margins" which the authorities are *not* committed to defending' (p. 65, italics in original).

A system of target zones is claimed to possess a number of advantages. First, it would promote greater policy co-ordination since target zones would be the outcome of negotiated agreements. Countries that adopted deviant policies would be identifiable even if the zones were wide and frequently revised. Second, target zones would impose some policy discipline since they would involve a constraint on countries' monetary and fiscal policies. Third, target zones would provide an anchor for exchange rate expectations. In brief, advocates of the target zones system maintain that its adoption would cure the ills of the current regime. Induced policy discipline and co-ordination would ensure greater exchange rate predictability and minimise, if not eliminate, exchange rate misalignments. Such a system, further, would command the support of the Third World countries. As already noted, the Group of Twenty-Four considered target zones involving the currencies of the main industrial countries as a potential basis for a system which could promote exchange rate stability.

The determination of target zones would depend on estimates of the 'equilibrium' real exchange rate. Williamson (1983b) identified this rate with the purchasing power parity (PPP) rate. However, as Frenkel and Goldstein (1986) observe, the use of PPP as the basis for computing the equilibrium exchange rate may involve a number of difficulties. First, real disturbances require that exchange rates deviate from their PPP values. Therefore, changes in equilibrium real exchange rates may not be as easy to calculate. Second, PPP-based estimates of the equilibrium exchange rate will not necessarily be credible to market participants. Finally, there are the difficulties associated with choosing between the various price indices and base periods when employing PPP.

Frenkel and Goldstein (1986) consider the possibility of estimating equilibrium exchange rates by using some structural model of exchange rate determination. The weakness of such an approach is that all structural models so far employed in the empirical literature have been shown to perform very poorly when used for forecasting purposes.

The third method of calculating the equilibrium exchange rate involves the underlying balance approach. It defines the real equilibrium exchange rate as that rate which would make the 'underlying' current account equal to 'normal' net capital flows. Frankel and Goldstein (1986) observe that the concept of 'normal' net capital flows is so ambiguous as to cast serious doubts on the usefulness of the underlying balance approach.

In brief, a major difficulty in the case for a system of target zones is the lack of a consensus on how the equilibrium exchange rate can be estimated with a reasonable degree of confidence. However, that the equilibrium exchange rate may not be easy to estimate accurately is not sufficient to dismiss the target zones system on the grounds that it is not feasible.

If a target zones system were to deliver exchange rate stability it should possess certain characteristics. First, if it were to serve as an expectations anchor then target zones should be publicly known. Second, the width of the zones should not be so large as to allow the emergence of significant exchange rate misalignments. Third, countries should be firmly committed to keeping the exchange rates within the agreed zones and accordingly adjust their fiscal and monetary policies. Fourth, revisions of the zones should not occur at predetermined intervals; instead, countries should resort to such revisions only when it is evidently necessary; that is, the system should be a form of pegging rather than a form of floating and bear a close resemblance to the EMS.

Conclusions

The current regime deserves the label 'non-system'. As such its perform-ance cannot be improved without major institutional changes. Exchange rate flexibility has proved to be a weak basis for international monetary relationships. The failure of the post-1973 regime contrasts sharply with the success of the EMS. But the latter reflects above all the *political* commitment of member countries to the system. However, though the case of an international system to replace the present non-system is over-whelming the political will is lacking. The USA, though no longer the dominant economy, continues to be the most powerful one. Therefore, there exist strong incentives for it to persist with its nationalistic policies. But the relative decline of the United States, in both economic and political terms, is likely to continue, particularly as Europe moves towards and beyond 1992. As the balance of political power alters, circumstances may develop which will generate the political will necessary for the establish-ment of a viable international monetary system. But it is difficult to see this occurring sooner rather than later.

Notes

1 See Friedman, 1953; Meade, 1955; Sohmen, 1961; and Johnson, 1972.
2 See also IMF, 1984. This study concludes that there is no robust evidence to support the

proposition that exchange rate variability has discouraged international trade.
3 For an excellent assessment of the performance of the EMS see Gros and Thygesen, 1988.
4 For a survey of this literature see Levich, 1985.
5 For a survey of the literature on the balance of payments and exchange rates see Frenkel and Mussa, 1985.
6 The respective positions and fully presented in Frenkel and Goldstein, 1986, and in Crockett and Goldstein, 1987.
7 Both reports are reprinted in Crockett and Goldstein, 1987, where they are fully discussed.
8 The Group of Twenty-Four also recommends the introduction of objective indicators; see Crockett and Goldstein, 1987.

References

Bilson, G. F. O. (1979). 'Why the Deutschmark could trouble the EMS', *Euromoney*, Euromoney Publications Ltd., London.

Crockett, A. and Goldstein, M. (1987). *Strengthening the International Monetary System: Exchange Rates, Surveillance, and Objective Indicators*, Occasional Paper 50, International Monetary Fund, Washington, DC.

Cushman, D. O. (1983). 'The effects of real exchange risk on international trade', *Journal of International Trade*, vol. 15, pp. 45–63.

De Grauwe, P. (1988). 'Exchange rate variability and the slowdown in growth of international trade', *International Monetary Fund Staff Papers*, vol. 35, pp. 63–84.

European Communities (1984). *Five Years of Monetary Cooperation in Europe*, Communication from the Commission to the Council, Brussels, COM(84), Final.

Frenkel, J. A. (1983). 'Turbulence in the foreign exchange markets and macroeconomic policies', in D. Bigman and T. Taya (eds), *Exchange Rate and Trade Instability: Causes, Consequences and Remedies* (Cambridge, Mass.: Bullinger).

Frenkel, J. A. and Goldstein, M. (1986). 'A guide to target zones', *International Monetary Fund Staff Papers*, vol. 33, pp. 633–73.

Frenkel, J. A. and Mussa, M. (1980). 'The efficiency of foreign exchange markets and measures of turbulence', *American Economic Review*, vol. 70, pp. 374–81.

Frenkel, J. A. and Mussa, M. (1985), 'Asset markets, exchange rates, and the balance of payments', in R. W. Jones and P. B. Kenen (eds), *Handbook of International Economics*, vol. 2 (Amsterdam: North-Holland).

Friedman, M. (1953). 'The case for flexible exchange rates', in *Essays in Positive Economics* (Chicago: University of Chicago Press).

Gros, D. (1987). 'On the volatility of exchange rates: tests of monetary and portfolio balance models of exchange rate determination', Centre for European Policy Studies Working Document, no. 31, Brussels.

Gros, D. and Thygesen, N. (1988). *The EMS: Achievements, Current Issues and Directions for the Future*, Centre for European Policy Studies Paper, no. 35, Brussels.

International Monetary Fund (1984). *Exchange Rate Volatility and World Trade*, Occasional Paper 28, Washington, DC.

Johnson, H. G. (1972). 'The case for flexible exchange rates, 1969', in H. G. Johnson (ed.), *Further Essays in Monetary Economics* (London: Allen & Unwin).

Laidler, D. (1982). 'The case for flexible exchange rates in 1980', in M. Sumner and G. Zis (eds), *European Monetary Union* (London: Macmillan).

Lanyi, A. (1969). *The Case for Flexible Exchange Rates Reconsidered*, Essays in International Finance, no. 72, Princeton University, International Finance Section, Princeton, New Jersey.

Levich, R. M. (1985). 'Empirical studies of exchange rates: price behaviour, rate deter-
   mination and market efficiency', in R. W. Jones and P. B. Kenen (eds), *Handbook of Inter-
   national Economics*, vol. 2 (Amsterdam: North-Holland).
Ludlow, P. (1982). *The Making of the European Monetary System* (London: Butterworth
   Scientific).
McKinnon, R. I. (1981). 'Exchange rate instability, trade imbalances and monetary policies in
   Japan, Europe and the United States', in P. Oppenheimer (ed.), *Issues in International
   Economics* (Boston: Routledge & Kegan Paul).
McKinnon, R. I. (1982). 'Currency substitution and instability in the world dollar standard',
   American Economic Review, vol. 72, pp. 320–33.
Meade, J. (1955). 'The case for variable exchange rates', *Three Banks Review*, pp. 3–27.
Sohmen, E. (1961). *Flexible Exchange Rates* (Chicago: Chicago University Press).
Triffin, R. (1982). 'The world monetary scandal: sources...and cures', *Economic Notes*,
   pp. 1–19.
Williamson, J. (1983a). *The Open Economy and the World Economy* (New York: Basic
   Books).
Williamson, J. (1983b). *The Exchange Rate System* (Washington, DC: Institute for Inter-
   national Economics).

5

Integration into the EMS: the UK debate

Michael Artis

Introduction

At the heart of the European Monetary System is the commitment of the member countries to maintain their bilateral exchange rates within relatively narrow bands. To enable them to do this, the system disposes of various credit facilities and offers the opportunity for a regulated breach of this commitment in the form of agreed realignments. Given the critical role of this 'exchange rate mechanism' (ERM) it has become customary to refer to the prospect of the pound sterling being put into it as that of 'the UK joining the EMS', though in fact the UK already is formally a member of the system and participates in full in other aspects of its operation.

As is well known, the UK has displayed a long-standing reluctance to integrate fully into the EMS in this sense, a policy stance which in 1987 came to be seen as substantially modified as membership of the ERM was then for a period simulated in an experiment in which sterling was kept within an ERM-style ($\pm 2\frac{1}{4}\%$) band *vis-à-vis* the DM, with £1 = 3DM as the top of the band. Official confirmation of what was observable in the market as a new policy was made available by the Chancellor of the Exchequer, only to be decisively rejected in a statement from the Prime Minister reiterating the customary British position on formal membership; early in 1988 the DM peg was removed and sterling appreciated sharply through the top of the previous band.

The DM-pegging policy might be seen as a genuine experiment designed to test for the implications of a formal commitment; as a political action designed (if successful) to quell remaining doubts about the wisdom of a formal commitment; or as an episode in independent policy-making, a full commitment waiting on other developments. Whatever the precise intentions behind the policy it is clear that it was in tune with what has been a considerable conversion of opinion at all levels in the UK towards a more favourable attitude on formal entry into the ERM. A landmark was the publication in 1983 of a report from the House of Lords which concluded (ibid., p. xxiv) that 'the balance of advantage lies in early, though not necessarily immediate entry'. The perpetuation of the doctrine of 'unripe time' was becoming increasingly less acceptable.[1]

This change in opinion, though real, should not be allowed to conceal the fact that formal membership of the ERM appeals to different groups for different reasons. Some see in it a means to stabilise the real rate of exchange, others the means to stabilise the nominal rate of exchange against a low-inflation country. In opposition, there are, equally, those who see participation in the ERM as resigning the UK's ability to control its own competitiveness and those who see in it an unacceptable erosion of monetary independence.

All these viewpoints have a foothold in reality and the changing balance of views reflects a combination of the evolving experience of the EMS in operation and the experience of the UK itself in executing a monetary policy which in 1979, at least, was seen as radically new, something indeed of a 'laboratory experiment', to use Tobin's (1981) description.

In the next section of the paper we review what appear to be the central achievements of the EMS to date. But there are a number of reasons for thinking that the EMS may be at something of a crossroads in terms of its future development, so the subsequent section is devoted to a consideration of this question. After that we briefly review the evolution of the experiment in monetary policy conducted in the UK since 1979. We then broach the chief issues around which opinions in favour of, and opposed to, UK participation in the EMS have collected. This leads on to a speculative conclusion which reviews possible developments or variations of the terms of membership, which might decisively influence a British decision on integration.

I The EMS to date

The three most arresting claims made for the EMS (apart from the fact that in surviving it has defied the many predictions of its early demise!) are that

it has reduced the volatility of exchange rates for its members;
it has reduced the extent of exchange rate misalignment suffered by its members;
it has provided a framework for successful counter-inflation policies.

The *volatility* of exchange rates is a short-run, 'high-frequency' concept, referring to the short-run variability of exchange rates. Since the EMS provides for realignments (and such realignments have taken place on eleven occasions so far – see Table 5.1), it is not a foregone conclusion that

Table 5.1 Realignments of EMS central rates, per cent

						Dates of realignments					
	24/9 1979	30/11 1979	22/3 1981	5/10 1981	22/2 1982	14/6 1982	21/3 1983	21/7 1985	7/4 1986	4/8 1986	12/1 1987
Belgian franc	0.0	0.0	0.0	0.0	−8.5	0.0	+1.5	+2.0	+1.0	0.0	+2.0
Danish krone	−2.9	−4.8	0.0	0.0	−3.0	0.0	+2.5	+2.0	+1.0	0.0	0.0
West German mark	+2.0	0.0	0.0	+5.5	0.0	+4.25	+5.5	+2.0	+3.0	0.0	+3.0
French franc	0.0	0.0	0.0	−3.0	0.0	−5.75	−2.5	+2.0	−3.0	0.0	0.0
Irish punt	0.0	0.0	0.0	0.0	0.0	0.0	−3.5	+2.0	0.0	−8.0	0.0
Italian lira	0.0	0.0	−6.0	−3.0	0.0	−2.75	−2.5	−6.0	0.0	0.0	0.0
Dutch guilder	0.0	0.0	0.0	+5.5	0.0	+4.25	+3.5	+2.0	+3.0	0.0	+3.0

it has stabilised exchange rates. The standard test for whether or not it has done so is to compare some measure of variability of EMS exchange rates before and after the formation of the system with a similar measure of variability for a 'control group' of non-EMS currencies. This approach was popularised by Ungerer *et al.* (1983) and extended more recently (Ungerer *et al.*, 1986). It has also been used by a large number of other researchers, so that a mass of results is available involving a variety of measures of variability, data frequency, control groups and timing. A technical problem with the approach is that the variability measures commonly employed (variance-related measures) assume that the distribution of exchange rate changes is normal, whereas there is good evidence that such distributions in fact tend to have fatter tails and are more highly peaked than the normal. In the light of this consideration, Artis and Taylor (1988) have deployed a semi-nonparametric ranking test approach to the question which, though not distribution-free, is executed for a variety of candidate leptokurtic distributions as well as the normal. A convenient summary of their results is given in Tables 5.2–5.

Tables 5.2 and 5.3 give the results of the volatility tests when these are applied to effective exchange rate indices where the weights are restricted to currencies participating in the exchange rate mechanism of the EMS: thus, for an ERM participant, these are indices of intra-ERM exchange rates. As a significantly positive value of the statistic indicates a reduction in volatility and a negative one an increase,[2] it can readily be seen that the EMS has on this test exerted a powerful stabilising influence on exchange rates within the participating countries, contrasting with the position for UK sterling and, even more strongly, with that for the US dollar where a strong increase in volatility is indicated. When, as in Tables 5.4 and 5.5 the full effective (MERM) exchange rate indices of the IMF are used, the force of this conclusion is moderated somewhat: indeed for *nominal* IMF effective rates only the Italian lira and West German mark seem to show a marked reduction in volatility (by contrast there is a significant rise in dollar and UK sterling volatility), though for *real* rates, a significant reduction in volatility is exhibited for *all* ERM currencies (with only slightly less marked increase in volatility for the US dollar).

These results are in line with those of the mass of tests conducted using the standard approach, so it seems fair to say that there is massively convincing unanimity about the claim that the EMS has stabilised bilateral real and nominal intra-EMS exchange rates for its members, though it has not been so successful in stabilising effective exchange rate indices where there is some suggestion that the stabilising effect on intra-system exchange rates has been partially offset, at least, by increased variability in exchange rates *vis-à-vis* non-member currencies.[3]

Table 5.2   Test statistics for a shift in exchange rate volatility after March 1979: nominal effective (ERM) rates

Currency	Normal	Logistic	Double exponential	Cauchy
Danish krone	4.97 (0.34 E-6)	4.15 (0.16 E-4)	4.01 (0.30 E-4)	3.84 (0.61 E-4)
Belgian franc	5.29 (0.61 E-7)	4.54 (0.27 E-5)	4.52 (0.30 E-5)	5.14 (0.13 E-6)
French franc	5.28 (0.60 E-7)	4.37 (0.61 E-5)	4.32 (0.72 E-5)	4.38 (0.60 E-5)
Italian lira	5.26 (0.73 E-7)	4.32 (0.78 E-5)	4.29 (0.92 E-5)	4.17 (0.15 E-5)
Dutch guilder	5.64 (0.86 E-8)	4.66 (0.16 E-5)	4.57 (0.25 E-5)	4.32 (0.49 E-5)
West German mark	5.80 (0.33 E-8)	4.78 (0.85 E-6)	4.80 (0.81 E-6)	4.74 (0.10 E-5)
US dollar	−2.17 (0.01)	−1.95 (0.02)	−2.01 (0.02)	−2.75 (0.03 E-2)
Canadian dollar	0.01 (0.49)	0.03 (0.49)	0.004 (0.49)	0.17 (0.43)
Japanese yen	0.51 (0.30)	0.37 (0.35)	0.36 (0.36)	0.13 (0.45)
UK sterling	−1.03 (0.15)	−0.88 (0.19)	−0.96 (0.17)	−1.32 (0.09)

All test statistics are distributed as standard normal under the null hypothesis of no shift in volatility. Figures in parentheses are marginal (two-sided) significance levels. A significantly positive statistic indicates a reduction in volatility; a significantly negative statistic indicates an increase in volatility. The data sample consists of monthly data from January 1973 to December 1986.

Moreover, although the question has been less intensively studied, these findings of reduced *unconditional* variance appear also to be supported by findings of reduced *conditional* variance – that is, exchange rate change seem to have become more predictable as a result of the EMS (cf. Rogoff, 1985; Artis and Taylor, 1988). (Again, the counterfactual is that in the absence of the EMS, EMS exchange rate predictability would have behaved, over time, as that of the non-EMS control group.)

The volatility-reducing effects of the EMS may not be its most signifi-

Table 5.3 Test statistics for a shift in exchange rate volatility after March 1979: real effective (ERM) rates

Currency	Normal	Logistic	Double exponential	Cauchy
Danish krone	5.07 (0.20 E-6)	4.44 (0.45 E-5)	4.37 (0.61 E-5)	5.21 (0.93 E-7)
Belgian franc	2.21 (0.01)	1.85 (0.03)	1.79 (0.04)	1.72 (0.04)
French franc	3.52 (0.21 E-3)	2.86 (0.21 E-2)	2.87 (0.20 E-2)	2.81 (0.26 E-2)
Italian lira	5.08 (0.19 E-6)	4.19 (0.14 E-4)	4.11 (0.19 E-4)	4.06 (0.25 E-4)
Dutch guilder	3.26 (0.55 E-3)	2.78 (0.27 E-2)	2.68 (0.37 E-2)	2.82 (0.24 E-2)
Irish punt	6.34 (0.12 E-9)	5.33 (0.48 E-7)	5.24 (0.80 E-7)	5.52 (0.17 E-7)
West German mark	6.17 (0.33 E-9)	5.17 (0.11 E-6)	4.99 (0.30 E-6)	5.06 (0.20 E-6)
US dollar	−1.15 (0.12)	−1.15 (0.12)	−1.30 (0.1)	−2.28 (0.01)
Canadian dollar	−0.50 (0.31)	−0.51 (0.30)	−0.53 (0.30)	−1.06 (0.14)
Japanese yen	−0.04 (0.48)	−0.14 (0.44)	0.20 (0.42)	−0.67 (0.25)
UK sterling	0.02 (0.01)	−1.90 (0.03)	−1.93 (0.02)	−2.65 (0.41 E-2)

See note to Table 5.2.

cant exchange rate impact, however. Williamson (1985) has stressed the importance of distinguishing between exchange rate *volatility*, a 'high-frequency' measure in which, due to the sluggishness of prices the distinction between real and nominal rates is hardly relevant and exchange rate *misalignment*, a low-frequency real rate phenomenon. By misalignment Williamson means to refer to the departure, for a prolonged period of time (say 1–2 years), of a country's real exchange rate from its putative equilibrium level. The welfare costs associated with the two concepts of exchange rate variability differ. Whereas forward markets allow hedging of risk over short horizons, such markets may not exist for longer horizons; as a result,

*Table 5.4   Test statistics for a shift in exchange rate volatility after March 1979:
nominal effective (MERM) rates*

Currency	Normal	Logistic	Double exponential	Cauchy
Danish krone	−0.59 (0.28)	−0.48 (0.31)	−0.60 (0.27)	−0.95 (0.17)
Belgian franc	1.95 (0.06)	1.28 (0.10)	1.26 (0.10)	1.01 (0.16)
French franc	1.33 (0.09)	0.99 (0.16)	0.88 (0.19)	0.23 (0.41)
Italian lira	3.35 (0.4 E-3)	2.51 (0.60 E-2)	2.45 (0.71 E-2)	1.32 (0.09)
Dutch guilder	0.66 (0.25)	0.39 (0.34)	0.33 (0.37)	−0.40 (0.34)
West German mark	2.09 (0.02)	1.55 (0.06)	1.46 (0.07)	0.57 (0.28)
US dollar	−2.62 (0.43 E-2)	−2.25 (0.01)	−2.31 (0.01)	−2.92 (0.17 E-2)
Canadian dollar	2.03 (0.02)	1.74 (0.04)	1.76 (0.04)	2.05 (0.02)
Japanese yen	−0.94 (0.17)	−0.62 (0.27)	−0.66 (0.25)	−0.12 (0.49)
UK sterling	−1.84 (0.03)	−1.62 (0.05)	−1.66 (0.05)	−2.06 (0.02)

See note to Table 5.2.

and in contrast with exchange rate volatility, the costs of (real) exchange
rate misalignment can be substantial, involving avoidable shut-down and
start-up production costs, misallocation of investment between time and
place, losses occasioned by protectionism and so on. It is sufficiently well
known not to need demonstration that the EMS currencies have not experienced misalignments on the scale experienced, first by the pound
sterling in the early 1980s, and secondly by the US dollar a little later. This
relative absence of misalignment seems a strong point in favour of the
system. However, movements in real exchange rates in the ERM are
bigger over long periods than might be expected or seems desirable. After
all, the EMS can be regarded as the exchange rate union expression of a
customs union; as such, it might be expected to obey an implicit duty to

Table 5.5   *Test statistics for a shift in exchange rate volatility after March 1979: real effective (MERM) rates*

Currency	Normal	Logistic	Double exponential	Cauchy
Danish krone	4.36 (0.65 E-5)	3.61 (0.15 E-3)	3.57 (0.18 E-3)	3.45 (0.27 E-3)
Belgian franc	1.92 (0.03)	1.61 (0.05)	1.62 (0.05)	1.95 (0.03)
French franc	2.17 (0.01)	1.78 (0.03)	1.81 (0.03)	1.72 (0.04)
Italian lira	3.14 (0.85 E-3)	2.45 (0.71 E-2)	2.49 (0.63 E-2)	2.09 (0.02)
Dutch guilder	1.78 (0.03)	1.45 (0.07)	1.41 (0.08)	1.81 (0.12)
West German mark	3.35 (0.41 E-3)	2.54 (0.50 E-2)	2.49 (0.63 E-2)	1.32 (0.09)
US dollar	−1.31 (0.09)	−1.32 (0.09)	−1.36 (0.08)	−2.48 (0.65 E-2)
Canadian dollar	1.39 (0.08)	1.17 (0.12)	1.11 (0.13)	1.11 (0.13)
Japanese yen	0.10 (0.46)	0.11 (0.45)	0.11 (0.45)	0.22 (0.41)
UK sterling	−1.44 (0.07)	−1.12 (0.13)	−1.10 (0.13)	−0.91 (0.18)

See note to Table 5.2.

stabilise real rates of exchange on pain of provoking on the part of those countries which suffer declines in competitiveness attempts to restore it by devices which would undo the achievements of the customs union. In Artis and Taylor (1987) the evidence that is obvious to the eye (especially for Italian lira and Irish punt real rates) is given a more technical expression in the form of testing whether a random walk for EMS real rates of exchange can be rejected. Since it cannot, and since the random walk simply says that today's exchange rate is determined by yesterday's, the implication seems to be that real exchange rates can drift anywhere. Even if this implication is dismissed as somewhat too strongly drawn,[4] the evidence on real rates is not as reassuring as perhaps it ought to be. Technically, the subject could stand greater research.

   The third major claim made for the EMS is that it has provided a frame-work for successful counter-inflation policy. By this has to be meant some-thing more than that inflation inside the EMS has fallen during the life of the system, since it has also fallen in countries outside the system, sometimes more dramatically.

   Rather, the claim must be that the system made possible a counter-inflation strategy not feasible otherwise (or not feasible to the same (desired) extent) and/or that the costs of reducing inflation were reduced by using the system as a framework. The literature on the value of pre-commitment in monetary policy might be used to support both claims in that, by committing to the EMS governments 'tie themselves to the mast' of the DM exchange rate and provide themselves with a punishment in the event of reneging; at the same time, more power passes to the central bank which may be more independent and less prone to the use of 'discretion' than the government. A different, but complementary, argument, relies on the greater transparency of the exchange rate as opposed to the money supply. A commitment to stabilise the DM-exchange rate, if credible, can be relatively easily translated by relevant price and wage setting agents into acceptable wage and price changes and into unemployment costs (at least, this is true for agents in the 'open' sector of the economy); then, the process of reducing inflation incurs a lower unemployment cost because expectations are reduced by incorporating a component relating to German inflation. Of course, a commitment to the EMS is not automati-cally and *per se* credible. Governments have to show that this is a serious commitment by taking appropriate action domestically to reduce inflation (reducing the extent of wage-indexing, for example) and by showing that the exchange rate peg is taken seriously. Almost certainly this will result in periods, before realignments, when not-fully-successful policies issue in overvalued real exchange rates – this is a form of punishment and discipline for the private sector just as the realignment itself is in effect a punishment for the monetary authorities. The central question nevertheless is whether as a result of all this, the costs of reducing inflation are decreased. The evidence on these issues is still somewhat sparse; however, data presented in Giavazzi and Giovannini (1987) are consistent with the proposition that the EMS framework produced a reduction in the costs of reducing inflation (using the UK as a control), and Artis and Ormerod (1987) find that inflation expectations generators for the principal EMS countries are improved by adding in expectations of German inflation during the EMS period, though not before, with the notable and provocative exception of the UK which has not participated in the critical ERM feature of the system. These findings suggest that the costs of reducing inflation were cut by membership of the EMS (ERM).

It is implicit in this, of course, that Germany is the dominant country and the leader by virtue of its low inflation record and reputation. It is an observed fact that the measures built into the EMS to ensure symmetry of adjustment (the divergence indicator and the surrounding presumption that action should be taken by the country triggering the threshold) have fallen out of fashion. At a time when the policy priority was to beat inflation it was positively not desired to have symmetrical adjustments which would have raised German inflation towards the EMS average; rather, the objective was that of ensuring the convergence of the average on the German standard.

II   The EMS at a crossroads

The relevance of the *past* performance of the EMS to a UK decision to participate fully in the system would stand to be eroded if it seemed as though the system itself was about to undergo a change; and it is important to note that there are pressures for substantial changes in the operation of the system. These pressures stem from three important factors and the changes they indicate are not only technical in nature, though technical changes are not insignificant.

The three factors that stand out as requiring an adaptation of the system are the following: the decision by the Community to 'complete the internal market' by 1992; the widespread and substantial reduction in inflation achieved and the prospect of recessionary or slump conditions developing; and the attempts at the world level (uncertain as these are) to promote the international co-ordination of economic policy.

The first of these factors is significant because it is part of the process of completing the internal market that the controls on flows of foreign exchange that exist in Italy, France and Belgium should be abolished. The role of capital exchange controls in the two leading non-German countries has been examined in a number of places (but see especially the papers by Giavazzi and Giovannini, 1986, Giavazzi and Pagano, 1985, and the collection in the European Commission, 1988) and it can be argued that these controls have played a critical role in the past functioning of the system in at least two ways: they have allowed the authorities to hold the whip hand in the timing and size of realignments, thus sustaining the counter-inflationary policy of underindexing and delaying the exchange rate adjustment; and they permit countries a degree of independence in interest rate policy which would not otherwise be available.[5] In the absence of such controls the obligation to defend the exchange rate against the DM in effect requires that a country should match German interest rates plus a premium to compensate for the inflation differential against Germany; the controls yield an extra degree of freedom which central banks enjoy. It is arguable that the reduction in inflation that has been achieved makes it less important to preserve the use of exchange controls for the sake of strengthening counter-inflationary policies; but it is not especially easy to imagine the Banca d'Italia or the Banque de France accepting the diminution in interest rate discretion with complete equanimity.

The removal of the protection afforded by exchange controls calls for a mix of technical and substantive reforms. The technical reforms needed comprise such things as limitations on the size of realignments, so as to prevent them from causing discrete shifts in market rates, widening the bands (or less provocatively, the greater use of existing bands), and extending the size of intervention facilities. These are all matters upon which the system's managers have already made a start, in the package of changes announced in September 1987. The provision of borrowing rights for system currencies to be used in intra-marginal intervention is a technical change with a more far-reaching political implication, since it does imply – in principle – a dilution of the power of the strong currency country whose currency may now be borrowed in large amounts to sustain a weaker one, thus threatening a weakening of the strong currency country's control over its own money supply. The qualification that these implications only flow *in principle* from the technical provisions implies a suspicion that in practice a substantiation of these claims would merely lead to a suspension of the credit facilities. Thus a more deliberate and less haphazard move towards a dilution of the German dominance of the system may be required in the longer run as a means of making good the loss of independence implied in the abolition of exchange controls: the argument is that countries will be more willing to relinquish sovereignty if they can be persuaded that what they have done is, in effect, to pool it. In this way the loss of independent discretion would be compensated by the acquisition of a say in EMS-wide policy.

The second major factor picked out as promising a change in system behaviour points in the same direction. While the policy priority remained so firmly that of reducing inflation, the dominance of Germany as a low-inflation country was positively desirable and at any rate could hardly be disputed. As concern about inflation recedes, however, the same rationale no longer applies: once again, it seems likely that a solution must be found in more co-operative decision-making.

Finally, a similar conclusion seems to flow from the momentum towards a greater degree of policy co-operation at the world – or G-7 – level. The point here is that however tidy and sensible a G-3 solution might seem, the actions of the countries concerned have made it rather clear that the formal channels of co-operation will involve G-5 and G-7 groupings. No less than four of the G-7 are members of the EMS; none of the other three seems in the least likely to delegate its responsibility to Germany, but there is a premium on some agreement between them.

To sum up so far, then: to date, the EMS has operated very successfully to stabilise its members' exchange rates and has provided a counter-inflation framework which its members have found useful. As a consequence the provisions for symmetrical adjustment which the founders of the system had laboured to introduce have largely remained unused, as unwanted. The circumstances favoured the hegemony of one country; not accidentally, the most successful exchange rate systems have been hegemonic. Another consequence of the counter-inflation preoccupation of the system has been that in some countries, at any rate, real exchange rates appear to have got out of kilter. At the end of this successful period of operation, however, the system appears faced with the need to modify its operations, both technically, and in terms of the degree of co-operation involved: pressures stemming from the decision to remove exchange controls, the waning of the 'inflation-first' policy priority and the momentum of world monetary co-operation all seem to point in the same direction.

III   The monetary policy experiment in the UK

The beginning of the EMS almost exactly coincides with the commencement, in Britain, of the 'Thatcher experiment'.

That experiment began with a formal commitment, later enshrined in the Medium Term Financial Strategy (MTFS), to bring down the rate of growth of a broadly defined money supply (£M3), over a period of five years. Alongside this commitment there was also a target for the progressive reduction of the Public Sector Borrowing Requirement as a proportion of GDP. It was argued that adherence to these objectives would bring down the rate of inflation and could cut the unemployment costs of doing so. In the initial statement of this grand design the exchange rate was quite explicitly cast as the object of 'benign neglect'.

Experience with this strategy was deeply disillusioning; in retrospect it appears that the decision to target the broad money supply coincided with the onset of a period of financial innovation which increased the demand for broad money relative to narrow money and made the targets inappropriately restrictive. Yet, the nature of the policy experiment laid stress on the value of commitment, presenting the government with a distinct dilemma: would an overrun of the monetary target be seen as ruining the government's credibility, or would it be seen by the public as covered by an implicit escape clause permitting the suspension of the targets in the event of certain contingencies? To sharpen the dilemma, there was at the same

time the second oil price shock, which in and of itself was seen as a reason
for expecting a rise in the real sterling exchange rate. Since both the
expected and the unexpected tightening of monetary policy also led to a
rise in the exchange rate, the fact that it did rise was hardly surprising; the
real appreciation was – to that date, which was of course before the dollar
appreciation – in fact on a scale unprecedented in the history of indus-
trially developed countries. At the time, it was not easy to see to what
extent the exchange rate appreciation correctly reflected the 'permanent'
part of the oil price rise, to what extent it reflected the intended restrictiveness of monetary policy, and to what extent it represented an 'excess'
appreciation. The fact that the 'overshooting' phenomenon – despite
Dornbusch's (1976) analysis of it – was not widely understood was a further
contributor to the diagnostic problem for the policy makers.[6]

The upshot of the tensions created by the massive exchange rate
appreciation occurring even while the monetary targets were being overrun
was twofold: first, the target ranges were extended to other definitions of
the money supply both narrower (M0, M1) and broader (PSL1, PSL2), on
the basis that these should not be so prone to distortion as £M3. Second, a
progressively more formal and explicit role was given to the exchange rate;
at first this was done without public announcement, though it was clear to
those near the markets that the policy of benign neglect had already been
cancelled. Eventually, the formal statement of the MTFS was changed so
that in effect the monetary targets were conditionised on the exchange
rate; later still, the broad monetary aggregate was abandoned altogether
in the face of continued and more pronounced innovation in the financial
markets. More emphasis has been placed on the MTFS as a statement
about nominal income ('velocity-corrected money supply') targets, with
narrow money as a short-run (leading indicator) target, along with the exchange rate. Then, in 1987, with the Louvre Accord marking the initiation
of the policy, a phase of DM-targeting was introduced (see Figure 5.1).
This seemed to bring the MTFS full circle from a policy of monetary
growth targets and benign neglect of the exchange rate to one of exchange
rate targeting with benign neglect of the monetary aggregates. However,
after this policy had held for approximately a year, the peg was removed.
By the time of the 1988 Budget the exchange rate was again reduced to the
role of a conditioning variable. (Some of these developments are summarised in Table 5.6 which lists the variables for which target ranges were
explicitly quoted in successive restatements of the MTFS.)

IV   Participation in the ERM

Given the evolution of British economic policy up to 1987 as described in
the previous section and the terms on which the success of the EMS has

Figure 5.1 Sterling/DM rate, 10 August 1984 to 13 May 1988

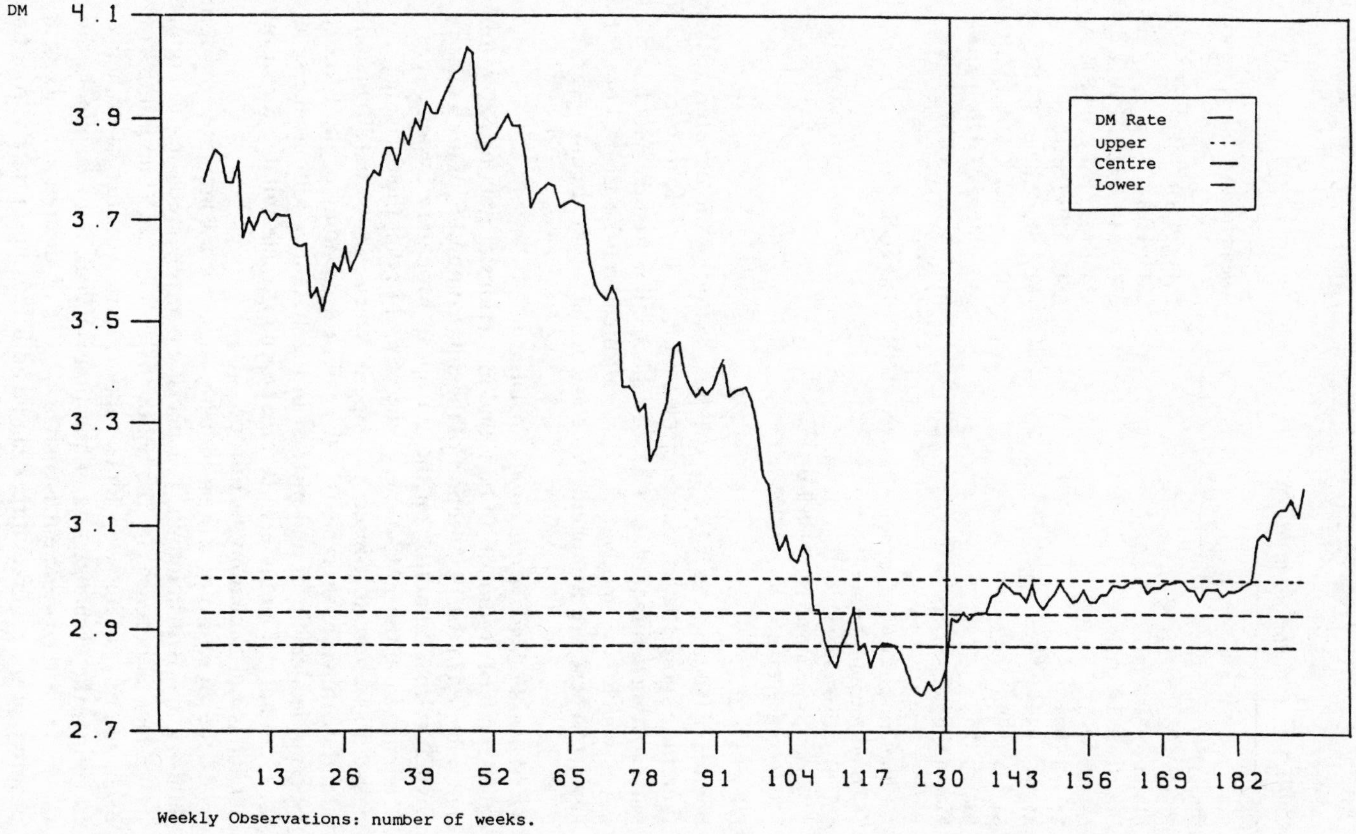

DM

4.1

3.9

3.7

3.5

3.3

3.1

2.9

2.7

13 26 39 52 65 78 91 104 117 130 143 156 169 182

DM Rate   ___
Upper   ......
Centre   ___
Lower   ___

Weekly Observations: number of weeks.

Table 5.6   Content of the MTFS

	4-year forward ranges quoted[a]
March 1980	£M3; PSBR
March 1981	£M3; PSBR
March 1982	£M3, M1, PSL2; PSBR
March 1983	£M3, M1, PSL2; PSBR
March 1984	£M3; M0; PSBR
March 1985	£M3; M0; Money GDP;[b] PSBR
March 1986	M0;[c] Money GDP; PSBR, £M3
March 1987	M0;[d] Money GDP; PSBR
March 1988	M0;[e] Money GDP; PSBR

[a] Target ranges except as noted below, PSBR as % GDP.
[b] 'Broad medium term objective.'
[c] 'Illustrative ranges' for 1987/8 on.
[d] 'Illustrative ranges' for 1988/9 on.
[e] 'Illustrative ranges' for 1989/90 on.

been achieved, as described in the first section of the chapter, it seemed then little more than a natural progression for the UK to become a fully participating member of the EMS. In this section, we take a look at the key issues which have motivated British attitudes on the EMS, both for and against. These are arranged, in no particular order, below.

The real exchange rate and competitiveness
One strand of argument, to be found in sections of Labour Party opinion, and reflected in the 1985 Report of the Sub-Committee of the Treasury and Civil Service Committee on the European Monetary System, sees independence from the EMS as necessary to ensure that the exchange rate can be used as a tool to conserve competitiveness. In its 'hard' version, this strand of thinking suggests that the political economy of the EMS is that German leadership of and interest in the system conditions the securing, for Germany, of an undervalued real exchange rate suitable for sustaining her industrial hegemony in Europe.

As the structure of British industry makes it a competitor of German industry, the British interest is especially poorly served, on this argument, by formal adherence to the EMS. Although the importance of the exchange rate on this view lends support to the practice of exchange rate targeting, the exchange rate in question is a real, not a nominal, rate and the logic of the argument is that a degree of discretion is necessary to ensure that the real rate target can be adjusted appropriately from time to time. Surprisingly, the same view of the essential importance of securing a degree of stability in the real exchange rate simultaneously motivates support for UK entry into the EMS from those who (as in the Report of the Public Policy Centre) view the system as capable of supporting a 'crawling peg' pattern of adjustment; the over-appreciation of the real exchange rate in the early 1980s is regarded as an example of an evil to be avoided by abandoning independent monetary policy in favour of joining the EMS.

The history of the system shows why there is merit in both these (albeit contradictory) views.

First, it is clear that an important motivation for Germany in supporting the system is to stabilise the real DM exchange rate and, since Germany is a low-inflation country and exchange rate changes within the system are discouraged,[7] it seems fair to conclude that a degree of bias towards under-valuation of the real DM is likely to eventuate. In fact, as argued earlier, this can be regarded as a cost of using the system as a counter-inflationary framework.

On the other hand, it is clear that exchange rate changes inside the ERM, at realignments, have always been in the direction indicated by real rate stabilisation considerations whereas in some long-run sense it seems plausible to argue – as we noted earlier – that the EMS as the exchange rate union counterpart of a customs union must aim to prevent changes in competitiveness which in the limit might lead to the undoing of the achievements of the customs union. It does seem to mistake the character of the EMS, though, to suggest that it can now be used as a 'crawling peg'; although the perception that it was so used in the early stages of its history may be accurate enough,[8] subsequent developments have highlighted its nominal rigidity and counter-inflationary purpose.

Monetary sovereignty and independence
Viewed as a means to the control of inflation, adherence to an exchange rate target against a low-inflation currency has much to recommend it. As against a monetary growth target, exchange rate targeting is not vulnerable to money demand shocks and arguably commands greater transparency. Indeed, since in an open economy the transmission mechanism of monetary policy appears to work through the exchange rate, logic suggests that weaknesses in the transmission between money and exchange rates can best be made good by targeting the exchange rate. MacKinnon's 'currency substitution' world (see, e.g. MacKinnon, 1981), where the source of apparent instability in national money demand functions is to be found in currency switching, is only a particular example where exchange rate targeting is superior. In this case, stabilising an exchange rate implies automatically supplying more of the currency in greater demand, so

accommodating the harmless switch in tastes which gives rise to the problem in the first place. More generally, a consequence of exchange rate targeting is to endogenise the money supply which is obliged to accommodate demand; this in itself implies a loss of independence in the sense that the money supply cannot be chosen with some other end in view. The loss of independence is inevitably more keenly felt if the exchange rate target itself cannot be unilaterally modified.

For some proponents of British membership of the EMS, the loss of independence would be desirable since it would 'buy' the anti-inflation reputation of the Bundesbank, and so provide a rather straightforward form of pre-commitment. This view is to be found, also, in the Report of the Public Policy Centre on the EMS.

A contrary view clearly prevailed with the government in 1979, anxious to indulge in its own monetary experiment. At the end of that experiment it may be questioned whether, despite the volte-face on the intermediate variable chosen for targeting, the government has any need to 'buy' a counter-inflationary reputation. It is not difficult to argue that the government has established a reputation for being hard on inflation, even if it has not established a reputation for hitting its monetary targets. In this case, the added value of formal membership of the system might seem small. What *would* be added would perhaps be more valuable for *future* governments than for the present one. It can, for example, be argued that a future possible Labour government and perhaps almost any plausible future (post-Thatcher) Conservative government will have a less positive counter-inflationary reputation than the present government and, accordingly, more to gain from a pre-commitment of the kind involved in formal membership.

*Asymmetrical aspects of sterling: the 'petrocurrency' and
'bipolarity' problems*
There are at least two reasons why the adherence of sterling to the ERM represents a proposition qualitatively different from that of the present participation of the French franc and Italian lira (apart from the absence of exchange control in the British case). First, the UK economy is self-sufficient in oil. This implies that the sterling real exchange rate *vis-à-vis* the oil-poor countries of the EMS should correctly appreciate in respect of 'permanent' oil price rises. Generally, a desired characteristic of a currency union is that member countries should be symmetrically affected by common external shocks; the EMS is not a full currency union, however, so what is required here is that realignment 'rules' should acknowledge the need for a specific adjustment in the event of oil 'shocks'. Given such an acknowledgement the oil asymmetry need not be an issue: in fact, member-

ship of the EMS could reduce the excess adjustment which some observers would claim has been a consequence of sterling's 'petrocurrency' status in the past. The second important differentiating characteristic is that sterling still remains a widely held currency, so that the possibility of destabilising movements between sterling and the DM in what would be a 'bipolar' system has struck some observers as constituting a potential obstacle or at least as requiring a high degree of co-ordination between the relevant monetary authorities and/or some other form of accommodation (wider bands being a possibility mentioned in Artis and Miller, 1986, for example).

'The rate upon entry'

An especially vexatious issue in past discussions of UK membership of the EMS has concerned the rate upon entry. Because the rationale of the system is to discourage sharp changes, the rate upon entry exerts a special role. It seems important to ensure that this rate should be acceptable on grounds both of competitiveness and of inflation control. Past exercises in calculating the rate upon entry have exhibited that this can be a nice dilemma. If, for example, the ECU-rate of sterling is currently felt to be too high on grounds of competitiveness, it seems obvious that a fall in the rate of exchange should be engineered prior to joining. Yet, if the principal argument for membership is a control-of-inflation argument, the devaluation move would hardly make the package as a whole very credible. A possible resolution (illustrated in Artis and Miller, 1986) is the adoption of wider bands, which allow for the eventual desirable devaluation without excessively compromising the counter-inflation impact of EMS membership.

Conclusions

British hostility to the EMS in the past has probably been unfortunate. Quite a number of observers would probably agree, in retrospect, that a decision to participate in the ERM in 1979 would have made for better outcomes, for Britain, than those actually attained by the exercise of independent monetary sovereignty: the sterling misalignment of the early 1980s would have been avoided (or at least attenuated) and inflation could still have been brought down to acceptable levels. The conversion of British attitudes to the EMS in recent years suggests that this scenario might be widely shared.

Nevertheless, bygones are bygones. The counter-inflation episode in EMS (and global) economic policy is over and other issues are claiming attention. Some of the new developments in the EMS can only make British entry more likely: the removal of exchange controls and the accompanying changes in intervention arrangements make the system more acceptable. On the British side, policy has simulated membership of the system for a time, and at the September 1987 meetings of the International Monetary Fund the Chancellor of the Exchequer went so far as to offer as a recipe for the efficient regulation of exchange rate zones at the global level the EMS realignment model (where the central rate change is calculated not to disturb market rates and so not to reward speculation). The comparatively easy passage of the system even when a number of capital exchange controls in France and Italy have been removed suggests – so far – that the threats perceived to the system's stability from this new departure may have been exaggerated, whereas the sustained simulation of British membership, while it lasted, involved none of the problems that observers had suggested might accompany formal membership and was not terminated for any of these reasons.[9]

Although it is necessary to caution against too complacent an interpretation of these successes, they are, certainly, favourable to the eventual prospect of British participation in the system.

Appendix: the volatility test

The volatility test deployed in Artis and Taylor (1988), on which the results quoted in Tables 5.2–5 depend, proceeds from the observation that economists are far from certain about the distribution of exchange rate changes. In order to circumvent this problem a non-parametric approach may be adopted, based on the ranking, in order of size, of exchange rate changes. Intuitively, if a significant number of lower-ranked percentage changes were recorded in the latter half of the sample (after the formation of the EMS), a reduction in volatility is indicated. The exact procedure is as follows.

Let Δe_t be the change in the (logarithm of the) exchange rate at time t; then the maintained hypothesis is:

$$\Delta e_t = \mu + \sigma_t \varepsilon_t,$$
$$\sigma_t = \exp(\alpha + \beta z_t), \tag{5.1}$$

where μ, α and β are unknown constant scalars, ε_t is independently and identically distributed with distribution function F and density function f, and z_t is a binary variable reflecting the hypothesised change in volatility, that is:

$z_t = 1$, $t \leq$ March 1979,

$z = 0$, otherwise.

Given (5.1), the null hypothesis of no shift in volatility is then:

$$H_\alpha : \beta = 0. \tag{5.2}$$

Hajek and Sidak (1967) (henceforth HS) developed a number of non-parametric rank tests for dealing with problems involving this kind of framework, which, under appropriate regularity conditions, are locally most powerful (HS, pp. 70–1). The test statistics take the form

$$\xi = \sum_{t=1}^{T} (z_t - \bar{z}) \, \alpha(u_t) \tag{5.3}$$

where $\bar{z}$ is the arithmetic mean of the z_t sequence of T observations ($\bar{z} = T^{-1} \sum_{t=1}^{T} z_t$) and u_t is defined as follows. Let $r(\Delta e_t)$ be the rank of Δe_t, that is, Δe_t is the $r(\Delta e_t)$th smallest change in the total sequence considered; then

$$u_t = r(\Delta e_t)/(T + 1).$$

Clearly, u_t must lie in the closed interval $[1/(T+1), T/(T + 1)]$ (for no ties in rank). The function $\alpha(.)$ in (5.3) is a score function defined in HS (p. 70), depending upon the assumed density of ε_t, namely f, Hajek and Sidak define a class of functions which can be used in place of the score function in large samples, since $\alpha(.)$ may in practice be difficult to evaluate. If F is the assumed distribution function of ε_t, then

$$F(x) = \int_{-\infty}^{x} f(y) \, dy$$

and $F^{-1}(u)$ is the inverse of F:

$$F^{-1} = \inf(x | F(x) \geq u)$$

then the asymptotic score function, $\psi(.)$ is defined (HS, p. 19):

$$\psi : (0, 1) \rightarrow [\mathrm{R} \tag{5.4}$$

Under the maintained hypothesis (1), the statistic

$$\eta = \sum_{t=1}^{T} (z_t - \bar{z}) \, \psi(u_r) \tag{5.5}$$

(i.e. as in (5.3) with $\alpha(.)$ replaced by $\psi(.)$ will be asymptotically normally distributed. Under the null hypothesis (5.2), η will have mean zero and variance ϱ^2 given by (HS, pp. 159–60):

$$\varrho^2 = \left\{ \sum_{t=1}^{T} (z_t - \bar{z})^2 \right\} \int_0^1 \{\psi(u) - \bar{\psi}\}^2 \, du \tag{5.6}$$

where

$$\bar{\psi} = \int_0^1 \{\psi(u) \, du$$

The test is now as follows. For a given choice of f, η can be calculated as in (5.5) and referred to the normal distribution, to construct a test of any given normal size, of the null hypothesis (5.2) (no change in volatility). Significantly negative values of η reflect a negative value of β in (5.1), that is, an increase in volatility post-March 1979, whereas significantly positive values of η imply a reduction in volatility post-March 1979. The statistic η in (5.5) provides the locally most powerful test among the class of all possible tests (HS, p. 249).

Note that although the test procedure just outlined is non-parametric in the sense that no volatility measures are actually estimated, in implementing the procedure one cannot avoid choosing an appropriate distribution for changes in the exchange rate. In order to try and minimise the damage due to choosing an inappropriate distribution four well-known ones were selected – hopefully, the true distribution of exchange rate changes is close to one of them. The densities used correspond to the normal, logistic, double exponential and Cauchy distributions. The density and asymptotic score functions (as defined in (5.4)) for these distributions are shown in Artis and Taylor (1988). All of the chosen distributions are symmetric and both the double exponential and Cauchy distributions have fat tails.[10]

Notes

1 Successive British governments have maintained that they would put sterling into the ERM 'when the time was ripe'.
2 The basis of the test is discussed in the appendix.
3 Fratianni, 1988, using a parametric method on OECD effective exchange rate data finds that for Belgium and The Netherlands at least the destabilising effect is more important than the stabilising effect.
4 Since we would not be able to reject a number of other 'near random walk' hypotheses for real exchange rates if we tested them, and these would imply that the exchange rate would settle down in the long run. It is also possible that this long run is so long that the data slice used in our experiments was inadequately short.
5 The maintenance of the legislative apparatus required to make the controls work also provides protection to the domestic banking industry and to methods of monetary control which amount to a 'tax' on domestic banking. The removal of such barriers to free trade in services is of course a primary goal of the Community's 1992 project.
6 Of course, in subsequent analysis of the experience the Dornbusch model played a prominent role – cf. Buiter and Miller, 1981, for example (though Buiter and Miller, 1983, is notably more cautious about assigning blame to monetary policy).

7 Realignments of the system are multilateral decisions, not unilateral as in the Bretton Woods system. A single country may then not 'get its own way'. A standard exhibit in this connection is the thwarted Belgian desire to devalue by 11% in 1982, when the actual devaluation allowed was 8.5%.

8 Cf. Sam Brittan's description of the system at this time in his 'How the EMS has become a mere crawling peg', *Financial Times*, 24 March 1983.

9 But it would be naive to overlook the fact that not being a formal member, and thus avoiding the possibility of agreed realignments, presents quite a different subject for speculation, from full formal membership.

10 Another relevant distribution would have been Student's *t*. However, the score function (4) for this distribution would have been very difficult to compute. A possibility not considered is that there was a change in distribution of ERM exchange rate changes post-March 1979 (e.g. a shift from normal to Cauchy). Tests for this kind of behaviour could conceivably be based on likelihood ratio tests, although one might suspect that the discriminatory power of such procedures would be low.

References

Artis, M. J. and Miller, M. H. (1986). 'On living with the EMS', *Midland Bank Review*, Winter, pp. 11–20.

Artis, M. J. and Ormerod, P. (1987). 'Converging on the German Standard: wage-price processes in Western Europe', University of Manchester Economics Department, mimeo.

Artis, M. J. and Taylor, M. P. (1988). 'Exchange rates and the EMS: assessing the track record', CEPR Discussion Paper.

Buiter, W. H. and Miller, M. H. (1981). 'The Thatcher experiment: the first two years', *Brookings Papers in Economic Activity*, 2.

Buiter, W. H. and Miller, M. H. (1983). 'Changing the rules: economic consequences of the Thatcher regime', *Brookings Papers in Economic Activity*, 2, pp. 305–65.

Dornbusch, R. (1976). 'Expectations and exchange rate dynamics', *Journal of Political Economy*, vol. 84, pp. 1161–76.

European Commission (1988). 'The creation of a European Financial Area', *European Perspectives*.

Fratianni, M. (1988). 'The European Monetary System: how well has it worked?', paper presented at a Cato Institute Conference, February.

Giavazzi, F. and Giovannini, A. (1986). 'The EMS and the dollar', *Economic Policy*, April, pp. 455–73.

Giavazzi, F. and Giovannini, A. (1987). 'The role of the exchange rate regime in a disinflation: empirical evidence on the European Monetary System', paper presented to the American Economic Association meetings, Chicago, December.

Giavazzi, F. and Pagano, M. (1985). 'Capital controls and the European Monetary System', *Euromobiliare*, Milan, June.

Hajek, J. and Sidak, Z. (1967). *The Theory of Rank Tests* (New York and Prague: Academic Press).

MacKinnon, R. I. (1981). 'The exchange rate and macroeconomic policy: changing post-war perceptions', *Journal of Economic Literature*, 19, June, pp. 531–57.

Public Policy Centre (1986). 'The need for an exchange rate policy and the option of full UK membership of the EMS', *Report* of the Exchange Rate Committee reprinted in *Marcus Wallenberg Papers on International Finance*.

Report of the House of Lords Select Committee on the European Communities (1983). 'The

European Monetary System', July.

Report of the Sub-Committee of the House of Commons Committee on the Treasury and Civil Service (1985). *The European Monetary System*, October.

Rogoff, K. (1985). 'Can exchange rate predictability be achieved without monetary convergence?', *European Economic Review*, May, pp. 93–115.

Tobin, J. (1981). Evidence presented to the House of Commons Committee on the Treasury and Civil Service, *Monetary Policy* vol. II, (Minutes of Evidence) (London: HMSO).

Ungerer, H., Evans, O. and Nyberg, P. (1983). 'The European Monetary System: the experience 1979–1982', IMF *Occasional Papers*, No. 19, May.

Ungerer, H., Evans, O., Mayer, T. and Young, P. (1986). 'The European Monetary System: recent developments', IMF *Occasional Papers*, No. 48, December.

Williamson, J. (1985). 'The exchange rate system', rev. ed., *Policy Analyses in International Economics*, 5, Institute of International Economics, Washington, June.

6

Is the business cycle real or monetary, Keynesian or classical?

Michael Parkin

I Introduction

This paper develops and implements tests that discriminate between three leading theories of the business cycle. These theories are:

(1) 'Real', proposed by Kydland and Prescott (1982), Long and Plosser (1983) and King and Plosser (1984);
(2) 'Equilibrium monetary', proposed by Lucas (1972, 1973, 1975);
(3) 'New Keynesian', proposed by Fischer (1977), Phelps and Taylor (1977) and Taylor (1979, 1980).

The alternative theories make contrasting predictions about the effects of monetary policy actions on aggregate fluctuations. The real theory predicts that the course of real output is independent of the behaviour of nominal magnitudes. The equilibrium monetary theory predicts that fore-castable components of monetary policy have no real effects but that the variability of output will be influenced by the monetary policy regime and by the predictability of the growth of nominal aggregate demand. The new Keynesian theory predicts that fluctuations in nominal demand, even if foreseen, generate fluctuations in output; according to this theory, appro-priately designed monetary policy feedback rules lower the variability of output.

No decisive tests have so far been offered that are capable of eliminating one, or more, of these theories. Each theory has its proponents and each can draw some comfort from the casual empiricism that often passes for hypothesis testing in macroeconomics.[1] The tests implemented here are clean and, as it turns out, decisive. The real and new Keynesian models are rejected. The monetary equilibrium model is not rejected.

I do not want to proclaim, on the basis of those tests, the death of either real business cycle theory or Keynesian macroeconomics. What is reported here is one set of tests on one body of data. The robustness of the conclusions with respect to other data sets needs to be checked before such a conclusion would be warranted.

The paper is organised as follows: Section II describes the institutions and history that generates the data employed; Section III develops the models; Section IV sets out the statistical tests performed and reports their results; Section V summarises the conclusions and offers suggestions for further work on this topic.

II   The data base – institutions and history

The economy is that of Japan; the time period is 1965–85; and the key element of the data base is the quarterly time series of aggregate real gross domestic product.[2]

The first feature of the Japanese economy that is crucial for present purposes is an unusual set of wage determining arrangements. During a period of a few weeks at the end of March and the beginning of April each year (effectively the end of calendar quarter one), virtually all labour market contracts are negotiated and wages set for the coming year. This spring wage round, known as *Shunto* (spring labour offensive) (see Shimada *et al.*, 1983, pp. 49–51), greatly simplifies the specification of the new Keynesian model of the labour market. The relevant new Keynesian model is one with multi-period wage contracts (multi-quarter) where all the contracts run for the same period of time (Fischer, 1977) rather than one in which contracts overlap (Taylor, 1979, 1980). In Taylor's labour model the persistence of shocks arises from the overlapping contracts, whereas in Fischer's model persistence within the contract period arises from the multi-period contracts themselves while persistence from one contract period to the next emanates from some other source.

Although wages are determined each spring, bonuses are an important component of labour income in Japan, and this creates an ambiguity concerning the importance of contractually predetermined wages. There are two views among students of the Japanese labour market concerning the effects of bonuses. One view is that bonuses inject sufficient flexibility into real wages to ensure that the labour market is always cleared (see, especially, Hashimoto, 1979). This view corresponds to both the real and equilibrium monetary views of the working of the labour market. Other scholars, observing that bonus payments are relatively constant over the cycle, suggest that wage fluctuations depend primarily on the wage rates decided on through collective bargaining (see Shimada *et al.*, 1983).

The models set out here exploit these features of the Japanese labour market. One model (Keynesian) treats the wages determined at the time of

Shunto as being contractually fixed for the forthcoming year. The other models (real and equilibrium monetary) assume that bonuses inject sufficient flexibility into wages to render the wage determined at *Shunto* irrelevant. In this second case the bonus is assumed to adjust to offset any errors made at *Shunto* so that real wage movements achieve continuous labour market clearing.

A second feature of Japan's macroeconomic history in the sample period is a switch, in mid-1975 (1975:2), from exchange rate and interest rate targeting to money supply control. This switch represented a clear, abrupt and well-understood change in monetary policy regime (see Suzuki, 1980). Such a switch in monetary policy regime has different predicted effects in the three alternative models of the business cycle and this provides a further important source of discriminating power between them.

These two features of the Japanese economy, *Shunto* and the change in monetary policy regime in 1975, enable us to discriminate between all three theories of the cycle. The labour market arrangements enable us to discriminate between the real and equilibrium monetary theories on the one hand and the Keynesian theory on the other. The monetary policy regime switch enables us to discriminate between the real theory on the one hand and the equilibrium monetary and Keynesian theories on the other. The combination of the features of Japan's labour market and monetary policy enable us to discriminate between all three theories.

Much more, of course, could be said about the Japanese economy during the sample period employed. The foregoing selective account focuses only on those features that are exploited in this study.[3]

The next section sets out three models of the business cycle.

III   Alternative business cycle theories

It is convenient to begin with a real model of the business cycle since this model forms the basis for the other two models. The model set out below, though not identical to any of those suggested in the earlier literature, is the simplest real model capable of displaying the key characteristics of fluctuations in aggregate output. The central focus here is on aggregate output – especially in the empirical work – but the model makes predictions about other variables as well.

The economy is open and small. It takes the real rate of interest and international relative prices of goods and services as given and is free to import and export capital and goods and services at those prices. The model is real but it contains money. It will turn out though that money is irrelevant to the paths of real variables.

Micro-foundations – the choices of firms and households

The economy consists of a large number of representative firms, each of which seeks to maximise profits by choosing the paths of output, labour and capital inputs, and net imported inputs. That is, firms seek to:

$$\operatorname*{Max}_{\{Y_t, L_t, K_t, X_t\}} \Pi_t = Y_t - \frac{W_t}{P_t} L_t - R_t K_t - \Theta_t X_t \tag{6.1}$$

where Π is profit, Y is output, L is labour input, K is capital input, X is net imports, W is money wage rate, P is price level, R is real rental rate, Θ is relative price of net imports, and t is time.

Firms are visualised as renting all their inputs and having no essential intertemporal dimension to their problem. They choose output, labour, capital and imported inputs, to maximise (6.1) subject to a production function:

$$Y_t = Z_t F(L_t, K_t, X_t) \tag{6.2}$$

where Z is a random technology shock. A particular form is assumed for the production function, which is:

$$F = L^\alpha K^\beta X^\gamma \qquad \alpha, \beta, \gamma > 0; \ \alpha + \beta + \gamma < 1. \tag{6.3}$$

The first-order necessary conditions for the maximisation of profits are

$$\left.\begin{array}{l} Z_t \alpha L_t^{(\alpha-1)} K_t^\beta X_t^\gamma = W_t/P_t, \\ Z_t \beta L_t^\alpha K_t^{(\beta-1)} X_t^\gamma = R_t, \\ Z_t \gamma L_t^\alpha K_t^\beta X_t^{(\gamma-1)} = \Theta_t. \end{array}\right\} \tag{6.4}$$

Taking logarithms of (6.4) enables us to write a set of linear input demand functions of the form

$$\begin{bmatrix} (\alpha-1) & \beta & \gamma \\ \alpha & (\beta-1) & \gamma \\ \alpha & \beta & (\gamma-1) \end{bmatrix} \begin{bmatrix} \ell_t^d \\ k_t^d \\ x_t^d \end{bmatrix} = \begin{bmatrix} -z_t & -\log \alpha & +(w_t-p_t) \\ -z_t & -\log \beta & +r_t \\ -z_t & -\log \gamma & +\theta_t \end{bmatrix} \tag{6.5}$$

where a lower-case letter denotes the logarithm of the relevant upper-case letter and the superscript d denotes demand.

The central focus of the present study is the behaviour of aggregate output. Output may be determined recursively, given the optimal inputs in (6.5), by substituting those optimal inputs into the production function. Though the focus of this study is on the cyclical behaviour of output, the alternative theories compared differ in the way in which they treat the labour market. It is essential, therefore, to focus also on that market.

The solution to system (6.5), together with the production function, gives rise to the demand for labour and supply of output functions:

$$\ell_t^d = D_t + \alpha \log \alpha - (1 + \alpha \phi)(w_t - p_t), \tag{6.6}$$

$$y_t^s = D_t - \alpha \phi (w_t - p_t), \tag{6.7}$$

where $D_t \equiv \phi(z_t - \beta r_t - \gamma \theta_t + (\alpha \log \alpha + \beta \log \beta + \gamma \log \gamma))$
and $\phi \equiv (1 - \alpha - \beta - \gamma)^{-1}$.

The composite variable D is an exogenous random variable encompassing production function shocks as well as real interest rate and relative price shocks emanating from the rest of the world; it is the impulse that generates fluctuations in output and other aggregates. Next consider the behaviour of households. The economy consists of N_t representative (dynastic) households which seek to maximise a time-separable, infinite-horizon utility function subject to initial holdings of assets and to a sequence of budget constraints. Specifically, the problem solved by the representative household is to

$$\max_{\{C_{t+i}, L_{t+i}, A_{t+i}, M_{t+i}\}_{i=0}^{\infty}} U_t = E_t \sum_{i=0}^{\infty} b^i u (C_{t+i}, L_{t+i}), \tag{6.8}$$

subject to:

$$C_{t+i} \leq (1 + R_{t+i-1}) A_{t+i-1} + (1 + R_{t+i-1}^M) \frac{M_{t+i-1}}{P_{t+i-1}} - A_{t+i}$$

$$- \frac{M_{t+i}}{P_{t+i}} + \Pi_{t+i} + \frac{W_{t+i}}{P_{t+i}} L_{t+i} - T_{t+i} \left(\frac{M_{t+i}}{P_{t+i}}, Y_{t+i} \right), \tag{6.9}$$

given A_{t-1}, M_{t-1}, and where C is consumption, A is assets, M is nominal money balances, R^M is real rate of return on money, $T(\ )$ is transactions costs. Restrictions on the utility function are

$$u_C > 0, \ u_{CC} \leq 0, \ u_L < 0, \ u_{LL} \geq 0, \ u_{CL} \leq 0, \ 0 < b < 1.$$

The budget constraint states that in each period consumption may not exceed total resources available and those resources are the assets brought forth from the previous period (including money balances), together with the interest earned on them, labour and profit income, minus assets carried forward into the next period and also minus transactions costs. Transactions costs (the final term in the budget constraint), depend on the total scale of transactions, Y_t, and on real balances. The restrictions on the transactions technology are:

$$T_M < 0, \ T_{MM} > 0, \ T_Y > 0.$$

The rates of interest on both assets and money are real rates.

Necessary conditions for the maximisation of utility are the two Euler equations:

$$u_C(C_{t+i}, L_{t+i}) - b(1 + R_{t+i})E_{t+i}u_C(C_{t+i+1}, L_{t+i+1}) = 0, \quad i=0,1,2\ldots$$
$$\tag{6.10}$$

$$\left[1 + T_{M_{t+i}}\left(\frac{M_{t+i}}{P_{t+i}}, Y_t\right)\right]u_C(C_{t+i}, L_{t+i}) - b(1 + R_{t+i}^M)$$

$$E_{t+i}u_C(C_{t+i+1}, L_{t+i+1}) = 0, \quad i=0,1,2\ldots, \tag{6.11}$$

the two transversality conditions,

$$\lim_{T\to\infty} b^T E_{t+i}u_C(C_T, L_t) = 0, \tag{6.12}$$

$$\lim_{T\to\infty} b^T E_{t+i}\left[1 + T_{MT}\left(\frac{M_T}{P_T}, Y_T\right)\right]u_C(C_T, L_t) = 0, \tag{6.13}$$

and the static optimality condition

$$u_C(C_{t+i}, L_{t+i})\frac{W_{t+i}}{P_{t+i}} + u_L(C_{t+i}, L_{t+i}) = 0. \tag{6.14}$$

The difference equations (6.10 and (6.11), together with the terminal conditions (6.12) and (6.13), and given the initial values of A and M, determine the stochastic processes $\{A_{t+i}, M_{t+i}\}_{i=0}^{\infty}$. Constraint (6.9) (with equality) together with (6.14) determines consumption and labour supply.

To explore the properties of the solution first consider equations (6.10) and (6.11). Divide (6.11) by (6.10) to give (at $i=0$),

$$T_{M_t}\left(\frac{M_t^d}{P_t}, Y_t\right) = \frac{R_t^M - R_t}{1 + R_t} = V_t. \tag{6.15}$$

Equation (6.15) can be solved for the demand for real money balances, which depends positively on real income, positively on the own rate of return on money, and negatively on the rate of return on competing assets – a standard prediction.

It is assumed that there exists a competitive banking industry which ensures that the right-hand side of (6.15) is driven to a value that gives zero profit. Thus V is a technologically given exogenous random variable. Specialising (6.15) to the case in which T_M is homogeneous of degree one in Y and assuming money market equilibrium ($M^d = M$), enables us to write

$$m_t + v_t = p_t + y_t \tag{6.16}$$

where v is an exogenous stochastic process and lower-case letters, as before, are the logarithms of their upper-case counterparts.

A strong assumption about the instantaneous part of the utility function yields a useful special case of this household model that turns out to be adequate for the purpose of capturing the particular features of the business cycle on which the present study focuses. That assumption is that $u(.,.)$ is linear in consumption and separable in consumption and labour supply. Specifically:

$$u(C,L) = C - \left(\frac{g}{1+g}\right) L^{\left(\frac{g}{1+g}\right)}, g > 0. \tag{6.17}$$

Using (6.17) and (6.14) gives

$$\frac{W_t}{P_t} - L_t^{1/g} = 0 \tag{6.18}$$

and, taking the logarithms of (6.18) yields

$$\ell_t^s = g(w_t - p_t) + n_t \tag{6.19}$$

where n_t is the logarithm of population. Equation (6.19) is the aggregate supply of labour while (6.18) is the labour supply of the representative household.

The assumptions made on the utility function emphasise the lack of importance of intertemporal substitution in the supply of labour. By assuming a utility function that is linear in consumption and non-linear in labour, and separable in those two arguments, all the intertemporal substitution is placed on consumption and none of it on labour supply. I am not, of course, denying the possibility of intertemporal substitution in labour supply. I am simply assuming an extreme case but one that does not rule out fluctuations in the supply of labour and of output.

The model of household behaviour set out above predicts asset movements and consumption but the behaviour of those variables is irrelevant for present purposes. The assumption of a small open economy makes the international market for capital and assets as well as goods irrelevant for the determination of the course of the domestic business cycle. It is the domestic markets for labour, output and money that determine the paths of domestic output and the price level.

Predictions of the real model
The real business cycle model may now be solved for its predictions about employment, real wages and output. I shall focus only on the behaviour of output since that will be the subject of the subsequent empirical investigation.[4]

For convenience, the key equations will be repeated in summary form here. The demand for labour, given by equation (6.6) above is

$$\ell_t^d = D_t + \alpha\log\alpha - (1 + \alpha\phi)(w_t - p_t).$$

Fluctuations in the real variables, D_t, are the source of the business cycle. The supply of labour, given by equation (6.19) above, is

$$\ell_t^s = g(w_t - p_t) + n_t.$$

The labour market clears, that is,

$$\ell_t^d = \ell_t^s = \ell_t. \tag{6.20}$$

The above equations determine the levels of employment and real wages. The real wage together with the output supply function (equation (6.7)) gives the solution for output as

$$y_t = E_{t+i}q_t + (q_t - E_{t-i}q_t) \tag{6.21}$$

where $q_t \equiv \dfrac{1}{\Delta}((1 + g)D_t + \alpha\phi(n_t - \alpha\log\alpha),$

$$\Delta \equiv 1 + \alpha\phi + g.$$

I have written equation (6.21) in what appears to be an odd way to facilitate comparisons with subsequent models. To achieve this I have emphasised the role of random fluctuations to the exogenous variables that drive output – in this model production function shocks and rest-of-world real interest rate and relative price shocks are summarised in the random variable D.

As can be seen, output fluctuates as a result of fluctuations in technology, real interest rates and relative prices generated in the rest of the world, all summarised in the random variable D. Output also fluctuates as a result of population changes captured in the (assumed non-stochastic) variable n. Money market equilibrium [equation (6.16)] is irrelevant for the determination of the path of output.

The role played in this model by money depends on the exchange rate regime. With flexible exchange rates the money stock, M, is determined by the monetary authority and (6.16), together with (6.21), determines the price level. The relationship between domestic and world nominal prices as well as the real exchange rate, θ, determines the spot exchange rate. That is, the spot exchange rate is determined by

$$p_t = p_t^* + s_t - \theta_t \tag{6.22}$$

where s is the spot exchange rate and p^* is the nominal price level of the rest of the world.

Under a fixed exchange rate regime, the monetary authority determines the exchange rate in (6.22) and that value of s, together with the world-determined nominal price level p^* and real exchange rate θ determines the domestic price level. The money market equilibrium condition (6.16) then determines the money stock. In either case, money market equilibrium conditions are irrelevant for the behaviour of output. The classical dichotomy holds.

Equilibrium monetary model

The equilibrium monetary model is closely related to the real model. The key difference is that households are located on a series of informationally isolated 'islands' and do not have complete contemporaneous information about the price level of consumer goods. When making labour market decisions, they base their actions on a rational expectation of the current price level based on the information available at the end of the previous period together with their local information. As a consequence, the labour supply function becomes:

$$\ell_t^s = g(w_t - E_{t-i}p_t) + n_t \tag{6.19'}$$

where E is the expectations operator and the subscript $t-1$ dates the information set on which expectations are conditioned.

The rest of the equilibrium monetary model is identical to the real model. Equation (6.6) determines the demand for labour, (6.7) the supply of output, the labour market clears (6.20), the money market is in equilibrium (6.16), and the relationship between domestic and foreign prices and the spot exchange rate is given by (6.22).

Although the structural difference between the first and second models is slight, the implications are quite far-reaching. First, the exchange rate regime affects the behaviour of output. Under fixed exchange rates, with the spot exchange rate, s, given by monetary policy and with the rest-of-world price level and terms of trade given, the domestic price level p is an exogenous random variable. In contrast, under flexible exchange rates, with m determined by the monetary authorities, p and y become joint endogenous processes driven by m and the random velocity technology variable v. The solutions for output under the two monetary policy regimes in the equilibrium monetary model are:

$$y_t = E_{t-i}q_t + (q_t - E_{t-i}q_t) + \frac{\alpha\phi g}{\Delta}(p_t - E_{t-i}p_t) \tag{6.23}$$

for fixed rates, and

$$y_t = E_{t-i}q_t + k(q_t - E_{t-i}q_t) + \frac{k\alpha\phi g}{\Delta}(m_t - E_{t-i}m_t + v_t - E_{t-i}v_t), \tag{6.24}$$

where $k \equiv (1 + \alpha\phi + g)/(1 + \alpha\phi)(1 + g)$, $0 < k < 1$. Notice that the deterministic part of output, $E_{t-i}q_t$, is identical under the two regimes. The stochastic components of output differ, however, under the two regimes.

Real disturbances $(q_t - E_{t-i}q_t)$ have a smaller effect on output under flexible rates than under fixed rates since the coefficient k lies between zero and one. Nominal shocks also have a smaller effect on output under flexible rates than under fixed rates. There is no guarantee, though, that the variability of nominal shocks themselves will be smaller under flexible exchange rates than under fixed exchange rates. The nominal shock that drives output when exchange rates are fixed is unpredicted movements in the price level while under flexible rates it is unpredicted movements in nominal aggregate demand. If, under flexible exchange rates, monetary control is very precise and velocity highly predictable, then output will be less variable under flexible exchange rates. It is possible, however, for domestic monetary aggregates and velocity to be so highly variable under flexible exchange rates that the resulting variability of real output is larger under flexible rates than under fixed rates.

In either situation, it is clear that the behaviour of output under the two exchange rate regimes does provide a means for discriminating between the real business cycle model and the equilibrium monetary model. In the real business cycle model the exchange rate regime is irrelevant for the path of output. In the equilibrium monetary model the exchange rate regime is irrelevant for the behaviour of the deterministic part of output but does affect its variance.

Keynesian theory

The Keynesian theory of the business cycle does not sit quite as easily with the firm and household maximisation problems set out above as does the equilibrium monetary model. It would, in principle, be desirable to derive a Keynesian model from some explicit characterisation of the costs of setting wages and trading labour that make the assumptions of that model optimal. The literature has not developed along those lines and I shall not seek to make such a development here. Rather, I shall suppose, in admittedly loose terms, that the above optimisation problems may be viewed as relevant for the purpose of specifying the Keynesian model. The problem solved by firms is exactly relevant in the Keynesian case and the quantity of labour employed will equal the quantity of labour demanded. That is,

$$\ell_{t,\tau} = \ell_{t,\tau}^{d}. \tag{6.27}$$

I have modified the time notation for the Keynesian model[5] to keep certain matters clear in what will follow. The subscript t for the Keynesian model denotes a year, the subscript τ denotes a quarter $t = 0, 1, \ldots; \tau = 1, 2, 3, 4$.

The problem solved by households, in the Keynesian model, does not lead to a labour supply decision rule. Rather, it leads to an expression of labour supply plans that somehow feature in a bargaining process. That bargaining process results in the determination of a sequence of money wages which the parties expect, at the time of the bargining, will clear the labour market. Thus, instead of labour-market clearing, the Keynesian model assumes *expected* labour-market clearing where those expectations are conditioned on the information available at the time of negotiations. That is,

$$E_w \ell_{t,\tau}^s = E_w \ell_{t,\tau}^d \qquad (6.28)$$

where E_w denotes an expectation conditional on information available when wages are agreed at $t-1$, 4.

These are the only modifications that the Keynesian model makes to the equilibrium monetary model. The supply of labour remains as (6.19′) and the rest of the system contained in the first model applies to the Keynesian model.

The remark made above in the context of the equilibrium monetary model concerning the effects of monetary policy regimes applies to the Keynesian model. Thus, there are two output solutions – one for fixed exchange rates and one for flexible rates. Those solutions are, for fixed rates:

$$y_{t,\tau} = E_w q_{t,\tau} + k(1 + \alpha\phi)(q_{t,\tau} - E_w q_{t,\tau}) + \alpha\phi(p_{t,\tau} - E_w p_{t,\tau}) \quad (6.29)$$

and for flexible rates

$$y_{t,\tau} = E_w q_{t,\tau} + k(q_{t,\tau} - E_w q_{t,\tau}) + \frac{\alpha\phi}{1 + \alpha\phi}(m_{t,\tau} - E_w m_{t,\tau} +$$
$$v_{t,\tau} - E_w v_{t,\tau}). \qquad (6.30)$$

As in the case of the real model, the movements in output that are fore-castable at the time wages are set are independent of the monetary regime. In this case, though, output will vary as a result of the evolution of real and nominal shocks relative to their expectations at the time that labour market contracts were last negotiated.

Real shocks in the form of unforecasted variations in q have an unambi-guously larger effect under fixed exchange rates than under flexible rates. We have already established that k lies between zero and one. The coef-ficient $k(1+\alpha\phi)$ is larger than one. Thus, under flexible exchange rates real shocks have a damped effect on output while under fixed rates they have an amplified effect. The effects of nominal shocks on output are also larger under fixed rates than under flexible rates (for a given size of shock). The comparison in this case is similar to that of the equilibrium monetary model but the two cases are identical only for $g = \infty$.

Equations (6.29) and (6.30) look similar to (6.23) and (6.24) and the task of discriminating between the equilibrium and Keynesian models does not appear straightforward. There are some key differences though. First, in the Keynesian model it is forecast errors that have accumulated since the previous wage-setting period that drive output while in the equilibrium monetary model it is one-period-ahead forecast errors that drive output. Second, as will become apparent in the next section, the precise form of the difference equation driving output under the Keynesian model as well as its variance, is exchange rate regime-specific.

I have now developed three alternative models of the business cycle and generated their implications for the behaviour of aggregate output. The next task is to examine the behaviour of output and to test the hypotheses generated by these three competing theories.

IV   Testing and discriminating

It is convenient to begin by looking at the time series to be explained – Japan's real gross domestic product between 1965:1 and 1985:1. Figure 6.1 sets out the path of that variable. It is immediately apparent that the primary concern of this paper, the business cycle, is not the major feature of the data. A strong upward trend and a strikingly regular seasonal pattern are the dominant features. These two features of the data are captured in the models set out above by the production function shock variable, z, as well as the other exogenous variables summarised in the random variable, q_t.

In view of the dominance of trends and seasonality in the data the statistical model of the q_t process clearly is important. The proponents of real and monetary equilibrium business cycle theories have typically favoured modelling trends and seasonal factors with deterministic variables (smooth time trends and linear seasonal shifts).[6] More recently, Nelson and Plosser (1982) have proposed that the trends and seasonals be modelled stochastically. Specifically, they have proposed that a random walk in the seasonal difference of output is the appropriate model.[7]

If tests capable of discriminating between these two alternative methods for modelling trends and seasonality were available there would be little problem. A general model could be set out that incorporated both as special cases and the restrictions implied by each formulation could be tested. That approach, however, is not straightforward. Nelson and Heejon Kang (1981, 1984) have shown that spurious autoregressions may be found in data generated by unit root processes. Dickey and Fuller

Figure 6.1 Japan's real GDP, 1965–85

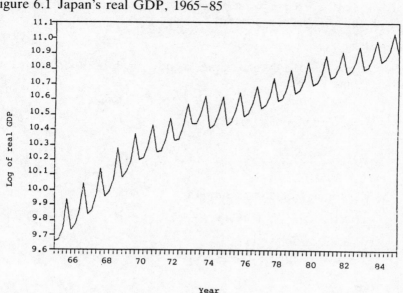

(1981) have calculated, using Monte Carlo methods, tables of test statistics for detecting unit roots. These tests, however, are for special-case processes.

In the light of this situation, I model the q_t process in two alternative ways. First, I employ a model that embodies both deterministic trends and seasonals and a first-order autoregressive process. Second, I use the first difference of the seasonal difference.

The first assumption, which will be called model A, is:

$$q_t = f(t,\tau) + ay_{t-1} + u_t \tag{6.31}$$

where $f(t,\tau)$ is a deterministic function of the year (t) and the season (τ) and where[8]

$$u_t \sim \text{iid } (0,\sigma_u^2).$$

The random component on (6.31), u, is associated with the random variable D in the definition of q. Specifically, it can be seen that

$$D_t - E_{t-1}D_t = \frac{\Delta}{1 + g} u_t.$$

Using (6.31), we may obtain solutions for output under the three alternative business cycle models. Those solutions are: for the real model,

$$y_t = f(t,\tau) + ay_{t-1} + u_t, \tag{6.32}$$

regardless of the exchange rate regime; for the equilibrium monetary model under fixed exchange rates,

$$y_t = f(t,\tau) + ay_{t-1} + u_t + \xi_t^r \tag{6.33}$$

where r represents the exchange rate regime which is either fixed, i, or flexible, ℓ, and where

$$\xi_t^i = u_t + \frac{\alpha\phi g}{\Delta}(p_t - E_{t-1}p_t), \tag{6.34a}$$

$$\xi_t^\ell = ku_t + \frac{k\alpha\phi g}{\Delta}(m_t - E_{t-1}m_t + v_t - E_{t-1}v_t). \tag{6.34b}$$

For the Keynesian model the solution is

$$y_{t,\tau} = f(t,\tau) + aE_w y_{-1} + ak_1^r(y_{-j} - E_w y_{-j}) + \xi_{t,\tau}^r \tag{6.35}$$

where $j = \begin{cases} t-1, 4 & \text{for } \tau=1 \\ t, \tau-1 & \text{for } \tau=2,3,4 \end{cases}$

and where

$$k_1^i = \Delta/(1 + g) > 1, \tag{6.36a}$$

$$k_1^\ell = \Delta/(1 + g)(1 + \alpha\phi) < 1, \tag{6.36b}$$

and

$$\xi^r = k_1^r u_{t,\tau} + k_2^r(m_{t,\tau} - E_w m_{t,\tau} + v_{t,\tau} - E_w v_{t,\tau}), \tag{6.37}$$

$$k_2^i = \alpha\phi, \tag{6.38a}$$

$$k_2^\ell = \alpha\phi/(a + \alpha\phi). \tag{6.38b}$$

The solutions to the real model (6.32) and the equilibrium monetary model (6.33) are stochastic difference equations with iid disturbances, the disturbances being the forecast errors of exogenous variables – real shocks, prices, or nominal aggregate demand. The Keynesian solution (6.35) needs some further work. It includes expectations of the dependent variable conditional on information available at the time of wage determination.

To solve (6.35) we need to calculate $E_w y_{t,\tau}$, which is

$$E_w y_{t,\tau} = f(t,\tau) + aE_w y_{-j} \tag{6.39}$$

and which, given $y_{t-1,4}$ has the solution

$$E_w y_{t,\tau} = g(t,\tau) + a^\tau y_{t-1,4}. \tag{6.40}$$

Using (6.40) in (6.35) gives

$$y_{t,\tau} = h(t,\tau) + a^\tau k_1^r y_{-j} + a^\tau (1 - k_1^r) y_{t-1,4} + \xi_{t,\tau}^r. \tag{6.41}$$

The key distinctions between the three theories are now transparently clear. The real theory predicts that output follows an autoregressive process that is independent of the exchange rate regime. The equilibrium monetary theory predicts that output follows an autoregressive process, the variance of which changes when the exchange rate regime changes. In this case, the deterministic part of the process is exchange rate regime-invariant. The Keynesian theory, like the equilibrium monetary theory, predicts that the variance of output changes with the exchange rate regime. It also makes two other predictions. First, output in the fourth quarter of the previous year affects current output in a systematic way. Second, the coefficients of the autoregressive process change when the exchange rate regime changes. More strongly, since k_1^r is greater than one under fixed rates and less than one under flexible rates, the coefficient on output in the fourth quarter of the previous year will be negative under fixed exchange rates and positive under flexible exchange rates. Thus, if the model of q_t assumed in (6.31) is true, we have a potentially powerful way of discriminating between these three theories of the business cycle.

The key differences in the predictions of the three models are summarised in Figures 6.2 and 6.3. Figure 6.2 contrasts the real model (frame a) with the monetary and Keynesian models (frame b). In the real model aggregate supply (AS) is inelastic. Under fixed exchange rates aggregate demand (AD) is perfectly elastic while, under flexible rates, aggregate demand is downward sloping. A shock to nominal demand measured by a vertical displacement from AD to AD′ (under either exchange rate regime) raises the price level from p_0 to p_1 but has no effect on output. A shock to aggregate supply from AS to AS′ raises output from y_0 to y_1 regardless of the exchange rate regime. Under fixed rates the price level stays constant at p_0 (the equilibrium being at D) and under flexible exchange rates the price level falls (the equilibrium being at C).

In the monetary and Keynesian models aggregate demand is the same as in the real model but aggregate supply has positive elasticity. The initial equilibrium is at A. A shock to aggregate demand that raises the AD curve to AD′ (moving the curve through point F under either fixed or flexible rates) raises output. Output raises to y_2 under fixed rates (point C) and y_1 under flexible rates (point B). A shock to aggregate supply which shifts the aggregate supply curve to AS′ lowers output. Under fixed rates output falls to y_4 (point E) and under flexible rates to y_3 (point D).

Thus if the variability of output is invariant with respect to the exchange rate regime, the real model is not rejected and the monetary and Keynesian models are rejected. Conversely, a change in the variability of output when the exchange rate regime changes leads to a rejection of the real model and

Figure 6.2 Real v. monetary and Keynesian models

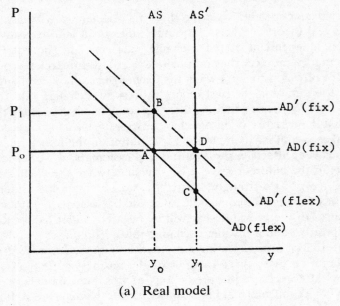

(a) Real model

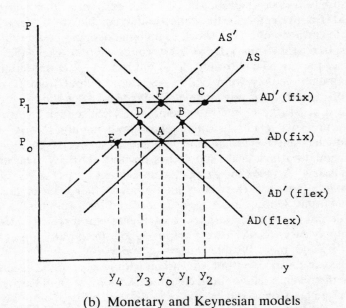

(b) Monetary and Keynesian models

Figure 6.3 Real and monetary v. Keynesian model

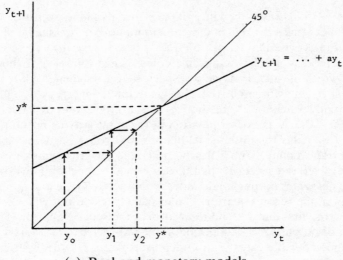

(a) Real and monetary models

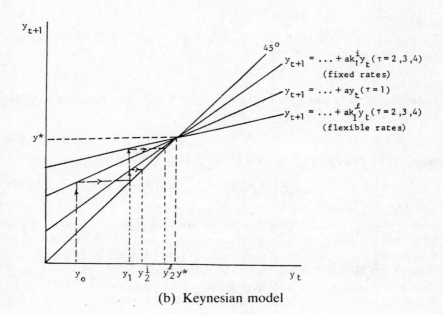

(b) Keynesian model

a non-rejection but no discrimination between the monetary and Keynesian models.

Figure 6.3 illustrates the difference in the dynamic adjustments predicted and contrasts the real and monetary models on the one hand (frame a) with the Keynesian model on the other (frame b). The real and monetary models predict monotonic convergence following a shock, the path of which is invariant with respect to the exchange rate regime. Starting at y_0, and with no further shocks, output converges through y_1 and y_2, eventually reaching y^*. In the Keynesian model output moves in the first quarter after wage determination in the same way as in the real and monetary models. In subsequent quarters the response depends on the exchange rate regime. Under flexible rates the reaction function is flatter and under fixed rates steeper than the quarter-one reaction function. Thus under flexible rates output would move from y_0 to y_1 in the first quarter and then to y_2^{ℓ} in the second quarter. Under fixed rates output will move from y_0 to y_1 in the first quarter and then to y_2^{i} in the second quarter. The convergence of output to y^* is still monotonic but the speed of adjustment is higher under flexible rates than under fixed rates. (Figure 6.3b excludes some features of the actual adjustment path that would show up as shifts in the reaction functions.)

An alternative model of q_t, called model B, is the first difference of the seasonal difference of output. Specifically, assume that

$$q_t = y_{t-4} + (y_{t-1} - y_{t-5}) + u_t. \tag{6.42}$$

Using (6.42) instead of (6.31) yields the following predictions for output. In the case of the real model,

$$(1 - L)(1 - L^4)y_t = u_t, \tag{6.43}$$

regardless of the exchange rate regime. In the case of the monetary equilibrium model,

$$(1 - L)(1 - L^4)y_t = \xi_t^r \tag{6.44}$$

where ξ_t^r is given by (6.34). And in the case of the Keynesian model,

$$(1 - L)(1 - L^4)y_{t,\tau} = (1 - k_1^r)(1 - L^4)(y_{t-1,4} - y_{-j}) + \xi_{t,\tau}^r \tag{6.45}$$

and where $\xi_{t,\tau}^r$ and k_1^r are given in (6.36) and (6.37).

It is evident that the same general distinctions apply to the three business cycle models in the case of this alternative model of q_t. Again, in the real model the output process is exchange rate regime-invariant; in the equilibrium monetary model only the variance of output process changes with the exchange rate regime, and in the Keynesian model the autoregressive parameters as well as the variance of output change when the exchange rate regime changes. The A and B versions of the three alternative models are summarised in Table 6.1. It is now possible to discriminate between the alternatives.

The key prediction that distinguishes the real business cycle theory from the other two concerns the behaviour of the random component of output across the two exchange rate regimes. The real business cycle theory predicts a homogeneous process while the other two theories predict a specific type of heteroskedasticity, namely that the variance of the disturbance term in output is lower under flexible exchange rates than under fixed rates.

To test for heteroskedasticity in the output process an equation of the form of (6.32) was estimated and the residuals recovered for model A, and the first difference of the seasonal difference was calculated as an estimate of the shocks driving output for model B. These series are plotted in Figures 6.4 and 6.5 respectively. The frequency distributions of the estimated shocks are set out in Table 6.2. The figures in Table 6.2 are, of course, just another way of looking at the data in Figures 6.4 and 6.5.

The data presented in these figures and table suggest that random fluctuations in real GDP are indeed drawn from a tighter distribution post-1975 than pre-1975. Is that impression statistically significant?

Table 6.1 Summary of predictions

Model A: Deterministic trend and seasonals		
Real	$y_t = f(t,\tau) + ay_{t-1} + u_t$	(6.32)
Monetary equilibrium	$y_t = f(t,\tau) + ay_{t-1} + \xi_t^r$ $\mathrm{var}(\xi^i) > \mathrm{var}(\xi^\ell)$	(6.33)
Keynesian	$y_{t,\tau} = h(t,\tau) + ak_1^r y_{-j} + a^\tau(1 - k_1^r)y_{t-1,4} + \xi_t^r$ $\mathrm{var}(\xi^i) > \mathrm{var}(\xi^\ell)$ and $k_1^i > 1 > k_1^\ell > 0$	(6.41)
Model B: Unit roots		
Real	$(1 - L)(1 - L^4)y_t = u_t$	(6.43)
Monetary equilibrium	$(1 - L)(1 - L^4)y_t = \xi_t^r$ $\mathrm{var}(\xi^i) > \mathrm{var}(\xi^\ell)$	(6.44)
Keynesian	$(1 - L)(1 - L^4)y_{t,\tau} = (1 - k_1^r)(1 - L^4)(y_{t-1,4}) - y_{-j}) + \xi_{t,\tau}^r$ $\mathrm{var}(\xi^i) > \mathrm{var}(\xi^\ell)$ and $k_1^i > 1 > k_1^\ell > 0$	(6.45)

Table 6.2 Frequency distributions of output shocks (percentages)

Size of shock	Version A		Version B	
	Fixed	Flexible	Fixed	Flexible
$x < -3\%$	10.0	—		
$-3\% \leq x < -2\%$	10.0			
$-2\% \leq x < -1\%$	10.0			
$-1\% \leq x < 0$	15.0			
$0 \leq x < 1\%$	20.0			
$1\% \leq x < 2\%$	25.0			
$2\% \leq x < 3\%$	7.5			
$3\% \leq x$	2.5			

Testing for the effects of th
handled with some care. The
random variable – a dummy
when the regime changes. The
variable interacts with the ex
cesses that drive output clearly
way in which to model the re
particular, if the regime is infl
that interdependence between
supply and the policy regime –
  I shall assume that no such int
shall assume that the change in tl
to the shock process driving out
switch was unanticipated but, h
indefinitely. The actual history c
geting and the adoption of mone
with this assumption. Exchange r
period of the worldwide inflatio
Japan. This fact appears to have
firm monetary targeting (see Suz
way prompted by any aspects of .... stochastic behaviour of real output.
  Adopting these assumptions makes it possible to model the regime
switch in a clean and rigorous way by simply allowing the relevant parameters to take on different values in the two exchange rate regimes and by
testing hypotheses of homogeneity across the two regimes, using standard
procedures.
  To test for the equality of the variances of the output shocks F-tests

Figure 6.4 Random shocks to output, deterministic trend and seasonals

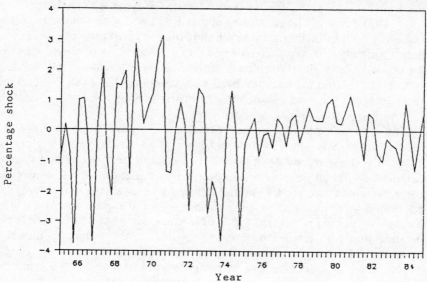

Figure 6.5 Random shocks to output, unit root model

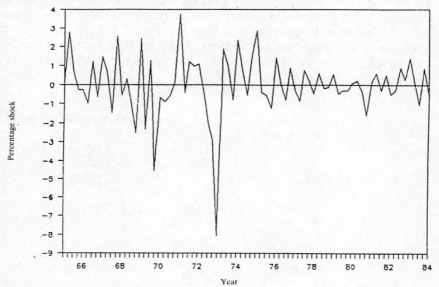

were computed which are summarised in Table 6.3. Because the shock of the fourth quarter of 1973, associated with the large rise in the price of oil in 1973:3 was so large, it was decided to test for the equality of the variances both by including and excluding the effects of that single observation. Evidently, the hypothesis of equality of variances is strongly rejected for model A and clearly rejected at the 5% level for model B.[9]

I conclude from the tests reported and summarised in Table 6.3 that the real business cycle model is inconsistent with the behaviour of real GDP in Japan during this sample period.

The next task is to discriminate between the equilibrium monetary and Keynesian models, the key differences between which are highlighted in Table 6.1. First, focus on model A. The monetary model is given by equation (6.33) and the Keynesian model by equation (6.41). Inspecting these two equations reveals that the difference between the two models can be summarised in terms of propositions about the parameters k_1^r. The Keynesian model predicts the string of inequalities; $k_1^i > 1 > k_1^\ell > 0$. It can be seen that the Keynesian model specialises to the monetary model if $k_1^i = k_1^\ell = 1$.

Next look at model B. The monetary model is described by equation (6.44) and the Keynesian model by equation (6.45). Again, the same distinction holds. It is the values of the parameters k_1^r that distinguishes between the two models and again the same restrictions characterise the monetary equilibrium model.

There is, thus, a ready way of testing the Keynesian model and of discriminating between the Keynesian and monetary models. For the Keynesian model to be true the restriction that $k_1^i > 1$ and $k_1^\ell < 1$ must be true. If those two parameters are not significantly different from each other and not significantly different from 1 then the restrictions of the monetary

Table 6.3   Tests for difference in variance of output shocks across policy regimes

Version	Oil shock 1973:4	Test statistic	Conclusion and significance
		F(1,78)	
A	included	16.11	reject equality 0.001
A	excluded	13.33	reject equality 0.005
		F(1,73)	
B	included	4.90	reject equality 0.03
B	excluded	4.31	reject equality 0.04

Table 6.4 *Tests of restrictions of the Keynesian model*

		Prediction: $k_1^i > 1 > k_1^\ell > 0$		
Version	Oil shock 1973:4	Test statistic	Conclusion	Significance
A	included	$F(1,69) = 2.674$	reject	0.11
A	excluded	$F(1,68) = 2.211$	reject	0.14
B	included	$F(1,73) = 0.747$	reject	0.39
B	excluded	$F(1,72) = 1.561$	reject	0.22

model cannot be rejected but the predictions of the Keynesian model are rejected.

Tests of the inequality restrictions implied by the Keynesian model are set out in Table 6.4. For model A a regression based on equation (6.41) including the non-linear restrictions on the parameters a, k_1^i, k_1^ℓ, was estimated and the null hypothesis of equality of k_1^i and k_1^ℓ was tested. In the case of model B equation (6.45) was estimated and the same null hypothesis tested on the parameters k_1^i and k_1^ℓ in that formulation. The results, set out in Table 6.4, decisively reject the predictions of the Keynesian model. We can confidently accept the restriction that k_1^i is equal to k_1^ℓ, thereby rejecting the Keynesian model.

To test the monetary model we need to test the hypothesis that the additional restriction that $k_1^i = k_1^\ell = 1$ is satisfied. Table 6.5 summarises the tests of these restrictions. For model A these restrictions are tested by comparing equation (6.41) with equation (6.33). Equation (6.41) has two additional free parameters. For version B the comparison is made between equations (6.45) and (6.44) and again, (6.45) has two additional para-

Table 6.5 *Tests of restrictions of the monetary equilibrium model*

		Prediction: $k_1^i = k_1^\ell = 1$		
Version	Oil shock 1973:4	Test statistic	Conclusion	Significance
A	included	$F(2,69) = 2.490$	accept	0.09
A	excluded	$F(2,68) = 1.786$	accept	0.18
B	included	$F(2,73) = 0.401$	accept	0.67
B	excluded	$F(2,72) = 0.261$	accept	0.77

Table 6.6   Residuals analysis

Version	Oil shock 1973:4	DW	Q(24)	Significance of Q
A	included	1.591	77.675	0.14 (E-06)
A	excluded	1.692	82.138	0.27 (E-07)
B	included	2.113	29.283	0.21
B	excluded	2.404	34.655	0.07

meters. As the results shown in Table 6.4 reveal, we are not able to reject the restriction of the monetary equilibrium model.

In discriminating between the three models I have used two different statistical representations of trends and cycles as a check on the robustness of the conclusions reached. It is clear that for all the crucial tests performed, the outcome is identical (though the strength does vary), regardless of which trend and seasonal model is employed. Some features of the results obtained do point in the direction of rejecting, however, the deterministic model. The residuals in that model are significantly autocorrelated (at some order) as indicated by the Box–Pierce Q statistic (see Table 6.6). We cannot reject the hypothesis that the stochastic process described by the first difference of the seasonal difference is white noise, however (again, see Box–Pierce Q statistics in Table 6.6).

V   Conclusions

This chapter has reported the results of implementing simple but decisive tests, that discriminate between real, equilibrium monetary and new Keynesian theories of the business cycle. For this particular economy and time period, the tests are decisive, and lead to a rejection of real and Keynesian theories and to a non-rejection of the monetary equilibrium theory.

It is premature to conclude that Keynesian theory has been an unfortunate blind alley and that it should now be banished from the textbooks and from policy discussions, or that the recently renewed interest in real business cycle theory is misplaced. Clearly, much more testing is required. Even those who previously believed the Japanese economy to be a prime example of new Keynesianism can legitimately argue that the bonus system is responsible for equilibrium behaviour and that, since most other countries do not have the same type of bonus arrangements that are present in Japan, these same conclusions will not apply to those other countries. That conjecture needs to be checked out. It will, though, be less than straight-forward to perform that task. The key difficulty lies in the fact that most countries do not have well-defined wage rounds of the type found in Japan. Wages are set for periods that vary from perhaps a year to as much as three years into the future. Some contracts are indexed and some are not. Some times of the year are more popular for negotiating wage settlements but significant fractions of contracts are renewed in each and every quarter of the year. Thus, finding strong predictions concerning the autoregression pattern of output (or of other aggregates) and of the error processes that are implied by the alternative models will be harder and less clear-cut in the case of these other economies. Nevertheless, the careful writing down of models similar to that employed here (but with appropriately more complicated timing patterns for the Keynesian versions) does promise success.

One feature of the work reported here is that exclusive focus has been placed on the behaviour of output. Clearly, the behaviour of employment, money wages, real wages and the price level, all provide, in principle, additional information concerning the validity of each of the three alter-native models. Further work that checks out the predictions of the three models for these other variables and examines whether the conclusions reached on the basis of the behaviour of output apply to those other variables would also be desirable. The results of this work could go either way, for the behaviour of other variables would depend crucially on some of the (perhaps subsidiary) assumptions employed in the current analysis. Further work along these lines needs to be pursued.

Notes

Work on this paper has been supported by a grant from the Social Sciences and Humanities Research Council of Canada. I am grateful to Robin Carter, Zvi Hercowitz, Peter Howitt, Chris Robinson, Aman Ullah and Michael Veall for comments on an earlier draft. The usual disclaimer applies.

1 Even careful attempts to discriminate between Keynesian and equilibrium monetary theories are capable of more than one interpretation. Perhaps the best examples of these are the series of papers Barro, 1977, 1978; and Barro and Rush, 1980. My own earlier effort (Parkin, 1984) was also inconclusive.
2 My earlier study (Parkin, 1984) provides a comprehensive survey of the previous literature on the Japanese business cycle. That paper and this have been heavily influenced by Grossman and Haraf, 1983.
3 For a much richer account of that history see Komiya and Yasui, 1984.
4 As an aside, I should like to note that the measurement of labour market variables – employment and real wages – is, in my view, too unreliable to make the predictions of the model in that area empirically relevant.
5 This time notation was first used by Grossman and Haraf, 1983, whose work was very

influential in attracting me to this problem and episode.

6 As an aside, I should like to offer the suggestion that favouring a deterministic model of the trend arises from the fact that traditional growth models were couched in deterministic terms with the consequence that the random fluctuations were thought of as being *the* 'business cycle'.

7 Wasserfallen, 1985, provides a useful review of the two alternative approaches.

8 The function $f(t,\tau)$ employed is:

$$\beta_0 + \beta_1 t + \beta_2 s_2 + \beta_3 s_3 + \beta_4 s_4 + \beta_5 d_1 + \beta_6 d_1 t + \beta_7 d_2 s_4 + b_8 d_3$$

where t is time, s_i is 1 in quarter i and zero elsewhere, d_1 is 1 after 1973:3 and zero elsewhere, d_2 is 1 before 1969 and zero elsewhere, and d_3 is 1 in 1973:4 and zero elsewhere.

9 The details of these and the other calculations are set out in an Appendix available on request. All the computations were performed using RATS (Doan and Litterman, 1981).

References

Barro, R. J. (1977). 'Unanticipated money growth and unemployment in the United States', *American Economic Review*, vol. 67, no. 1, pp. 101–15.

Barro, R. J. (1978). 'Unanticipated money, output and the price level in the United States', *Journal of Political Economy*, vol. 86, no. 4, pp. 549–80.

Barro, R. J. and Rush, M. (1980). 'Unanticipated money and economic activity', in S. Fischer (ed.), *Rational Expectations and Economic Policy* (Chicago and London: University of Chicago Press).

Dickey, D. A. and Fuller, W. A. (1981). 'Likelihood ratio statistics for autoregressive time series with a unit root', *Econometrica*, vol. 49, pp. 1057–72.

Doan, T. A. and Litterman, R. B. (1981). User's Manual RATS Version 4.1, Minneapolis, Minn. VAR Econometrics.

Fischer, S. (1977). 'Long-term contracts, rational expectations, and the optimal money supply rule', *Journal of Political Economy*, vol. 85, no. 1, pp. 191–206.

Grossman, H. I. and Haraf, W. S. (1983). 'Shunto, rational expectations and output growth in Japan', Brown University, Department of Economics, Working Paper No. 83–5, May 1983.

Hashimoto, M. (1979). 'Bonus payments, on-the-job training, and lifetime employment in Japan', *Journal of Political Economy*, vol. 86, no. 5, pp. 1086–1104.

King, R. G. and Plosser, C. I. (1984). 'Money, credit and prices in a real business cycle model', *American Economic Review*, vol. 74, no. 3, pp. 363–80.

Komiya, R. and Yasui, K. (1984). 'Japan's macroeconomic performance since the first oil crisis: review and reappraisal', in K. Brunner and A. H. Meltzer (eds), *Carnegie–Rochester Conference Series on Public Policy*, vol. 20, pp. 69–114.

Kydland, F. E. and Prescott, E. C. (1982). 'Time to build and aggregate fluctuations', *Econometrica*, vol. 50, no. 6, pp. 1345–70.

Long, J. B. and Plosser, C. I. (1983). 'Real business cycles', *Journal of Political Economy*, vol. 91, no. 1, pp. 39–69.

Lucas, R. E. Jr. (1972). 'Expectations and the neutrality of money', *Journal of Economic Theory*, vol. 4, no. 2, pp. 103–24.

Lucas, R. E. Jr. (1973). 'Some international evidence on output–inflation tradeoffs', *American Economic Review*, vol. 63, no. 3, pp. 326–34.

Lucas, R. E. Jr. (1975). 'An equilibrium model of the business cycle', *Journal of Political Economy*, vol. 83, no. 6, pp. 1113–44.

Nelson, C. R. and Heejon Kang (1981). 'Spurious periodicity in inappropriately detrended time series', *Econometrica*, vol. 49, pp. 741–51.

Nelson, C. R. and Heejon Kang (1984). 'Pitfalls in the use of time as an explanatory variable in regression', *Journal of Business and Economic Statistics*, vol. 2, pp. 73–82.

Nelson, C. R. and Plosser, C. I. (1982). 'Trends and random walks in macroeconomic time series', *Journal of Monetary Economics*, vol. 10, pp. 139–62.

Parkin, M. (1984). 'Discriminating between Keynesian and classical theories of the business cycle: Japan, 1967–1982', *Bank of Japan Monetary and Economic Studies*, vol. 2, no. 2, pp. 23–60.

Phelps, E. S. and Taylor, J. B. (1977). 'Stabilising powers of monetary policy under rational expectations', *Journal of Political Economy*, vol. 85, no. 1, pp. 163–90.

Shimada, H., Seike, A., Furugori, T., Sakai, Y. and Hosokawa, T. (1983). 'The Japanese labor market: a survey', *Japanese Economic Studies*, vol. 11, pp. 3–84.

Suzuki, Y. (1980). 'Why Japanese macroeconomic performance was better in 1959', Bank of Japan Mimeograph. Paper presented to the World Congress of the Mont Pelerin Society, Stanford, Calif.

Taylor, J. B. (1979). 'Staggered wage setting in a macro model', *American Economic Review, Papers and Proceedings*, vol. 69, no. 2, pp. 108–13.

Taylor, J. B. (1980). 'Aggregate dynamics and staggered contracts', *Journal of Political Economy*, vol. 88, no. 1, pp. 1–23.

Wasserfallen, W. (1985). 'Trends, random walks and the Phillips curve: evidence from six countries', mimeo, University of Bern, January.

Part II
Industry, trade and investment

7

Manufacturing industry, economic growth and the balance of payments

Sir James Ball

Introduction

It is over a quarter of a century ago since I joined the economics department of the University of Manchester and met Dennis Coppock. We were *nearly* all Keynesians then. Keynes had solved the problem of how to maintain full employment – so it seemed. However, there were seen to be problems with the rate of economic growth. Attempts by government to expand output through fiscal expansion led to balance of payments crisis, in a world in which the exchange rate was a central policy focus. 'Stop–go' was the way in which alternate bouts of policy expansion and contraction were described. There grew up the idea that, as immediately after the Second World War, the economy was 'balance of payments constrained'.

The existence of North Sea oil over the last decade shifted attention away from the problem of the balance of payments. However, the issue of the balance of payments as a constraint on future economic growth has been returning. It was raised in its most dramatic form by the House of Lords Report from the Select Committee on Overseas Trade in 1985 (House of Lords, 1985a).

To oversimplify, the problem is posed – what do we do when the oil runs out? Initially this appears as a 'balance of payments' problem. Both the reduction in the oil price and the peaking of North Sea oil production mean that receipts have fallen rapidly and are likely to continue to fall into the 1990s. Moreover, during the years of major oil production there was initially a sharp fall in manufacturing employment and output, although output has recovered substantially since 1981. This is expected to have at least two important and related effects: there could be serious problems with the balance of payments (harking back to the 1960s) and important consequences for economic growth. Thus the future of manufacturing industry is seen as *crucially* at the heart of Britain's economic future. This is a theme that has occurred in the late 1960s and the early and late 1970s. It now comes again.

The remainder of this chapter is devoted first to the question, to what extent is there something unique about manufacturing industry which makes it so crucial to our future? Secondly, it is concerned with the significance of the idea that the balance of payments does impose and is likely to impose some constraint on economic growth which is also related to the UK's manufacturing future.

Economic growth and manufacturing industry

It was Nicholas Kaldor who first focused on the link between economic growth and manufacturing growth in his influential inaugural lecture on the 'Causes of the Slow Rate of Economic Growth of the United Kingdom' (Kaldor, 1966). The general thesis was that differences in rates of economic growth were largely attributable to differences in the *stages of development* 'rather than in the realm of personal (or rather individual) abilities or incentives' (p. 3). In particular, a fast rate of growth was primarily associated with a fast rate of growth of the secondary sector of the economy, mainly the manufacturing sector. The trouble with the United Kingdom economy, it was asserted, was that in terms of sector balance it had reached 'premature maturity' ahead of other countries.

The unique importance of manufacturing industry in the growth pocess was dependent on 'the existence of economies of scale or increasing returns, which causes productivity to increase in response to, or as a by-product of, the increase in total output' (p. 8). The interplay of static and dynamic factors caused returns to increase with an increase in the scale of industrial activities. The centrepiece of this phenomenon was the 'learning curve' down which the economy had to travel – 'which means that productivity tends to grow, the faster output expands' (p. 9). It is of the utmost importance to understand that this process is seen as a 'macro-phenomenon': 'just because so much of the economies of scale emerge as a result of increased differentiation, the emergence of new processes and new subsidiary industries, they cannot be discerned adequately by observing the effects of variations in the size of an individual firm or of a particular industry' (p. 10). Thus manufacturing industry was seen as the 'engine' of economic growth.

What therefore accounted for *differences* in the rates of growth between countries? 'The explanation in my view, lies partly in demand factors and partly in supply factors; and both of these combine to make fast rates of growth the characteristic of an intermediate stage in economic development' (p. 19). Kaldor hesitated as to how important was the widely held view that the balance of payments had been a constraint on postwar economic growth in Britain:

> It is certainly true that brief periods of relatively high growth during the last twenty years were increasingly attended by a rapid growth of imports resulting in balance of payments deficits; and it was the occurrence of these deficits as much as the labour shortages and the resulting inflation, which forced the introduction of deflationary measures which brought these periods to an end... But this does not necessarily prove that the balance of payments was the *effective* constraint on our rate of economic growth. (p. 24)

Ball and Burns argued shortly afterwards (1968) that

> While growth and the balance of payments are closely interrelated, the balance of payments is not the sole potential constraint on the rate of growth...the removal of this constraint is unlikely to result in any dramatic change in the UK's growth potential; equally important are the constraints imposed by the potential rate of investment and the growth of the capital stock, and the rates of growth of the labour supply and productivity. These are internal constraints. Even given some solution of the balance-of-payments problem, there is no promised land into which we can then naturally expect to pass. Recent excessive concentration on the payments account has tended to sweep these issues under the carpet.

Kaldor himself concluded that 'A higher rate of growth could not have been maintained unless more manpower had been made available to the manufacturing industry' (1966, p. 26). The shortage of labour thesis was criticised by Wolfe (1968) and Kaldor quickly retracted this part of his analysis (Kaldor, 1971). He now focused on the demand side of the economy in a second major paper to the British Association in 1970. Here Kaldor maintained the original idea of the importance of manufacturing industry for the reasons already given, but now emphasised the significance of one component of manufacturing output, namely exports. From this developed the idea of *export-led growth*:

> My main criticism of the philosophy underlying the White Paper [of 1944] and of the post-war policies of economic management that were built on it, is that it treated the problem of full employment and (implicity) of growth, as one of internal demand management, and not one of exports and of international competitiveness. (Kaldor, 1971, p. 5).

The new twist given to the analysis by Kaldor was to argue that fiscal policy was to be the key instrument for maintaining equilibrium in the *balance of payments*, while the exchange rate *via* the growth of exports was to determine the overall *rate of growth of output*. Inflation was left to some appropriate form of incomes policy. Thus the overall 'affordable' growth rate was determined by the growth of exports and the setting of the exchange rate. Fiscal policy was to fix the growth of domestic demand so as to generate the only rate of growth of imports consistent with the export growth rate and balance of payments equilibrium. The essence of this approach is that the exchange rate was seen as a policy instrument that might be manipulated to set the growth rate.

De-industrialisation

Events following the publication of Kaldor's (1971) paper conspired to put the issue raised on the back-burner. Monetary and fiscal expansion following the rise in the oil price was reflected in record inflation and a sharper recession than in the rest of the world. But as the dust began to settle in 1976 and some modest recovery became apparent, the questions of the performance and the future of manufacturing industry came back on to the agenda in the form of the so-called problem of *de-industrialisation*.

The general problem might be described as the progressive weakening of the manufacturing sector of the economy. How is weakness to be defined? A starting point might be to consider the share of manufacturing employment and output in total employment and ouput. They appear to be reasonable *domestic* measures of the *relative* importance of the manufacturing sector to the national economy. However, if falling ratios simply reflected slower growth in manufacturing relative to the rest of the economy why should that matter if total output was growing satisfactorily? (See Cairncross, 1978, p. 6.)

Over a decade ago Singh asked the question: what constitutes an 'efficient' manufacturing sector in an open economy such as the United Kingdom? (1977, p. 127) He emphasised the importance of not attempting to define de-industrialisation on a purely domestic basis. In his view,

> the manufacturing sector is the major source of foreign exchange earnings on the current account. More importantly...it is potentially the main means through which an improvement in the balance of payments could be thought sufficient to correct the existing disequilibrium. Therefore given *The normal levels of the other components of the balance of payments* we may define an efficient manufacturing sector as one which (*currently as well as potentially*) *not only satisfies the demands of consumers at home but is also able to sell enough of its products abroad to pay for the nation's import requirements*. This is however subject to the important restriction that *an 'efficient' manufacturing sector must be able to achieve these objectives at socially acceptable levels of output, employment and the exchange rate.*

(1977, p. 128, italics in original)

He went on to argue that

In operational terms, a structural problem can arise in this sense if the manufacturing sector, without losing price or cost competitiveness, is unable to export enough to pay for the full employment level of imports (1977, p. 128).

The chief difficulty with this definition is that it begs the central question that is at issue. In a neoclassical world with fully flexible prices and capital mobility there is no such thing as *the* 'full employment level of imports'. It is the assumption that there is which gives the definition its plausibility. Thirlwall (1982, p. 23) seems to make a similar point, arguing that the trouble with the definition is that it is not 'cause free': 'The cause is pre-judged before the analysis starts which is not satisfactory.' Thirlwall's own solution is to settle for the fact that it has been the *absolute* decline in manufacturing employment that should be the focus of concern. It is, however, clear that this by itself is not enough, important a figure as it might be. While it has been suggested that Singh's definition is question-begging, nevertheless the international dimension of the problem cannot be overlooked. It does matter whether performance, however measured, compares with the performance in other countries. Internal measures alone are not enough.

There would seem to be more agreement between Thirlwall and Singh as to why a progressive weakening of the manufacturing sector should be a matter of concern. It was seen as important as the engine of growth (Thirlwall, 1982, p. 27) for the reason put forward by Kaldor (1966) (see also Singh, 1977, p. 118). It was seen as important to the future of jobs and unemployment and because it constituted a major share of export earnings, with regard to the future of the balance of payments. (See also the contributions in Blackaby, 1979.)

The coming of North Sea oil was overlaid on the debate on de-industrialisation. At the end of the paper cited, Singh wrote (1977, p. 133):

But there is at least one component of visible trade (minerals, fuels etc) which may be expected to show an enormous improvement over the next few years as a consequence of North Sea oil. Depending on the size of the surplus the country could then have a balance of payments equilibrium at full employment and at desired levels of real income and exchange rate, even if the trading position of the manufacturing sector continued to decline. This however is not a sustainable position in the long run, since unless the manufacturing sector improves and become more dynamic, it may not be able to pay for the full employment level of imports at a later stage when the oil runs out.

For many people there is the belief that the latter situation will emerge in the 1990s if not before (see House of Lords, 1985a, 1985b). Before addressing the main issues that have emerged so far, some observations about the role and consequences of North Sea oil are in order.

Manufacturing industry, North Sea oil and the balance of payments

It is helpful from the point of view of exposition to follow the approach of
Eastwood and Venables (1982) in reviewing the benefits of North Sea oil in
terms of its effects on the potential flow of foreign exchange. (See also the
discussion in Ball, 1982, pp. 223–6.) For a country with no oil, the discovery of oil means that it is no longer necessary to purchase it from abroad.
True, there are real resource costs related to the production of the oil, but
relative to the other implications for real resources, they may as a first
approximation be netted out. This focuses attention on the *financial* consequences of North Sea oil development as opposed to the *real resource*
consequences. The replacement of imported oil (in dollars) by domestic oil
releases foreign exchange. It also increases national wealth – in the sense
that it augments existing producible and saleable resources and so increases real income for the community as a whole. There are two ways in
which the coming on-stream of North Sea oil affects the economy: through
the exchange rate and through the level of spending.

Given the existence of a windfall gain in foreign exchange earnings, how
can the benefits in foreign exchange terms be enjoyed? The answer is clear
and immediate. They can only be enjoyed by the purchase of a combination
of overseas assets and goods at a constant exchange rate or by shifting
resources from manufacturing into service industries if the exchange rate
rises.

In so far as all net foreign exchange arising from North Sea oil has been
immediately spent overseas in one form or another, there will be *no* change
in the real exchange rate, *no* change in either the internal or external
demand for domestically produced manufactured products, and so *no*
effect directly on the output and employment of manufacturing industry.

However, in the other polar case, namely that all the foreign exchange
surplus is saved by the community, the current account will show a surplus
(assuming for the sake of argument we start from near balance), which by
assumption is not offset either by increased imports or a capital outflow.
Exports which had previously financed the purchase of oil are now surplus
to requirements from a balance of payments point of view. As a result the
real exchange rate must rise, the profitability of exporting will therefore
fall, and the export side of the current account will be squeezed back into
balance with the level of imports. In this extreme case oil production will
crowd out an equal amount of manufacturing output, so leaving total
output unchanged, but in the short run at least leaving idle resources – the
unemployment resulting from the decline in manufacturing, or at least in
that part of manufacturing producing tradable goods. On this scenario,
the only way that any benefit can be obtained from North Sea oil is by the

reabsorption of the idle resources into alternative uses producing non-tradable goods. (For a discussion of the problem from this point of view see Forsyth and Kay, 1980.)

It is therefore possible to invent scenarios in which the consequences of North Sea oil for manufacturing industry range from zero to a complete crowding out of an equivalent manufacturing industry output by oil production. Neither extreme is inevitable. The actual outcome is an empirical matter. It depends primarily on the extent to which North Sea oil raised the real exchange rate and through that conduit reduced manufacturing output below what it would otherwise have been. Any empirical analysis must separate out the 'pure' effects of North Sea oil from other factors that affected the behaviour of manufacturing industry at the time, which includes the general state of the world economy and the fiscal and monetary environment determined by the government, together with the decline in the real rate of return on capital that preceded the rise in oil prices.

The facts are that the major decline in manufacturing industry relative to trend occurred in the period 1979–81. As shown in Figure 7.1 the trend of manufacturing industry in terms of output had been negative since 1973. Employment in manufacturing had declined from 7.85 million in 1973 to 7.16 million in 1979. Between 1979 and 1981 manufacturing production fell by 14% and a further million jobs were lost. By 1986 total employment in manufacturing had fallen to 5.6 million. The question that economists have addressed has been, how much of this was due to the special influences of North Sea oil, and how much to other factors? The principal other factor on which there has been a focus of attention has been the fiscal and monetary policy pursued by the government of the day.

The empirical evidence as summarised by Bean (1987, pp. 82–5) and his own estimates make it clear that the rise in the real exchange rate that occurred in the period 1979–81 was materially influenced by the coming on-stream of North Sea oil. It is, however, frequently argued that a material role was played by the tightening of fiscal and monetary policy by the incoming Thatcher administration in 1979 in the face of accelerating inflation.

It is certainly true that the fiscal and monetary policy of the period was a significant determining factor in raising the real exchange rate in the short term (i.e. during 1980). But it is hard to see that this resulted from the *tightness* of fiscal and monetary policy rather than its *laxity*. While nominal interest rates rose sharply in 1980, sterling M3 grew by nearly 16%. Real interest rates in terms of domestic currency were only 2.6%. Concurrently, public spending rose by 26% in nominal terms and by 1.6% in real terms compared with an overall fall in total real output of 2.8%. However, while there may be some agreement that fiscal policy was lax, it is generally accepted that monetary policy was tightened, if reference is made both to

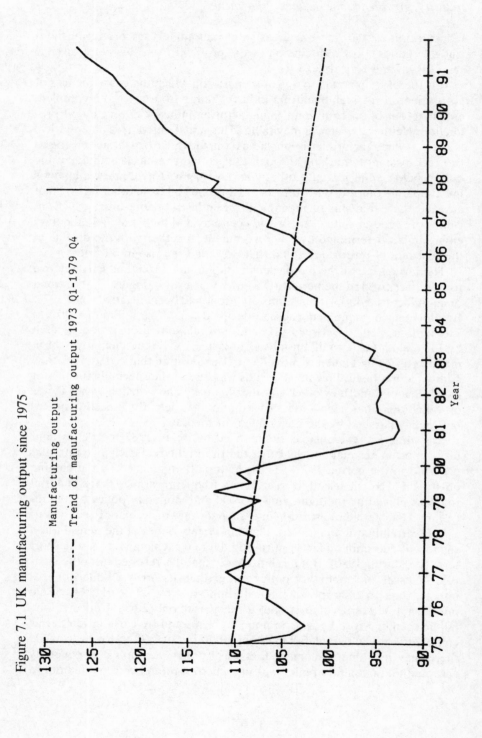

Figure 7.1 UK manufacturing output since 1975

——— Manufacturing output

—·—·— Trend of manufacturing output 1973 Q1-1979 Q4

the behaviour of the exchange and to the behaviour of the money supply as measured by M0. A final conclusion depends in part on why inflation accelerated over this period. To the extent that it was facilitated by monetary growth, monetary policy can hardly be described as restrictive.

All this suggests to me that far from tackling the problem of inflation, which reached 16% in 1980, both fiscal and monetary policy were out of control as a result of the ill-timed implementation of the promises contained in the Conservative Party's election manifesto of the previous year, in particular the implementation of the Clegg public pay awards and the rise in VAT. Control was only regained with the Budget of 1981. The combination of these events means that more damage was done to manufacturing industry than could simply be accounted for by the short-term adjustment problems associated with the development of North Sea oil. Having said that, there is a strong case for arguing that the decline in the non-oil trade balance, particularly in manufactures (see the House of Lords Select Committee Report, 1985a), resulted in large measure from the balance of payments adjustment process brought about by the contribution of oil to the current balance.

While correctly asserting that in the last analysis there was no reason why the discovery of oil logically entailed a major rise in the real exchange rate and a decline in manufacturing industry, the House of Lords Select Committee also wanted to know why a surplus on manufactured traded goods and oil could not coexist together (see House of Lords, 1985b, p. 558). The answer to the question was succinctly given by Mr Lawson, the Chancellor of the Exchequer, to whom the question was addressed (ibid p. 559). The other side of the coin to the current account surplus is of course the supply of savings. In the absence of a dramatic autonomous rise in the rate of saving it was in practice impossible to achieve what the Lords desired.

The role of manufacturing industry

The importance of manufacturing industry to the United Kingdom both in the present and in the past is not in question. It is equally not in question that there are serious matters of concern with regard to the historical performance of manufacturing in the United Kingdom, its current position and its future prospects. The important questions to be addressed relate first to the competitive position of manufacturing and the effects of that on relevant economic variables. Secondly and more fundamentally, much of the discussion of the role of manufacturing industry has suggested not simply that it is *a major and important sector* of the economy whose present and future is of profound interest to us, but that its future success has a

Table 7.1   *Share of manufacturing in GDP*

	1960	1970	1980	1985
USA	28.6	25.7	21.8	20.4
Japan	33.9	35.9	29.2	29.8
France	29.1	28.7	26.5	n.a.
West Germany	40.3	38.4	32.6	32.3
UK	32.1	28.1	24.0	22.6

Value added in manufacturing as percentage of current price GDP.

Source: *OECD Historical Statistics 1960–85*, Paris, October 1987 edition, Table 5.3.

unique significance. With the former it is easy to agree. The latter raises issues that require more examination.

The facts relating to the historical performance of manufacturing industry in the United Kingdom since the Second World War are well known. As shown in Table 7.1 the share of manufacturing in GDP declined from 32.1% in 1960, to 24.9% in 1979. Concomitantly as in Table 7.2 the share of manufacturing employment in civilian employment fell from 36% to 28.1%. To begin with at least it is appropriate to examine the historical record up to 1979 in view of the discussion of the last section. Prior to 1979 there may be greater agreement as to the causes of the fall in the share of manufacturing than for the period 1979 to date. As we have seen, much of recent discussion has sought to explain the behaviour of manufacturing since 1979 in terms of the effects of oil and the consequences of the fiscal and monetary policies pursued by Mrs Thatcher's government.

Table 7.2   *Employment in manufacturing*

	% of total civilian employment			
	1960	1970	1980	1985
USA	27.1	26.4	22.1	19.5
Japan	21.5	27.0	24.7	25.0
France	27.5	27.8	25.8	23.2
West Germany	37.0	39.4	34.3	32.0
UK	36.0	34.5	30.2	25.7

Source: *OECD Historical Statistics 1960–85*, Paris, October 1987 edition, Table 2.11.

Table 7.3   *OECD exports – shares by value*

	Manufactures					
	1960	1970	1983	1985	1986	1987
USA	21.6	18.5	17.2	16.8		
Japan	6.9	11.7	18.4	19.7		
France	9.6	8.7	8.9	8.5		
West Germany	19.3	19.8	19.0	18.6		
UK	16.5	10.8	7.9	7.9	7.6	8.0[a]

[a] estimate.

Source: *National Institute Economic Review* and *Monthly Review of External Trade Statistics*.

Over the period 1960–79 we also observe a decline in long-term competitiveness as measured by the share of manufactured exports in world manufactured exports as shown in Table 7.3. Some would point also to the increasing share of UK markets taken by imported manufactures as a further indicator of competitive decline. While this may have been substantially the case over this period, it is clear from the last section that a sharp rise in imports of manufactures will not necessarily reflect a decline in underlying competitiveness rather than an increase in international purchasing power relative to domestic capacity.

The figures for other countries in Tables 7.1 and 7.2 show that the decline in the *share* of manufacturing output and employment has been a general phenomenon in the OECD countries, at least since 1970. This suggests that whatever specific concerns there may be about the behaviour of manufacturing in the United Kingdom, part of what has been happening is related to a worldwide trend, reflecting changes in the underlying patterns of demand and productivity for and associated with manufactured products.

However, while this may be substantially the case, there have been matters of concern to the United Kingdom that transcend the general course of events. They relate to the fact that the share of manufacturing output, employment and export share have been declining more rapidly in the United Kingdom than elsewhere. Worse still, the United Kingdom represented the only example where manufacturing output actually declined in *absolute* terms between 1973 and 1981. It was only in 1986 that it regained its 1979 level. While the severe absolute reduction in manufacturing employment, both before 1979 and after 1979, raised severe social and economic problems, the decline in employment is not in itself a *prima facie* sign of reduced competitiveness. Paradoxically it might reflect the opposite. However, the behaviour of overall output would suggest that had the underlying competitive position of manufacturing output been better, the volume of employment would have declined far less.

The initial reason why manufacturing industry is regarded as unique in the economic process, stems from the contributions of Kaldor (1966, 1971) already discussed. The arguments reviewed in that discussion, it must be understood, are quite distinct from the arguments put forward in the last paragraph. The latter simply says that world manufactures constituted the fastest growing sector of the world economy overall, and so poor competitiveness resulted in a declining share of world demand for manufactures and so a relatively poor overall rate of economic growth. This in itself does not confer any uniqueness on the role of manufacturing. The uniqueness which characterises it as the 'engine of growth' is supposed to stem from the economies of scale, both static and dynamic, which generate macroeconomic effects for the economy as a whole (Kaldor, 1966).

There are two current difficulties with this hypothesis of uniqueness in the growth process and the conclusion that this presumably entails that 'special consideration' be given to manufacturing industry. The first is that, whatever the truth or falsity of the proposition in the past, it is not currently strictly relevant. The reason is simply that the long-term pattern of production, both at the world level and at the level of the individual country, will be determined by the pattern of demand and shifts in relative prices that originate from changes in supply conditions. The demand for manufactured goods has been interpreted as income-elastic. However, as incomes and standards of living rise, that elasticity may well be falling, giving rise at the margin to increased demand for other 'products' (not manufactured) and 'services'.

The second problem with the uniqueness argument turns on the importance of economies of scale and its interpretation at the microeconomic level. The argument put forward by Kaldor (1966) had a microeconomic analogue in the work done and the corporate policies advocated by the Boston Consulting Group (1968). At the industry level the learning curve was emphasised, and cost-focused corporate strategies advocated that permanent competitive advantage might be secured by sliding faster down the learning curve than competitors. The competitive position rested not on static economies of scale but on the cumulative output total. Competitors were required to relive the experience of the market leader.

This led to corporate strategy recommendations that focused on volume and market share as the key competitive variables which ultimately determined profitability as a natural outcome. Such ideas also to some extent underlay the importance of economies of scale in merger activity. They depended in large part on the importance of 'hardware' *versus* 'software' in economic performance (investment rather than organisation) and on relatively static technologies which set pre-ordained learning curves.

The modern strategy literature and studies of the competitive process over the last decade or so do not paint this picture of the world (Abernathy *et al.*, 1981; Baden Fuller, 1983; Hamel and Prahalad, 1985). Competitive strategies pursued by the Japanese (see Hamel and Prahalad, 1985) have not depended essentially on the presence of economies of scale or the existence of the learning curve. Success has been achieved in part by technological change (as in reprographics) where new technology has avoided the need to follow the leader, and by strong branding, the latter applying equally to service as well as manufactured products. There is little doubt that modern technology is substantially reducing the economic advantages of scale economies in production technology. The 'software' rather than 'hardware' has become more important (see the discussion of the US car industry in Abernathy *et al.*, 1981).

The second reason why attention is focused on the particular problems of manufacturing industry relates to the question, where are the jobs coming from? As shown in Figure 7.2, the employment experience in OECD over the last decade or more offers a sharp contrast between the experience of the USA and Japan on the one hand, and the United Kingdom and the European Community on the other. Between 1960 and 1974, natural wastage and absorption by other sectors roughly speaking matched the decline in manufacturing employment in the United Kingdom. Since 1974 some 2.65 million jobs have disappeared from manufacturing industry, while some 2.5 million new jobs have been created elsewhere. However, given the growth in the total labour force, new job creation has not been sufficient to prevent a major rise in unemployment. This is evidently a widespread problem in the European Community at large, although it came earlier and was of greater severity for the United Kingdom in the early 1980s.

The whole issue of job creation is a complex one, and a proper treatment is outside the scope of this chapter. The question here is to what extent is a relative and absolute expansion of manufacturing critically necessary for the elimination of current (April 1988) levels of unemployment and a return to what may be regarded as a more socially acceptable rate.

There seem to be two lines of argument. The first is that the job losses have occurred in manufacturing and been insufficiently offset by expansion elsewhere, notably in services. A *prima facie* case is therefore that unless manufacturing re-hires the unemployed, they will stay unemployed for

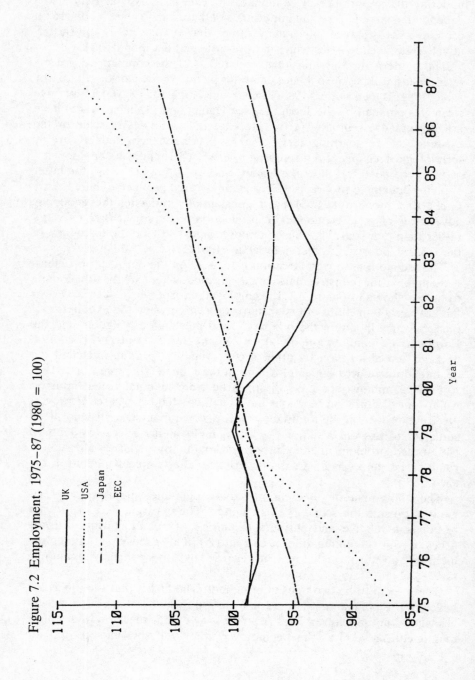

Figure 7.2 Employment, 1975–87 (1980 = 100)

ever. (This is the flavour of Thirlwall, 1982.) The second asserts that output and employment in economic activities outside manufacturing depend critically on the output of manufacturing industry itself. Hence not only will employment fail to grow if it does not grow in manufacturing itself, it will also fail to grow outside it – certainly as far as the private sector is concerned. This dependence of 'services' on manufacturing in a sort of parasitic way captures the flavour of much of the background to the discussion.

The House of Lords Committee (1985a) asserts that

> First the services sector is very dependent on manufacturing. As one witness said, 'The growth of the service area is not only tied to its own competitiveness within the service area itself...but it is totally dependent on the growth of the manufacturing industry to use those services it provides' [Cleminson Q112]. The ABCC stated that one fifth of all service industry output has manufacturing industry as its customer.

Taken literally, Sir James's statement is palpably untrue. As shown by Ray (1986, p. 30) sales of service outputs from non-industrial sources as a percentage of the gross output of manufacturing industry amount to only 8% by value (based on Census of Production data). The estimates of the ABCC (Association of British Chambers of Commerce) may or may not be correct – but they hardly indicate massive dependence. Sale of the output of services to the personal sector are clearly material as indicated by the fact that consumer spending on services accounts for 25% of GNP by value. The truth of the matter (following private communication with both the CSO and the DTI) is that we actually know remarkably little about the inter-sectoral flows. Much of the evidence is anecdotal. For example, sales of modern electronic equipment, including computers and telecommunications have been made to economic activities outside manufacturing industry on a large scale. Activities such as tourism lead to orders for cars, buses, ships and aeroplanes, and tourism is a major employer of the construction industry. It is difficult to quantify the position, but one thing is for sure, this is not a one-way street. To say that service industry depends on manufacturing may turn out to be no more or less true than the argument that in days gone by manufacturing was essentially dependent on economic activity in agriculture.

Recent research seems to suggest that even with a major expansion in the level of manufacturing output the prospects for more manufacturing jobs are not good – at least as far as large firms are concerned (see the IMS/ OSG Report, 1986). This has led in part to a focus on the ability of small business activity (in both manufacturing and services) to make a contribution to the reduction in unemployment. At a more general level, the overall behaviour of the labour market, whose inflexibility has been a feature of the European Community as a whole, may have been a far more important factor in restricting employment opportunities in the Community than changes in the composition of output – a problem that may continue to persist in the future.

The discussion now comes full circle as we return to the issue with which we started at the beginning, namely the idea of the current account of the balance of payments as a constraint on economic growth. There are two questions. What is the general nature of the constraint if it exists? What is the relationship of the performance of manufacturing industry to that constraint?

Starting from the point of view of the balance of payments we have already noted the definition of an efficient manufacturing sector as proposed by Singh (1977, p. 128). It is one in which there is a sufficient supply of manufactured exports to meet 'import requirements' at full employment. As pointed out earlier, the definition is question-begging in that it assumes that imports at full employment can be uniquely defined. In a world of perfect adjustments, however, there is no reason to suppose that any such 'requirement' exists. The most obvious way to make sense of it is to postulate a low rate of substitutability between domestic and imported output. The way in which this is usually done can be seen from the House of Lords Select Committee Report: 'Manufacturing even now represents over a fifth of all activity in the United Kingdom and it provides over 40 per cent of our overseas earnings. Its performance is therefore crucial in an economy which depends upon imports of food and raw materials' (House of Lords, 1985a, p. 11). This paints a picture of an economy which primarily exports manufactures to provide inputs of food and materials. As the following tables clearly establish, while that might have been true of the British economy in 1950, it is simply not true today. The structure of the current account of the balance of payments in terms of exports and imports is set out in Tables 7.4 and 7.5. In Table 7.6 we record the net balances of the different categories.

In Table 4 we see that in 1951 oil imports plus 'other goods', which include basic raw materials and food, accounted for 57% of the total value of imports of goods and services. If semi-manufactures are included, some 71% of imports of goods and services might be roughly classified as 'direct' inputs into economic activity. The value of oil plus 'other goods' was roughly equal to the value of exports of manufactures. It seems fair to say that at that time the UK exported manufactures to pay for food, materials and energy.

By 1986 the position had altered dramatically. Only 14% of the value of imports of goods and services was attributable to oil and 'other goods' and just over a quarter of the total by value could reasonably be attributed to

Table 7.4 *Visible and invisible exports 1951–86, £m (%)*

Exports	1951		1960		1970		1980		1986	
Visible exports (f.o.b.)										
Manufactures										
Semi-manufactures	1120.6	(26)	1131.0	(22)	2782.0	(21)	14152.0	(16)	20964.0	(14)
Finished manufactures	1066.4	(25)	1756.0	(30)	4100.0	(31)	20727.0	(23)	33540.0	(23)
Oil	35.3	(1)	104.2	(2)	180.0	(1)	6118.0	(7)	8221.0	(6)
Other goods	512.7	(12)	565.8	(10)	1088.0	(8)	6392.0	(7)	10136.0	(7)
Total visibles	2735.0	(64)	3737.0	(63)	8150.0	(62)	47389.0	(54)	72843.0	(49)
Invisible exports										
Services	913.0	(21)	1419.0	(24)	3379.0	(26)	15647.0	(18)	24992.0	(17)
Interest, profits and dividends	553.0	(13)	671.0	(11)	1494.0	(11)	23531.0	(27)	47370.0	(32)
Transfers	101.0	(2)	117.0	(2)	230.0	(2)	1881.0	(2)	3840.0	(3)
Total invisibles	1567.0	(36)	2207.0	(37)	5103.0	(38)	41059.0	(46)	76202.0	(51)
Total credits	4302.0	(100)	5944.0	(100)	13253.0	(100)	88481.0	(100)	149045.0	(100)

Balance of payments basis.

Sources: 1980–1986 UK Balance of Payments (1987). Pink book
1970–1980 UK Balance of Payments (1981). Pink book

For 1951, total visible balance plus all invisible balances are from Economic Trends Annual Supplement.
For 1951 and 1960 figures, visible trade by commodity estimates are on Overseas Trade Basis from Annual Abstract of Statistics (1961, 1969).

Definitions:
Other goods = food, beverages and tobacco, basic materials, other mineral fuels and lubricants, commodities and transactions not classified according to kind.
Semi-manufactured = SITC categories 5 and 6.
Finished manufactured = SITC categories 7 and 8.
i.e. semi-manufactured = chemicals and related products plus manufactured goods classified chiefly by material.
Finished manufactured = machinery and transport equipment and miscellaneous manufactured articles.

Table 7.5 Visible and invisible imports 1951–86, £m (%)

Imports	1951		1960		1970		1980		1986	
Visible exports (f.o.b.)										
Manufactures										
Semi-manufactures	648.4	(14)	922.0	(15)	2323.0	(19)	12561.0	(15)	21524.0	(14)
Finished manufactures	118.7	(3)	474.0	(8)	1997.0	(16)	16871.0	(20)	38453.0	(26)
Oil	306.9	(7)	480.0	(8)	676.0	(5)	5818.0	(7)	4165.0	(3)
Other goods	2350.0	(50)	2262.0	(37)	3188.0	(26)	10811.0	(13)	17164.0	(11)
Total visibles	3424.0	(73)	4183.0	(67)	8184.0	(66)	46061.0	(54)	81306.0	(54)
Invisible imports										
Services	907.0	(19)	1411.0	(23)	2963.0	(24)	11878.0	(14)	20002.0	(13)
Interest, profits and dividends	211.0	(5)	438.0	(7)	898.0	(7)	23750.0	(28)	42684.0	(28)
Transfers	129.0	(3)	185.0	(3)	412.0	(3)	3876.0	(5)	6033.0	(4)
Total invisibles	1247.0	(27)	2934.0	(33)	4273.0	(34)	39504.0	(46)	68719.0	(46)
Total debits	4671.0	(100)	6172.0	(100)	12457.0	(100)	85565.0	(100)	150025.0	(100)

Table 7.6 Trade balances (exports minus imports) £ million

	1951	1960	1970	1980	1986
Visible trade					
Manufactures					
Semi-manufactures	472.2	389.0	459.0	4002.0	−578.0
Finished manufactures	947.7	1282.0	2103.0	1455.0	−4914.0
Oil	−271.6	−376.0	−496.0	315.0	4056.0
Other goods	−1837.3	−1696.0	−2105.0	−4411.0	−7027.0
Visible balance	−689.0	−401.0	−34.0	1361.0	−8463.0
Invisible trade					
Services	6.0	8.0	481.0	3769.0	4990.0
Interest, profits and dividends	342.0	233.0	554.0	−219.0	4686.0
Transfers	−28.0	−68.0	−178.0	−1995.0	−2193.0
Invisible balance	320.0	173.0	857.0	1555.0	7483.0
Current balance	−369.0	−228.0	823.0	2916.0	−980.0

See footnote to Table 7.4.

'direct' inputs into economic activity. The value of manufactured exports was nearly three times as large as the value of food, materials and energy imported. The import side of the current account is largely unrecognisable compared with the position in 1951. This, as can be seen, is due to the major increase in the ratio of manufactured finished goods to total imports of goods and services from 3% in 1951 to 26% in 1986, and in overseas income paid out from 5% to 28%. Given this change in the structure of payments, the notion that at some time in the foreseeable future the United Kingdom will be unable to 'pay its way in the world' needs at best careful definition. At worst it is meaningless if it implies that we do not have the foreign exchange to buy more Japanese cars. (For some that will appear a blessing!) Confining ourselves to the trading account for goods and services alone, it is now more appropriate to say that we export manufactures in order to pay for other people's manufactures.

In his 1977 paper Singh stressed the size of exports earnings from manufactures as a token of the significance of the sector from a balance of payments point of view. He emphasised (p. 121) the relative stability of the ratio of manufactured earnings to earnings from services, and considered whether more resources should be allocated to the expansion of exports of private services. He concluded that 'Considering the balance of payments position alone, there are strong grounds for thinking that the latter course would at best produce no more than a minor improvement' (Singh 1977, p. 122). As can be seen from Table 7.3, the surplus on private services alone financed 70% of the deficit on food and raw materials by 1986 compared with zero in 1951.

Amongst other things, the data in Tables 7.4–6 make it apparent that we must distinguish clearly between the behaviour of the current account of the balance of payments on average and what happens at the margin. Since it is what happens at the margin that concerns us we focus on the behaviour of the net balances in Table 7.6 in the context of the question of what is likely to happen when the oil runs out. This question has two dimensions that need addressing. The first is the *magnitude* of the problem with which declining oil production (and price) presents us. The second is the *adjustment process* that is required to maintain balance of payments equilibrium and the consequences for the real level of output and the standard of living.

Since the House of Lords Select Committee Report (1985a) the dollar price of oil has fallen dramatically, giving rise to the well-known remark of the Chancellor of the Exchequer, Mr Lawson, in his 1986 Budget Speech: If we can survive unscathed the loss of half our oil revenues in less than 25 weeks, then the prospective loss of the other half over the remainder of the next 25 years should not cause us undue concern.' Since an oil price fall of such a magnitude was not foreseen by the House of Lords Select Committee (indeed why should it have been?) it seems a fair test of their concern to examine the magnitude of the problem arising from that source, rather than attempting to construct detailed forecasts for the 1990s.

The relevant basic facts concerning oil and the balance of payments can be summarised as follows. At a $15 price of oil net exports of oil produced an export surplus of roughly £4bn, as shown in Table 7.6. After allowing for payments of profits and interest abroad of about £1.3bn, we derive the net contribution to the overall balance of payments of £2.7bn.

Against this background, the magnitude of the problem and the likely process of adjustment has been examined by Budd *et al.* (1986). Using the permanent income approach (see Odling-Smee and Riley, 1985), they estimate that in 1986 prices there was an upper limit of about £2bn to the adjustment necessary as a result of the fall in the oil price from $26 to $15 a barrel. According to their analysis, the real exchange rate is the principal conduit through which the adjustment process takes place, and resources are shifted into net exports to replace the lost oil revenues:

> Thus the problem of the fall in oil prices is solved through an improvement in competitiveness which helps output and employment without harming inflation. The cost of the adjustment is a deterioration in the terms of trade which means that we can buy slightly fewer imports for a given quantity of exports. (Budd, *et al.*, 1986, p. 16)

The key to the implementation of the adjustment process is the supply response of the non-oil economy (whether in manufacturing or elsewhere) to the profitable opportunities provided by the fall in the real exchange rate. A major concern has been that a long-term decline in industrial capacity would make an adequate supply response difficult when the oil ran out. Loss of capacity, skills and markets are seen to be strongly asymmetrical in their effects, giving rise to the so-called 'hysteresis' effect. With regard to the 50% fall in oil revenues, Budd *et al.* (1986, p. 17) estimated that the adjustment process required an annual rate of growth of manufacturing output of about 4% per annum for a period of three years, a target they suggested is 'quite manageable'. If a shock of this size is remotely manageable it hardly seems impossible to deal with the further decline in North Sea oil revenues as production declines, partly as oil prices may well advance in the 1990s and current exploration and development suggests that, despite the inevitable decline, production from the North Sea is likely to take a lot longer dying than many currently suppose. As Robinson and McCullough have put it (1986, p. 20),

> It is now widely agreed that North Sea Production will decline from now on (though significant new fields are still being discovered). But it is certain that the

rate of decline will be much slower than the build up. Our estimate is that North Sea output could fall to about two thirds of its present level over the next ten years. (The pace of decline is little affected by the recent fall in the price.) Other things being equal this would require an expansion of non-oil output of about 2 per cent – hardly an insuperable problem given the time available for the adjustment.

It is reasonable to conclude that from the point of view of the balance of payments and declining oil revenues the fears of the House of Lords Select Committee and others as to the gloomy outlook for the 1990s are unproven to say the least and to describe the present situation as one of 'crisis' is nothing short of pure exaggeration. It is possible to make a case for the fact that while until the early 1980s the sad story with regard to the competitive position and performance of manufacturing industry is substantially true, as recorded above and by others, developments in the 1980s have moved on.

In Figure 7.1 we see the actual behaviour of manufacturing output set against the trend performance between the peaks of 1973 and 1979. While output did not regain its 1979 level until 1986, the level of output produced was then produced with one-third less people. The fall in the share of manufactured trade has been arrested, as shown in Table 7.3. Whether this represents a false dawn in British manufacturing remains to be seen. But there is little doubt as to the magnitude of the shake-out, the restructuring, and the redirection that has occurred.

In so far as change has come about it is attributable in my view to more effective management and labour performance within a stable financial and fiscal framework. The thesis that economic growth has been balance of payments constrained, reflects the underlying significance of supply side factors. The idea that manufacturing competitiveness in the 1960s and 1970s was a key determinant of economic growth as emphasised by Lord Kaldor (1971) was undoubteduly correct.

It was however followed by two errors. The first was to convert the idea into the thesis of balance of payments constrained growth. The underlying failure was the inability to supply an expanding world demand, resulting in a falling market share and lower-than-average growth. The loss of competitiveness also affects one's share of one's own domestic market. It is the ability to competitively meet demand wherever it arises, at home or abroad, that is crucial. To represent this as a balance of payments problem is to point the wrong way. It points among other things to protectionism rather than the underlying problem of competitiveness.

The second error was to suggest that the underlying problems of a lack of competitiveness at the micro level due to the behaviour of management and the labour force could be overcome at the macro level by the manipulation of the nominal exchange rate. Such an idea was a snare and a delusion, abandoned eventually by Kaldor himself (Kaldor, 1978, pp. 18–25, where protectionism seems to have taken over.)

Summary and policy

In this chapter I have summarised the history of ideas about the balance of payments as a constraint on economic growth and the notion that manufacturing industry plays a *unique* role in relation to the balance of payments, economic growth and job creation in the foreseeable future of the United Kingdom. The overall conclusion is that there is nothing particularly unique about the role of manufacturing. It has been and will continue to be a central and important sphere of economic activity. In the past, its competitive weakness has been a major contributing factor to economic decline as measured by our rate of economic growth relative to our competitors and our share of manufactured exports.

The 'uniqueness' hypothesis is rejected on three counts. As far as economic growth is concerned, dynamic economies of scale are no longer central to economic progress. Moreover the structure of economic output in the future will be determined by the pattern of demand which is likely to favour the expansion of 'services' relative to manufactured products in the industrial countries. As far as jobs are concerned, the future of employment in large-scale manufacturing industry will be limited by the fact that labour productivity will continue to outstrip or at least equal the growth of demand for manufactured products. As far as the balance of payments is concerned, it is no longer true that the UK exports manufactures to pay for food and raw materials. As the oil runs out, the shift in the exchange rate will not be associated with an inability to pay for the food and materials needed to keep the wheels of industry turning. It will encourage and facilitate the substitution of domestically produced for imported manufactures. Finally, while time prevents a fuller and appropriate exposition, there is sufficient evidence to suggest a *prima facie* case for the view that since the great fall of 1979–81, British manufacturing industry has undergone a major restructuring, emerging as a leaner and fitter beast than it started.

The position from which we began is that there were two central but related questions to be addressed. The first question was the unique role of manufacturing. The second was the existence of the balance of payments as a constraint on economic growth. The first we have just reviewed. The second stems from the error of seeing the behaviour of the current account of the balance of payments as a problem of demand rather than supply. Current account deficits have arisen repeatedly from the inability of supply

to meet expanding nominal demand. The underlying problem has therefore been one of *competitiveness*, which is not a function simply of the
exchange rate but also of the plethora of non-price competition elements
that determine the market share of the individual firm. It is firms that
compete in markets not countries.

The idea that the UK has been – and will again be – 'balance of payments constrained' leads to a variety of inappropriate policies. The policy
recommendation of Kaldor (1971) was that exchange rate policy should set
the nominal exchange rate at a rate that would deliver real export growth
at a desired or targeted rate. Such a policy is deficient on two grounds. First
it implies that *nominal* exchange rates can be used to set *real* exchange
rates in the long run, a highly contentious proposition. Secondly, such
policies in any event are doomed to failure if *all* countries attempt the same
thing at the same time. No proposed policy is *generally* feasible unless it
satisfies the condition that it can be pursued by all countries simultaneously.

The second class of policies that the 'constraint' hypothesis suggests is
that of protectionism. (For a recent survey of some of the issues involved
see Ball, 1987.) The idea that free trade is inhibiting to economic growth
and progress has been a key idea promoted by the Cambridge Economic
Policy Group, see again Singh, (1977). Apart from the fact that they do not
focus on the underlying problem (competitiveness) protectionist policies
also fail the general test referred to in the previous paragraph.

Finally, the 'liberal' reaction to the 'constraint' hypothesis focuses on
policies designed to promote exports (see Thirlwall, 1982). The idea of
promoting or encouraging exports is as fallacious as policies designed to
restrict imports. They neither of them address the fundamental underlying
problem of economic competitiveness. Indeed, in so far as underlying competitiveness is the determinant of economic growth and a rising standard of
living, the distinction between imports and exports is largely irrelevant
particularly in a world in which trade is predominantly in manufactured
goods. As already shown, 40% of United Kingdom exports and imports
are manufactured goods.

A central failing of economics, both at the macro and at the micro level,
has been its inability to take on board the functions of management and the
behaviour of the labour force. As emphasised by Littlechild (1986), the
traditional theory of market structure achieves determinate solutions to
market problems by dispensing with the active role of the manager or the
entrepreneur (namely, equilibrium under pure competition or monopoly).
Competitiveness in the real world is ultimately in the hands of management and the behaviour of the labour force. Of course the fiscal and
monetary regime which affects the financial and foreign exchange environment is of importance – but usually only in the short run. In the longer run,

relevant policies (some of which are proposed in House of Lords, 1985a) must be supply-side policies aimed at improving competitiveness, education, labour market flexibility and the encouragement of research and development. These are items that should be on anyone's agenda, although the question as to how government may make contributions in these areas will remain a contentious one.

None of this guarantees that either in the near future or later in the 1990s there will not be problems associated with the balance of payments and the exchange rate. But in so far as this is the case it will be for exactly the reasons that led to the mythology of the balance of payments constraint in the 1950s and 1960s. Attempts to combine over-expansionary fiscal policies in relation to supply capability are bound to end in tears. Poor economic performance, perhaps partly resulting from a disappointing performance in manufacturing could limit growth potential. But that is not a balance of payments story. Nor is the running out of oil.

Note

I am very grateful to Alan Budd, Terry Burns, Bill Robinson and Harold Rose for comments on an earlier draft of this paper. Keith Wade also read the draft and provided invaluable research support and Kathy Hammond statistical assistance. I am indebted to Ruth Warner for both secretarial and editorial contributions. All errors and omissions remaining are entirely mine.

References

Abernathy, W., Clark, K. B. and Kantrow, A. M. (1981). 'The new industrial competition', *Harvard Business Review*, vol. 59, Sept.–Oct., pp. 68–81.

Baden Fuller, C. F. (1983). 'The implications of the "learning curve" for firm strategy and public policy', *Applied Economics*, vol. 15, pp. 541–51.

Ball, Professor Sir James (1987). 'The causes of rising protectionism', BNARA Occasional Paper 7, November.

Ball, R. J. and Burns, T. (1968). 'The prospects of faster growth in Britain', *National Westminster Bank Review*, pp. 3–22.

Ball, R. J. (1982). *Money and Employment* (London: Macmillan).

Bean, C. (1987). 'The macroeconomic consequences of North Sea oil', in R. Dornbusch and R. Layard (eds), *The Performance of the British Economy* (Oxford: Oxford University Press).

Blackaby, F. (ed.) (1979). *De-industrialisation* (London: Heinemann).

Boston Consulting Group (1968). *Perspectives on Experience*, Boston.

Budd, A. P., Breedon, F. and Dicks, G. (1986). 'Adjustments to the oil price', *Economic Outlook*, October.

Cairncross, Sir Alec (1978). 'What is de-industrialisation', in F. Blackaby (ed.), *De-industrialisation* (London: Heinemann).

Eastwood, R. K. and Venables, A. J. (1982), 'The macroeconomic implications of a resource discovery in an open economy', *Economic Journal*, vol. 92, pp. 285–99.

Forsyth, P. J. and Kay, J. A. (1980). 'The economic implication of North Sea oil revenues', *Fiscal Studies*, vol. 1, no. 3, pp. 1–28.

Hamel, G. and Prahalad, C. K. (1985), 'Do you really have a global strategy?', *Harvard Business Review*, vol. 63, July–August, pp. 139–48.

House of Lords (1985a). *Report from the Select Committee on Overseas Trade*, Volume I – Report.

House of Lords (1985b). *Minutes and Evidence*.

Institute of Manpower Studies/Occupation Study Group Report (1986). *UK Occupation and Employment Trends to 1990: An Employer Based Study of the Trends and Their Underlying Causes*, A. Rajan and R. Pearson (eds) (London: Butterworths).

Kaldor, N. (1966). *Causes of the Slow Rate of Economic Growth of the United Kingdom* (Oxford: Oxford University Press).

Kaldor, N. (1971). 'Conflicts in national objectives', *Economic Journal*, vol. 81, pp. 1–16.

Kaldor, N. (1978). 'Comment', in F. Blackaby (ed.), *De-industrialisation* (London: Heinemann).

Littlechild, S. C. (1986). *The Falling of the Mixed Economy*, Hobart Paper, no. 80, IEA.

Odling-Smee, J. and Riley, C. (1985). 'Approaches to PSBR', *National Institute Review*, no. 113, pp. 65–80.

Ray, G. (1986). 'Services for manufacturing', *National Institute Review*, August, no. 117, pp. 30–32.

Robinson, P. W. and McCullough, A. (1986). 'Manufacturing prospects after OPEC III', *Economic Outlook*, October.

Singh, A. (1977). 'UK industry and the world economy: a case of de-industrialisation', *Cambridge Journal of Economics*, vol. 1, pp. 113–36.

Thirlwall, A. P. (1982). 'De-industrialisation in the United Kingdom', *Lloyds Bank Review*, April, pp. 22–37.

Wolfe, J. N. (1968). 'Productivity and growth in manufacturing industry: some reflections on Professor Kaldor's inaugural lecture', *Economica*, vol. 35, pp. 117–39.

8

Changes in British trade analysed in a pure trade theory framework

Lynden Moore

This contribution to Dennis Coppock's Festschrift will be an endeavour to use pure trade theory to analyse the changes in Britain's trading position. In general equilibrium analysis international trade is regarded as the exchange of one commodity, say manufacturers, for another, say agricultural products. The amount of manufactures offered in exchange for agricultural products depends on their relative price; the relationship can be represented by means of an offer curve, a device which at one time intrigued Dennis.

We will first consider the shift in trade that needs explaining. Then a brief pedagogic exposition of the theory will be given together with the modifications required to apply it to Britain. Tradable goods will be divided into three sectors: fuel, agriculture and manufacturing. The changes in each will be considered, their association will changes in Britain's commercial policy and finally the implications for the economy as a whole.

The shift in Britain's trading position

In 1950 Britain was a paradigm of an industrial power exporting manufacturers in exchange for food and raw materials. Four-fifths of her exports were manufactures: 35% were machinery and transport equipment, 34% semi-manufactures (16% textile), $6\frac{1}{2}$% chemicals. She was the second largest exporter of manufactures after the United States, accounting for 26% of world trade in them.

Obversely she was the largest importer and net importer of agricultural products in the world. Imports of food, beverages and tobacco accounted for 40% of her imports in 1950 and agricultural raw materials for 18%. Fuel in the form of petroleum products accounted for $7\frac{1}{2}$%. Only 4% of her imports were accounted for by finished manufactures, although an additional 11% were of semi-manufactures (Mansell, 1980).

By the 1980s, Britain's trading position had undergone a metamorphosis; she had become a net exporter of fuel and by 1983 had a deficit in manufactures.

This is generally attributed to the discovery of North Sea oil. Here it is argued that this is the most important of a number of changes in her fuel position which represent changes in her comparative advantage. But commercial policy has also contributed to her pattern of trade, initially her membership of the Commonwealth preference system up to its abandonment in 1973, and then the formation of preferential trading systems with other industrial countries, first the European Free Trade Area (EFTA) in 1959, and then the European Economic Community (EEC) in 1973. Britain now trades in a customs union of the twelve EEC countries and has free trade in manufactures with the remaining EFTA countries.

An endeavour will be made to consider this question in the context of pure trade policy. This is a theory of specialisation; trade in a commodity is regarded as being the difference between a country's production and consumption. Therefore it excludes intra-industry trade.

Analytical framework

Pure trade theory relates a country's specialisation in trade to the international prices it faces, and under the Heckscher–Ohlin–Samuelson theory, to the returns to factors of production. For instance, let us take a small country whose increasing cost production possibility curve for producing manufactures and agricultural products is shown by TT in Figure 8.1. If the country is closed to trade the maximum welfare attainable will be where the production possibility curve just touches the highest possible community indifference curve with domestic prices indicated by their slope at this point (not shown in the figure). Community indifference curves are here taken both as indicators of the responses of consumers to changes in price, and as levels of welfare; they are therefore assumed not to cross, and problems of the effect of the distribution of income on welfare are ignored.

If the world price of manufactures is greater than the domestic one (the price line is steeper), then when the country is opened to trade it will have an incentive to increase its output of manufactures and reduce that of agriculture. This will continue until the marginal rate at which agricultural products can be transformed into manufactures, as indicated by the slope of the production possibility curve, is just equal to the international relative price of manufactures to agricultural products as at point P_1 given by the slope of Y_4P_1 equal to that of Y_3P_2. The increase in the relative price of

Figure 8.1 Consumption and production with free trade and tariffs

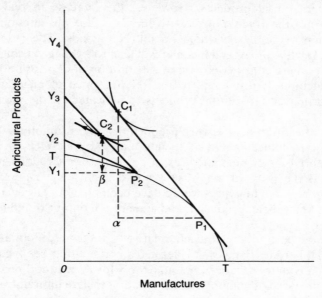

Free trade

The price of manufactures in terms of agricultural products is equal to the slope of $C_1 P_1$ and obversely.

Exports of manufactures $= \alpha P_1$.
Imports of agricultural products $= C_1 \alpha$.

With tariff on agricultural products, tariff revenue redistributed back to consumers

Domestic price of manufactures in terms of agricultural products slope of $C_2 P_2$

Domestic price of agricultural products with tariff $= \dfrac{Y_1 P_2}{Y_1 Y_2}$

International price of agricultural products $= \dfrac{Y_1 P_2}{Y_1 Y_3}$

Let tariff be a proportion t. Thus:

$$\frac{Y_1 P_2}{Y_1 Y_2} = \frac{Y_1 P_2}{Y_1 Y_3}(1 + t),$$

$$t = \frac{Y_1 Y_3 - Y_1 Y_2}{Y_1 Y_2} = \frac{Y_2 Y_3}{Y_1 Y_2}.$$

Exports of manufactures $= \beta P_2$.
Imports of agricultural products $= \beta C_2$.

manufactures will also encourage consumers to switch purchases from them to agricultural products. However, the increase in real incomes resulting from the trade will tend to increase the consumption of both goods assuming neither of them are inferior goods. The net result of changes in relative prices and incomes will lead to a change in consumption to point C_1 where consumers' rate of substitution of agricultural products for manufactures is just equal to the relative price of manufactures in relation to that of agricultural products as indicated by the international price line.

Trade is the difference between production and consumption. The trade triangle $C_1\alpha P_1$ indicates that at an international price C_1P_1 the country would export αP_1 of manufactures in exchange for $C_1\alpha$ of agricultural products. If the price of manufactures had been higher, the degree of specialisation in manufactures would have been greater still, even more of them would have been produced, and agricultural output would have been even lower.

The trade positon under each relative price can be obtained by a plotting of the trade triangles; it is termed an offer curve, see Figure 8.2. It represents a country's offer of manufactures for agricultural products. Of course, if the price of manufactures in relation to agricultural products fell sufficiently the offer might be reversed. A country's specialisation and offer on the world market would also change, and indeed might reverse, with a shift in its production possibility schedule.

Tariffs and subsidies destroy the equality between domestic and international prices, see Figure 8.1. If tariffs are imposed on imports of agricultural products both consumers and producers face a higher price of agricultural products indicated by the slope of Y_2P_2. This induces an increase in agricultural output at the expense of manufactures and production shifts from P_1 to P_2. This reduction in efficiency lowers real income, but the country as a whole can still trade at the international prices, and thus its consumption possibilities are along Y_3P_2. Consumers will equate their marginal rate of substitution indicated by the slope of their community indifference curve to the domestic tariff-distorted price but if the tariff revenue is redistributed back to them they will be able to consume along Y_3P_2, say at C_2. Then $C_2\beta$ agricultural products will be imported, βP_2 of manufactures exported. The overall effect has been a contraction of trade even though international prices remain the same.

Thus, a tariff has the effect of moving the offer curve depicted in Figure 8.2 inwards. If, as we have assumed, the country is small, the international price, equivalent to the rest of the world's offer curve, remains the same. But a large country will face a less than infinitely elastic curve on the part of

Figure 8.2 Offer curve of a country exporting manufactures

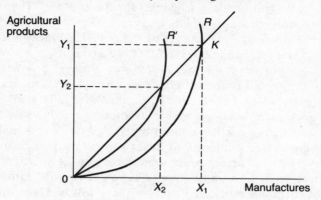

Relation between Figures 8.1 and 8.2

Free trade—offer curve *OR*	Fig. 8.1	Fig. 8.2
International price	$C_1P_1 = C_2P_2$	Line from origin *OK*
Exports	αP	OX_1
Imports	αC	OY_1

Tariff on imports of agricultural products—offer curve *OR'*

International price	$C_1P_1 = C_2P_2$	Lines from origin *OK*
Exports	βP_2	OX_2
Imports	βC_2	OY_2

the rest of the world and will be able to improve its terms of trade by such a shift.

Preferential trading is more difficult to incorporate. A preferential trading area is one in which a member country removes tariffs on imports from its partner countries but maintains them on imports from the rest of the world. Viner (1950) emphasised their discriminatory impact and regarded them as beneficial in so far as they led to trade creation, that is, transferred production from a higher-cost source (the home country), to a lower-cost source, but detrimental in so far as they led to trade diversion, that is, transferred production from a lower-cost source to a higher-cost source.

But it has been argued by Lipsey (1957) and others, that it is possible for the benefits to consumers in the form of lower prices to outweigh the loss of tariff revenue which represents the cost of trade diversion.

The partial equilibrium exposition of this for a market in which a country is a net importer is shown in Figure 8.3. Here S_H and D_H are the domestic supply and demand schedules for the product. There is an infinitely elastic foreign supply schedule to the market at price P_w. The initial tariff $t = P_1 P_w$, which equals a rate of $P_1 P_w \div O P_w$, raises the domestic price to P_1. And OQ_4 and OQ_3 are produced and consumed domestically with $Q_4 Q_3$ imported from the lowest-cost foreign producers. Tariff revenue is $Q_4 Q_3 . t$. Say the country now forms a customs union with a partner country which can supply the product at P_2. This will lower the domestic price to P_2 and domestic consumption will increase by $Q_3 Q_5$. Domestic production will be reduced by $Q_4 Q_6$, which as a transfer from the higher-cost home producers to the lower-cost partner country represents trade creation. Partner-country products without a tariff now appear cheaper than those from third countries even though the latter have the lowest cost of production and therefore there will be trade diversion of $Q_4 Q_3$ from the latter to the former. The cost of this trade diversion is the difference in actual cost of supply $P_2 P_w$ multiplied by the original quantity of imports $Q_4 Q_3$.

However, in order to estimate the effect on a country of entry into a customs union it is not sufficient to aggregate all the responses in her markets for importables and exportables; account must also be taken of the adjustment to any change in her exchange rate required for her to achieve current account or balance of payments equilibrium.

General equilibrium analysis has usually been applied to this theory in terms of the effects on a country's terms of trade. So far we have assumed that an individual country cannot affect its terms of trade. However, a customs union has the effect of integrating countries as a block in relation to the rest of the world. The total offer curve of a customs union can be obtained by radially summing the offer curves of its member countries. Because of the common external tariff it is of course distorted. If the customs union is a large entity it is likely to be able to affect international prices by its level of tariffs. A country faced with the question of whether it is worth joining should consider the effect on its terms of trade. As Ghosh (1974) has argued, a country might benefit from the formation of a customs union by staying out of it, if its formation lowered the price of its imports on the international market.

Dennis Coppock was interested in the elasticities of offer curves and the effect of tariffs on them, and soon after I arrived in Manchester supplied me with his handouts of them. Although appreciating their logical elegance I was sceptical about their practical usefulness; even the assumptions seemed unrealistic: had Britain for instance ever been on her production possibility curve. However, with time, I began to value the insights that the general equilibrium analysis of trade provides. Therefore in this article I

Figure 8.3 Effects of joining a customs union – trade creation and trade diversion

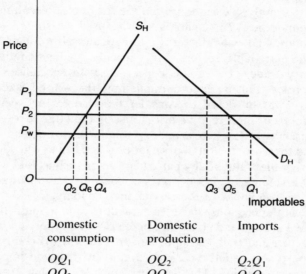

	Domestic consumption	Domestic production	Imports
Free trade	OQ_1	OQ_2	Q_2Q_1
Tariff on all imports	OQ_3	OQ_4	Q_4Q_3
Customs union	OQ_5	OQ_6	Q_6Q_5

Derived from C. P. Kindleberger (1973), *International Economics*, 5th edn (Georgetown, Ontario: Irwin Dorsey).

endeavour to apply this framework and these concepts to the changes in British trade since 1950.

Problems of application

There are many problems. We have to settle for the production possibility curve which represents the outer boundary of production within institutional constraints due to the influence of trade unions and the taxation of employment in the form of national insurance contributions, that is, labour cannot be regarded as receiving the value of its marginal product. Furthermore, one would expect economic expansion, that is, a movement of the production possibility schedule outwards over time. However, it should be pointed out that there has been very little increase in the supply of some of the factors of production; the acreage of cultivated land has actually declined, and the workforce has increased by only 0.5% per annum and employment only 0.1% per annum over the period 1960–86 (OECD *Historical Statistics*, 1960–86). Employment in the mid-1980s is at the same levels as it was in the late 1950s.

More importantly, we cannot retain the textbook presentation in terms of two commodities. The analysis will be used on three categories of tradable goods: fuel, manufactures and agricultural products.

In all three tradable sectors, but particularly manufactures, there is intra-industry trade. As we are concerned with specialisation the net balance of trade, that is, exports minus imports, will be taken.

Initially it was proposed to consider the changes between the three sectors in terms of their relative prices, taking the offer curve as a surface rather than a curve. But there is no long-run domestic price index of manufactures and therefore the retail price index was taken as a general deflator. In considering the trade of any particular sector such as fuel we therefore consider the volume of production and consumption and the change in relative price in relation to the rest of the economy.

The rest of the economy includes agriculture and manufacturing plus a large residual service and construction sector. The latter is a very heterogeneous sector, and trade is important to certain of its components. But overall exports are equal to 12% of output in 1986 and imports were a slightly lower production. This was very much lower than for agriculture, fuel and manufacturing. However, because this residual sector is so large its positive balance of £5 billion represented a significant element in the balance of payments. The rationale, none the less, for concentrating on agriculture, fuel and manufactures is that they have been more prone to external shocks and up to now most government intervention has been directed at them.

This intervention has not been as simple as the tariff analysis described above. In many cases it has been of the form in which consumers face different relative prices from producers. Subsidies to producers as under the Agricultural Act of 1947 raise prices to producers and thus encourage greater production as say in a movement from P_1 to P_2 in Figure 8.1. Consumption will be lower than at C_1 under free trade due to the lower real income resulting from intervention, but it will be higher than at C_2 because consumers will be facing world prices and therefore their community indifference curve will touch Y_3P_2. Therefore, the offer curve will not move inwards as much as with a tariff.

In addition, there are indirect taxes, which have increased as a proportion of revenue since Britain joined the EEC. These include excise duties particularly on petrol and fuel oil, and VAT which since 1979 has been at 15% but which is not imposed on food. Thus, there is often a considerable divergence between the prices consumers pay and producers receive and the rate at which each changes over time. Indeed, the most difficult aspect of the whole exercise is to select the appropriate price out of the limited statistical series available.

Periods being considered

In order to apply this comparative static analysis to the British situation, we must allow for economic expansion due to technical change and investment which increased the output that could be produced with the other primary factors which did not increase, such as employment and the area of land under cultivation. We need also to consider change in Britain's international environment. For convenience the whole period is divided into subperiods which generally coincide with those selected by the OECD.

(1) The period before 1968 was one of falling trade barriers on imports from industrial countries but in many cases rising barriers on imports from developing countries. Most OECD calculations are for 1960–8.
(2) 1968–73 was a period of rising inflation and difficulties in macroeconomic adjustment on the world market and the aftermath of Britain's devaluation of 1967. In June 1972 Britain abandoned her fixed exchange rate policy. In 1971 she introduced an import levy system on agricultural products in preparation for her accession to the Common Agricultural Policy (CAP).
(3) In 1973–9 the quadrupling of the oil price from 1973–4 was succeeded by a period of great macroeconomic instability in the world market as a whole. Between 1978 and 1980 the world price of oil was doubled again. In 1973 Britain entered the EEC and acceded to the CAP.
(4) 1980– The initial period of severe recession on the world market as well as in Britain as governments pursued policies designed to reduced inflation was followed by rapid growth in the USA and then in Britain.

Strictly speaking the international environment is only important in so far as it affects relative commodity prices or the rate of economic expansion. The shift in the whole production possibility curve cannot be identified. So instead we will consider the changes in consumption, production and trade that have occurred over the period and whether they have been associated with any change in relative prices.

Fuel

In recent years most of the malaise in manufacturing has been attributed to the development of North Sea oil. This is the most significant but not the only change that has occurred in the fuel sector. The fuel sector is considered in total because at the margin the fossil fuels – coal, oil and natural gas – and primary electricity (produced from hydroelectric and nuclear power plants) compete both in space heating and in the provision of power.

In 1950 domestically produced coal accounted for 90% of British fuel consumption and she also exported some. All oil was imported but her net imports of fuel were only 3% of consumption; she was approximately self-sufficient.

In the 1950s and 1960s new low-cost oilfields in the Middle East and then North Africa were brought into production. The real price of oil, that is, the realised price divided by a price index of manufactures, fell until in 1970 it was approximately half the level in 1950. The international real price of coal also tended to fall (World Bank, 1981). Government pricing policies for nationalised industries prevented these price reductions being passed on immediately and directly to domestic consumers and producers. Nevertheless, they provided the government with every incentive to induce the National Coal Board to close down its high-cost pits. A stylistic exposition of developments over the period is given in Figure 8.4 and Table 8.1.

From 1950 and 1970 British production of fuel fell from 221 to 176 million tonnes of coal equivalent (MTCE) – see Figure 8.5 – and this was entirely due to the contraction of the coal industry. There was an increase

Figure 8.4 Stylised exposition of the production and consumption of fuel and other goods and services (see Table 8.1)

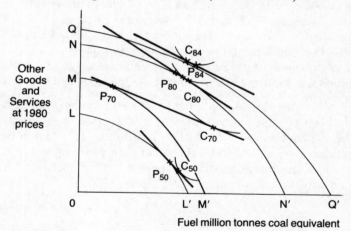

The production possibility schedule expands from *LL'* to *MM'* to *NN'* to *QQ'*. The relative price of fuel falls from $P_{50}C_{50}$ to $P_{70}C_{70}$. It then rises to $P_{80}C_{80}$ and then falls slightly to $C_{84}P_{84}$.

Table 8.1 Fuel – million tonnes of coal equivalent (MTCE), see Fig. 8.4

	Production $(P)^a$	Consumption (C)	Net exports P-C^b	Actual	Production of other goods at constant 1980 prices $1980 = 100$
1950	221	228	−74		53
1970	176	354	−178	−176	90
1980	338	341	−3	−25	100
1986	414	351	63	54	113

^{a} Including for non-fuel use.
^{b} Production minus consumption as on graph – no allowance made for changes in stock.

Sources:
Department of Energy, *Digest of United Kingdom Energy Statistics* 1980, 1983 and 1987.
Central Statistical Office, *Annual Abstract of Statistics* various issue.
Central Statistical Office, *Economic Trends Annual Supplement* 1988.

in consumption due to increased incomes from 228 to 337 MTCE or 354 MTCE including non-fuel use, almost all of this in oil. Thus, Britain became much more dependent on imports for her fuel supply, in particular on oil which by 1970 accounted for 45% of her consumption.

The first sign of the shift in Britain's comparative advantage was the discovery of North Sea gas. Output was very low in the early 1960s, but increased rapidly towards the end of the decade, reaching 16.6 MTCE by 1970 – see Figure 8.5.

By that time, the exploitation of North Sea oil had begun. Initially the output of North Sea oil increased only slowly; the cost of extraction was much higher than in the Middle East. After 1970 OPEC exerted pressure to raise the price of oil and it quadrupled between 1973 and 1974. In Figure 8.4 Britain is initially producing at P_{70} and importing the difference. The effect of such a rise in price of imports is to increase the slope of the international price line. Assuming production cannot be changed in the short run it must be pivoted downwards through P_{70} to provide the lower consumption possibility line. The immediate effect of the price rise was estimated to represent a reduction of about 2% in GDP (Governor of the Bank of England, 1980).

However, at that price, the exploitation of North Sea oil became profit-

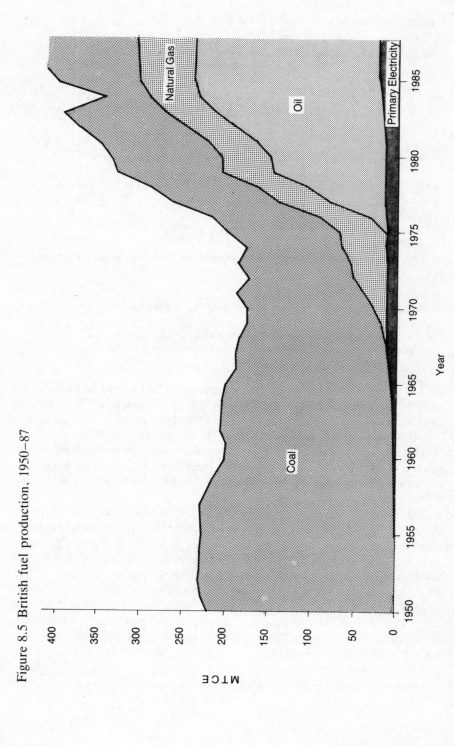

Figure 8.5 British fuel production, 1950–87

able and it attracted an inflow of a cumulative £20 billion of investment at 1980 prices (ibid). The production possibility curve moved horizontally outwards and vertically upwards to allow for increased productivity in the rest of the economy. By 1980 oil production had increased to 137 MTCE, coal production was 130, and total fuel production was 338 MTCE. However, prices to consumers had increased often sharply and erratically during the 1970s, at a rate well above the retail price index. Fuel conservation proceeded apace such that consumption fell between 1970 and 1980 to 341 MTCE. Britain was almost self-sufficient again. After 1984 the price of oil began to fall but production still continued and Britain became a net exporter of oil in 1981. By 1986 she was producing 216 MTCE of oil and 414 of fuel in total; subtracting consumption of 351 MTCE this left 63 MTCE for export (or building up stock).

Britain now exports about 13% of her output of fuel and 39% of her production of oil. So over the period being considered, Britain shifted from being slightly to being heavily dependent on imports of fuel by the late 1960s; subsequently the commercial policy of other countries in the form of the OPEC price rise made the extraction of North Sea oil economically feasibly and converted her into a net exporter of fuel.

Agriculture

The influence of government policy on agriculture is all-important. Thus, although on the world market the prices of all agricultural products and food have fluctuated in relation to manufactures the producers in Britain were largely shielded from them under the Agricultural Act of 1947. They received a guaranteed price which was generally higher than the world price. The price of certain inputs was also subsidised. But consumers could purchase products at the world price.

The result was an increase in food production. This could be measured in terms of total tonnage. For instance, the annual tonnage of cereals increased by 68% between 1950 and 1970. But it is less meaningful to discuss the whole of agricultural output in this way, particularly as it represents the result of a two-stage process, first of crops, then of livestock production, with most of the first going into the second. The only long-term measure is the index number of agricultural, forestry and fishing output, which shows an increase in output at constant factor cost of 59% from 1950 to 1970.

Expenditure on food increased by 15% at constant prices between 1950 and 1970. Between 1955 and 1970 Britain's net imports of food declined in monetary terms and even more in real terms. None the less by 1970 food still accounted for 20% of her imports, and 39% of them came from the Commonwealth and 29% from the EEC.

This all changed when after a brief transition with import levies from 1971 to 1973 Britain entered the EEC in 1973 and acceded to the Common Agricultural Policy (CAP). She had now moved from a system in which consumers could purchase products at world prices to one in which they faced the same prices as producers. 'Target' prices were set which were supposed to be maintained by a system of variable levies on imports from outside the EEC designed to bring them up to a set minimum import price. Should the price nevertheless fall below the target price there were provisions for buying for stock when the price reached a certain level. As the EEC production increased this provision was increasingly used.

These target prices were well above the world price and the White Paper of 1970 estimated that accession would involve an increase in consumer prices of 25% and producer prices of 10 points as producers were already receiving a 15% subsidy. However, world prices of food had begun to rise and this made the opportunity cost of entry appear lower in the White Paper of 1971 prior to entry. By 1979–80 the minimum import price was between 30% and 100% greater than the world price for grains, and was 311% greater for butter and 104% greater for beef and veal (Eurostat).

It has become increasingly difficult to calculate the effect of the CAP on producer and consumer prices as the EEC has introduced supplementary measures to reduce its expenditure. But in the period 1979–81 the prices to consumers were equivalent to a tax of 23% on sugar and milk and 12% on beef, whereas the effect of the system on producers was equivalent to a subsidy of 43% on average for all major crops and livestock products (OECD, 1987, pp. 117, 118).

An endeavour has been made to illustrate this situation between 1970 and 1984 in Figure 8.6. The value of home production and consumption, in terms of farm-gate or landed value to exclude the processing element, at constant 1980 prices, is shown in the accompanying Table 8.2. The overall result has been a persistent increase in output. Consumption has remained almost stationary over the period. The self-sufficiency ratio increased from 45% to 64%. The diagram does not reflect accurately the changes in prices. Over this period the real world price index of food (world unit value index in £ deflated by the retail price index) increased sharply from 1970 to 1973 and then declined; in 1984 it was below the level in 1970. A similar movement appears to have taken place for real producer prices. Consumer prices (including distributive margins) increased faster than the retail price index between 1970 and 1977; since then the increase has slowed down so that in 1984 they were only 5% greater in real terms than in 1970.

For Britain membership of the CAP has represented an adverse movement of her terms of trade; she pays higher prices whether her imports come from other EEC members, or from outside the EEC incurring vari-

Figure 8.6 Stylised exposition of the production and consumption of food and other goods and services (see Table 8.2)

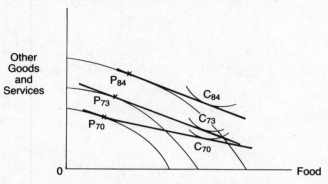

Production of food increases but consumption remains the same as production possibility curve shifts from *LL'* to *MM'* to *NN'*.

able import levies, because the levies themselves have to be transmitted to the EEC as part of its own resources. Her accession was regarded as a condition for membership of the EEC but the effect has been to add to the EEC surpluses; the volume of British imports of food, and oils and fats have increased by only 5% and 70% respectively whereas her exports have increased by 236% and 651% respectively between 1970 and 1987 – see Table 8.3. However, there has been a considerable amount of trade diversion towards the EEC as also can be seen from the area figures.[1]

Table 8.2   Food, see Fig. 8.6

	Home production	Home consumption	Degree of self-sufficiency	Real producer price	Real consumer price	Real world price[a]
	at 1980 prices £ million			(price indices: 1980 = 100)		
1970	5350	12,006	45	111	91	103
1973	5866	12,006	49	126	99	145
1984	7644	11,940	64	94	96	96

Sources:
[a] Unit values for food published in the *UN Monthly Bulletin of Statistics* converted to £s using current exchange rates and then deflated by the retail price index.

Other columns obtained from Central Statistical Office *Annual Abstract of Statistics*, various years.

Table 8.3 *Britain's balance of trade and changes in the volume of trade by product, and for exports (X) by destination and imports (M) by origin, 1970–87*

Category SITC (R2)	Overall balance 1970 £m	Overall balance 1987 £m	Volume Increase 1970–87 X%	Volume Increase 1970–87 M%	EEC X%	EEC M%	EFTA X%	EFTA M%	Commonwealth X%	Commonwealth M%
0 Food	-1,609	-4964	236	5	439	90	20	21	0	-50
1 Beverages & tobacco	76	431	62	206	252	399	4	-80	28	0
2&6 Crude materials, textile fibres	-1,059	-3251	102	-1	102	141	80	-24	19	-32
3 Fuels	-740	2648	372	46	487	-34	28	2181	690	-86
4 Animal & vegetable	-92	-194	651	70	1892	480	0	-38	-25	-53
5 Chemicals	242	2194	207	252	340	339	62	104	17	-59
6 Manufactures by material	57	-5077	33	116	70	375	-14	167	-19	-59
65 Textiles	158	-1638	13	289	91	424	-45	38	-51	3
67 Iron & steel	126	285	79	112	135	337	-17	8	-5	-70
68 Non-ferrous metals	-260	-441	10	21	24	409	35	92	-31	-71
69 Metal manufactures	165	-335	14	118	66	740	3	1126	-47	198
7 Machinery & transport equipment	1,822	-4017								
71–77 Machinery	1,044	-2074	60	422	111	450	8	132	-28	307
71–74 Mechanical[a]	871	1194	77	451	128	392	47	167	-18	382
75–77 electrical[b]	173	-3269	14	198	12	163	-12	71	-26	87
78 Road motor vehicles	700	-3933	222	300	512	1154	189	442	-2	841
781 Passenger cars	244	-3044	-10	640	(56)	(922)	(-65)	(121)	(-70)	(59)
8 Misc. manufactures	137	-2598	183	665	97	453	88	130	54	173
84 Clothing)	-13	-2396	149	423	410	393	46	19	16	193
85 Footwear)				454	-73	400	-60	-22	-53	-29
87&88 Scientific instruments and photo apparatus	55	54	214	475	279	563	100	202	-42	430
5–8 Manufactures	2,258	-9482	82	271	142	418	18	144	-12	-4
0–9 Total	-1,017	-14164	109	107	172	250	24	97	-28	-37

EEC ≡ France, Belgium, Luxembourg, Netherlands, W. Germany, Italy, Ireland, Denmark, Greece, Spain and Portugal in 1970 and 1987.
EFTA ≡ Iceland, Norway, Sweden, Finland, Switzerland and Austria in 1970 and 1987.

Sources:
HMSO *Annual Statement of the Overseas Trade of the United Kingdom 1970* (London, 1971)
Department of Trade and Industry *Overseas Trade Statistics of the United Kingdom* December 1987
Department of Trade and Industry *Monthly Review of External Trade Statistics* Annual Supplement No. 8, 1987 & Issue No. 150 July 1988

[a] less 716
[b] plus 716

An estimate of changes in the volume of trade with the different areas has been made by deflating monetary values by the unit values for that category. This shows British imports of food, and oils and fats from the Commonwealth have declined by 50% and 53% respectively, whereas from the EEC they have increased by 90% and 480% respectively.[2]

Manufactures

Throughout the period Britain's imports of manufactures have been increasing faster than her exports in real and money terms. She has exhibited a fundamental change in specialisation with manufacturing output as a proportion of GDP declining from the peak of 37% in 1951 (Brown and Sheriff, 1978), to 22% in 1986 (OECD *Historical Statistics*, 1960–86), although the volume of output continued to increase until 1973.

The question is the degree to which this represents a shift in Britain's comparative advantage or alternatively is the result of the commercial and protectionist policies she has pursued.

Let us consider briefly the various preferential schemes to which Britain has belonged. Initially she was a member of the Commonwealth preference scheme under which member countries gave preferential rates of duty on imports from each other. Britain's Commonwealth preference rate was generally four-fifths the manufacturing rate but for some products such as food and cotton yarn and fabric it was zero. She was the largest industrial power in the group and it accounted for 38% of all exports and around half of all her manufacturing exports in 1950. However, the value of this preference scheme became eroded as other members decided to raise their tariffs to encourage industrialisation. Furthermore, during the 1950s imports of cotton textiles from India, Pakistan and Hong Kong increased rapidly and by 1959 Britain's imports of cotton textiles were greater than her exports. Instead of accepting the shift in her comparative advantage she endeavoured to limit these imports by negotiating 'voluntary' export restraints with these member countries. These then had to be extended to other developing countries when their supply of imports also increased.

Britain found herself initially unable to accept the provisions of the Treaty of Rome signed in 1957 which established the EEC.

In 1959 Britain founded the European Free Trade Area which encompassed manufactures. It included some of the most advanced smaller industrialised countries such as Sweden and Switzerland and also less advanced countries such as Portugal. The EFTA secretariat calculated that one of the major benefits accruing to Britain arose from her increased imports of textiles from member countries. They classified this as trade creation, but in view of her restraints on imports from developing countries it appears more in the form of trade diversion. However, her exports of manufactures were increasing faster to the EEC than to EFTA (EFTA, 1969).

In 1973 Britain entered the EEC which comprised the other major industrialised West European countries. This involved removing trade barriers on imports of manufactures from member countries, and at the same time the EEC formed a free trade area in manufactures with the remaining EFTA countries; Commonwealth preference had to be abandoned. There was a Common External Tariff (CET) on imports from outside this area but on most of the items in which the industrialised countries specialised such as machinery and transport equipment, and chemicals, tariffs had been reduced under a series of GATT negotiations.

Over the period Britain had therefore moved from a membership of a preferential area of complementary Commonwealth countries to one of competitive European ones. The Vinerian analysis regarded the first as most likely to lead to trade diversion and therefore be detrimental. However, from Britain's point of view this was not important as most of the major suppliers of primary products were within the Commonwealth and imports of food from outside came in duty-free any way. However, the preferential rates in Commonwealth markets may have led to trade diversion towards her goods away from, say, Japanese ones. They may have contributed towards her very high initial degree of specialisation in manufactures. This system was bound to be eroded by the industrialised of other member countries.

On becoming a member of EFTA and then of EEC Britain faced increasing competition in machinery and transport goods in her own domestic market and in spite of the removal of tariff barriers had difficulty in expanding her exports to Europe. The member countries tried to impede the process of specialisation by directly or indirectly subsidising their 'champions'. Thus, the major European countries maintained their domestic car industries, although Ford and General Motors took advantage of this large tariff-free area to move production round. They also tried to maintain their steel industries although under the Davignon Plan production and subsidies were restricted in an endeavour to keep prices up.

Some idea of the effect of changes in trade preference on Britain's exports of manufactures can be obtained by considering her relative importance to her chief trading partners. Britain's exports to the EEC reached a low of 7.4% of total imports of other member countries in 1973;[3] since then her export proportion has increased, and in 1986 it was 7.8%. However, her market share in European countries in which she formerly had some protection against other EEC countries has declined quite markedly; in Denmark and Portugal, former EFTA countries, it has halved, and in Ireland, it has fallen by 40%. Her market share in the main non-European countries has also continued to decline, particularly in Canada with the abandonment of Commonwealth preference and Canada's moves towards a free trade area with the USA.

The proportion of Britain's imports supplied by other EEC countries has steadily increased from 29% in 1970 to 52% in 1986. In particular, West Germany, which only supplied 11% of her imports of manufactures in 1965 now supplies 21%. The share of EFTA countries Sweden and Switzerland has declined and so has that of the United States and Canada. But the share of Japan has continued to increase, reflecting her comparative advantage in sectors in which growth has been extremely rapid, namely electrical goods (SITC (R2) 716, 75–77), and scientific instruments and photographic apparatus (SITC (R2) 87 + 88) in which in 1986 the volume of imports were respectively 8 and $5\frac{1}{2}$ times their level in 1970 (Department of Trade and Industry, 1987).

In Table 8.3 estimates are made of the changes in the volume of exports and imports by commodity group in relation to the main areas. The EEC is defined for both years as in note 3 and EFTA is defined to exclude Denmark and Portugal. 1970 is chosen as a base to exclude the instability associated with 1973. The change in the volume of exports and imports to each area is made by deflating the value figures by the unit values for all exports or imports of that group.

On the eve of entry to the EEC in 1970 Britain was a net exporter of manufactures to all three trading areas with a positive balance in relation to the Commonwealth of £684 million, slightly greater than with the EEC. Her trade with the Commonwealth subsequently contracted with imports falling by a greater amount than exports. Exports of manufactures to the Commonwealth fell by 12% whereas imports increased by 4% mainly due to electrical goods but also due to clothing. Her exports of manufactures to the EEC grew by 142% but imports grew even more rapidly, quadrupling over the period. The increase in imports of manufactures was particularly large for electrical goods, metal manufactures, road vehicles and scientific instruments. A similar pattern emerges with EFTA although the increase in imports of manufactures is only 144% between 1970 and 1987.

Not all the present commercial policy is the result of the Treaty of Rome. Restrictions on imports of textiles and clothing from developing countries have arisen from the EEC's membership of the Multi Fibre Agreement (MFA) and the very limited 'voluntary' export restraints negotiated under it, particularly for imports from Asia. This has led to a considerable degree of trade diversion; imports of textiles from Commonwealth countries have scarcely increased whereas those from the EEC have risen by 422% and from EFTA by 38%. Imports of clothing have continued to rise from all areas but have risen much faster at 334% from the

EEC compared with 193% from the Commonwealth. This endeavour of Britain and now the EEC to protect the local cotton industry has not led to an increased output of the British industry but just a transfer of imports from developing countries to more expensive sources within the EEC. It is pure trade diversion and a direct efficiency loss. There is also an element of trade diversion in the increased imports of passenger cars of 650% from the EEC in so far as imports from Japan, the cheapest producer, have been restricted since 1977 by agreement between the industries to 11% of the domestic market. A similar situation now appears to be arising in electronic goods with the EEC imposing dumping duties on products from Japan and sometime South Korea which may not even be produced in Britain. British consumers have to pay higher prices for them and the tariff revenue goes to the Commission.

Thus, the general effect of commercial policy has been to expose British exporters of manufactures more directly to European competition. In a competitive system this would be expected to lead to a reduction in their relative price. This has to some extent occurred. However, the general presumption of economists working in Britain appears to be that manufacturers operate a mark-up system of prices based on labour costs. In that case, the effect of increased competition is reflected in a reduction in sales and also in profits.

In addition the CAP has operated to increase the price of agricultural products. Thus, the overall effect of commercial policy has been to discriminate against manufacturing in favour of agriculture. This has just intensified the de-industrialisation that occurred as the result of the exploitation of North Sea oil.

Manufacturing output fell after 1973 and in 1981 was 18% below the level in 1973. Many of the greatest reductions were in sectors taken to roughly correspond to the trade classification – see Table 8.4 – in which, from the trade figures, Britain appeared to be losing her comparative advantage and in particular appeared to be at a disadvantage in relation to the rest of the EEC, that is, metals, manufactures, mechanical engineering, motor vehicles and parts, and textiles. However, this excludes electrical and instrument engineering, the output of which has increased.

One would expect the changes in production to be associated with a transfer of factors of production from manufacturing to fuel and agriculture. With respect to investment this is what has happened. There was a rapid increase in investment in fuel (coal, petroleum and natural gas) from 1% of gross investment to 10% by 1976. Investment in agriculture remained about 3%, whereas investment in manufacturing fell from 22% in 1970 to 16% in 1973, it then fluctuated around 18% declining to 12% in the early 1980s. It was so low that net investment (net domestic fixed capital

Table 8.4   *Manufacturing output related to SITC categories*

SITC (R2)	Industry	Output at constant factor cost (1980 = 100)		
		1970	1973	1986
5	Chemicals	79	96	122.3
65	Textiles	135	147	98.8
67, 68	Metals	169	169	110.9
69	Metal goods not elsewhere specified	129	132	97.2
71–74	Mechanical engineering	111	113	92.7
75–77	Electrical engineering	74	89	} 129.9
87	Instrument engineering	78	86	
78	Motor vehicles	114	123	82.6
84, 85	Clothing, footwear	95	109	} 108.0
	Leather	148	150	

Indices in 1970 and 1973 obtained from that based on 1975 = 100 by dividing by index for 1980.

Source: Central Statistical Office, *National Accounts*, 1987 and *National Income and Expenditure*, 1981.

formation) in manufacturing was negative in the early 1980s (CSO, b, 1981, 1987).

However, the same cannot be said of employment. The extraction of North Sea oil has been a very capital-intensive process and coal mining has become more capital-intensive, so that total employment in the fuel sector has not increased. Employment has also continued to fall in agriculture. So the growing sectors did not employ more labour even though employment was falling in manufacturing. This has been the cause of the rise in unemployment which has only been modified by the increase in employment in the service sector.

Conclusion

In conclusion therefore, it is difficult to apply a general equilibrium analysis to the change in Britain's trading position since 1950 because of the lack of competitive conditions in the product and factor markets and the complexities of her commercial policies, which have only been touched on here. Nevertheless, the central tenet of the analysis, namely that a policy which favours one sector must discriminate against the others, is appropriate. The de-industrialisation of Britain is partly due to the exploitation of North Sea oil but it is also attributed to her change from membership of a preferential area of complementary economies to one of competitive economies in which agriculture is highly protected.

Notes

1 For the sake of consistency, the EEC is taken to include West Germany, The Netherlands, Belgium, Luxembourg, France, Italy, Denmark, the Irish Republic, Greece, Spain, Portugal and the UK in 1970 and 1986. EFTA is taken to exclude Denmark and Portugal.
2 This is inaccurate in so far as a unit value index averaged over all imports is used to deflate the monetary values for the two areas. As increasing proportions are coming from the higher priced source the index will show a faster increase than ones calculated for the individual areas. Thus, the measure of reduction of imports from the Commonwealth is too great and the increase in imports from the EEC is too low.
3 The EEC is taken to include West Germany, the Netherlands, Belgium, Luxembourg, France, Italy, Denmark, the Irish Republic, Greece, Spain and Portugal.

References

Brown, C. J. F. and Sheriff, T. D. (1978). 'De-industrialisation in the UK: background statistics', Discussion Paper no. 23 of The National Institute of Economic and Social Research.
Central Statistical Office. (a) Economic Trends and Annual Supplement; (b) UK National Accounts; (c) Annual Abstract of Statistics.
Commission of the European Communities. *The Agricultural Situation in the Community*, Annual Reports.
Department of Energy. *Digest of United Kingdom Energy Statistics*, 1980, 1983 and 1987.
Department of Trade and Industry, *Monthly Review of External Trade Statistics and Annual Supplement*, no. 7, 1986 and no. 8, 1987.
European Free Trade Association (1969). *The Effects of EFTA on the Economies of Member States*, Geneva.
Eurostat. *Yearbook of Agricultural Statistics* (1970, 1972, 1973).
Ghosh, S. K. (1974). 'Towards a theory of multiple customs unions', *American Economic Review*, March.
Governor of the Bank of England (1980). Ashbridge Lecture, *Bank of England Quarterly Bulletin*, December.
HMSO (1970). *Britain and the European Communities*, Cmnd. 4289.
HMSO (1971). *The United Kingdom and the European Communities*, Cmnd. 4715.
Lipsey, R. G. (1957). 'The theory of customs unions: trade diversion and welfare', *Economica*, vol. 24.
Mansell, K. (1980). 'UK visible trade in the post-war years', CSO *Economic Trends*, October.
Miller, M. H. (1971). 'Estimates of the static balance of payments and welfare costs of United Kingdom entry into the Common Market', *National Institute Economic Review*, no. 57.
Moore, L. (1985). *The Growth and Structure of International Trade Since the Second World War* (Brighton: Wheatsheaf) chs 5 and 11.

Organisation for Economic Co-operation and Development (1970). *The Growth of Output 1960–1980* (Paris: OECD).

Organisation for Economic Co-operation and Development (1987). *National Policies and Agricultural Trade* (Paris: OECD).

Organisation for Economic Co-operation and Development. *Historical Statistics* 1960–84, 1960–85 and 1960–86.

Viner, J. (1950). 'The economics of customs unions', republished in P. Robson (ed.) (1972), *International Economic Integration* (London: Penguin).

World Bank (1981). *Commodity Trade and Price Trends* (London: Johns Hopkins).

9

Inventory investment: plans and realisations

Michael Sumner

Introduction

Students of Dennis Coppock (1959, 1965) will scarcely need reminding of the central role of inventory investment in the propagation of business fluctuations. It stems in part from the short time-horizon of inventory decisions and their corresponding sensitivity to short-run variations in demand; but even in the absence of an accelerator, Metzler's (1941) 'pure' inventory cycle would ensure that unanticipated changes in demand generated an oscillatory response, at least in suitably simple models, when firms attempted to restore stocks to their target levels.

The distinction between planned and unplanned changes in inventories, while of crucial theoretical importance, poses an obvious practical problem in empirical studies. The standard procedure is to assume a mechanism for the generation of sales expectations, and to identify unplanned inventory investment with discrepancies between this proxy and actual sales. The typical result is that obtained by Coppock (1965, p. 31) who assumed static expectations for illustrative purposes, but inferred from the relative performance of current and lagged sales in his estimated stockbuilding functions that 'it would be more accurate to assume that expected sales are identical with actual sales for the current period, which would imply the absence of any unplanned changes in stocks'. This result is not confined to studies of US data, nor is it contingent on the assumption of static expectations. Hall *et al.* (1986) provide a particularly interesting British example because of their sophisticated treatment of expectations; they nevertheless find that the innovation in sales makes no contribution to their explanation of manufacturing stocks. The generality of this finding is illustrated by its place at the top of Blinder's catalogue (1981, p. 452) of embarrassing stylised facts about inventory investment.

The present chapter attempts to shed some clearer light on the magnitude and volatility of unplanned inventory investment by exploiting a hitherto unused data source, the CBI Survey of Industrial Trends in the manufacturing sector.[1] The crucial feature of this enquiry is its inclusion of questions about past experience as well as future intentions, so that unplanned changes can be inferred from successive surveys. For present purposes the data source also suffers from several weaknesses, however; hence the results of this investigation can only be regarded as provisional.

Limitations of the data

The most immediate problem is the brevity of the series. Questions on changes in the values of stocks of raw materials and finished goods have been included since the survey was initiated in 1958, but the questions were rephrased in terms of volume changes only in mid-1977. At the same time a question about work in progress was added. After allowing for differencing and requirements for lagged values of the survey observations, the main sample period is reduced to 1978:4 – 1986:2.

Secondly, there is an inconsistency between the time-horizon of the questions, which refer to actual changes over the past four months and expected changes over the next four, and the frequency of the surveys, which were changed from a triannual to a quarterly basis in 1972. If the questions are interpreted literally, a discrepancy could arise between the change predicted in one survey and the actual change recorded in the following enquiry, even if developments over the three months between the surveys had been predicted with complete accuracy. This inconsistency of timing introduces an additional source of measurement error in the inferred series of unplanned stockbuilding, and an element of automatic serial correlation through the overlapping of successive observations. It also blurs the comparison between the survey results and the official series of measured stockbuilding.

A final and familiar difficulty is that the survey responses are purely qualitative, indicating only the direction of actual or expected change. The most commonly used method of translating the survey information into a quantitative series is to define the expected change in the variable of interest as the mean of a probability distribution whose location can be inferred, up to a scaling factor, from the proportions of survey respondents expecting an increase, decrease and no change respectively. Pesaran (1984) proposed an alternative method which avoids the need to assume anything about the respondents' probability distribution, and instead uses the information collected by the CBI on past changes: the actual rate of change in the variable as measured by the CSO is regressed on the proportions of firms reporting increases and decreases in the period just ended, and the estimated parameters are then applied to the proportions expecting increases and decreases in the future. Wren-Lewis (1985) also used the information on firms' perceptions of past changes, but in a probabilistic setting, to determine the scaling factor, or just noticeable difference, without resorting to an additional arbitrary assumption. His comparison of these alternatives suggested that for quantity though not price variables, specifically the rate of change of output, there was little difference between the results of his preferred method using a logistic distribution and those of Pesaran's regression method. Moreover, the coefficients estimated in the latter procedure were so close in absolute value that the separate series of 'ups' and 'downs' could be replaced without loss of information by the 'balance' which records the difference between them, and which is frequently quoted in the financial press as a convenient summary statistic. In terms of the probabilistic approach, the balance statistic is proportional to the mean of a rectangular distribution with a constant variance.

Preliminary regressions of the CSO measures of output and inventory change on the corresponding CBI series of reported 'ups' and 'downs' showed that no significant loss of information resulted from using the balance statistic, which was therefore adopted as the unit of survey measurement for the purposes of this investigation.

The characteristics of inventory investment

The period examined in this study is not only short but also unrepresentative of earlier experience. Table 9.1 sets the sample period in a longer perspective so as to bring out the important differences.[2]

In the longer term, changes in inventory investment made only a tiny contribution to the average change in real GDP, but they contributed as much to the variance of output change as all the other components of aggregate demand in combination. Final sales grew more smoothly than GDP, rendering the standard characterisation of inventories as a buffer stock totally implausible. Blinder and Holtz-Eakin's claim (1986, p. 183) that 'business cycles *are* inventory fluctuations' is equally applicable to the UK.

The more recent past has in one sense been very different. In conditions

Table 9.1 Composition of change in GDP (%)

Period	1963–1985		1978:4–1986:2	
	Mean	Variance	Mean	Variance
Final sales	99.4	40	107.5	115
Inventory investment	0.6	37	−7.5	47

Table 9.2   Variance decomposition of inventory investment

1978:4–1986:2		% Total
Manufacturing		35
Materials and fuel	6	
Work in progress	6	
Finished goods	9	
Energy and water supply		6
Wholesale		10
Retail		5
Other		10

of severe depression, change in inventory investment has played a modestly stabilising role in reducing the variance of change in GDP relative to final sales. It remains, however, a highly volatile component of aggregate demand in comparison with the other individual constituents. Its contribution to the average change in GDP has been even smaller than before, in fact negative.

A second preliminary question concerns the share of the manufacturing sector, which is the focus of this study, in inventory investment. As the decomposition reported in Table 9.2 makes clear, manufacturing makes much the largest sectoral contribution to the variance of total stock-building. Within manufacturing, change in stocks of finished goods is the most volatile category. For both the manufacturing sector and the aggregate, the whole is greater than the sum of its parts in the sense that the covariance terms, which are not tabulated, are predominantly positive; in particular, fluctuations in manufacturers' stocks of finished goods are not offset but actually reinforced by fluctuations in the stocks of wholesale and retail traders.

It is worth observing in passing that the temptation to compare this decomposition with that presented by Blinder (1981) for the United States should be resisted. In the UK information on stocks of motor vehicles is collected only annually (CSO, 1985) and is included, presumably by interpolation, in the residual category of the quarterly data. In the USA, automobiles make a disproportionate contribution to the pronounced volatility of retail stockbuilding, which is Blinder's primary concern.

The characteristics and consistency of the CBI data

The changes in stocks and output reported *ex post* by the CBI respondents are separated in Table 9.3 into a planned component, recorded in the

Table 9.3   Decomposition of reported changes (%)

	Mean		Variance	
	Planned	Unplanned	Planned	Unplanned
Materials and fuel	145	−45	56	27
Work in progress	190	−90	66	20
Finished goods	206	−106	74	45
Output	−364	464	70	20

preceding survey, and a residual error term, which with qualifications represents unanticipated changes in stocks and unpredicted changes in output. The qualifications include errors introduced by variations in the sample and, as already noted, the possibility of contamination by the inconsistency between the time-horizon and the frequency of the surveys. In addition, taking the difference between the balance of perceived changes in one survey and the balance of expected changes in the previous survey assumes, with Pesaran and Wren-Lewis, that the scaling factor is the same for the *ex ante* as for the *ex post* responses; fortunately the latter cites a CBI survey of answering practices which suggests that the questions are indeed answered in the same way by almost all firms.

The first half of the table provides striking evidence of systematic mistakes in firms' planning and forecasting procedures. Unplanned increases in all categories of stocks offset a substantial proportion of the planned average decrease, and the expected increase in output stubbornly failed to materialise. The common assumption that expectations are unbiased on average (e.g. Carlson and Parkin, 1975) is clearly unwarranted in this turbulent sample. The variance decomposition in the second half of the table confirms that unplanned changes are most pronounced in the finished goods category of stockbuilding; but surprises are far from negligible in the other categories of survey response.

The consistency between the CBI balance statistics and the CSO measures of inventory investment and of quarterly rates of change of manufacturing production is examined in Table 9.4.[3] All the intercepts are appropriately insignificant, and each of the planned changes makes a significant contribution to the explanation of the corresponding CSO measure. For changes in output and stocks of finished goods, there is no significant difference between the coefficients of the planned and unplanned changes reported to the CBI, and the point estimates are close in both cases. The standard errors of the unplanned changes are higher than those of the planned changes, as expected given the additional sources of error intro-

Table 9.4   Consistency of CSO and CBI measures

	Inventory investment (£M at 1980 prices)			
	Materials and fuel	Work in progress	Finished goods	Output change (% per quarter)
Intercept	16.70 (0.84)	22.07 (0.59)	56.81 (1.19)	−0.07 (0.22)
Planned change	10.37 (9.89)	6.23 (2.92)	12.60 (3.76)	0.08 (4.63)
Unplanned change	5.64 (3.73)	−0.88 (0.23)	11.14 (2.60)	0.08 (2.54)
$\bar{R}^2$	0.82	0.18	0.35	0.50
D-W	2.19	2.38	2.09	2.37
F	5.45	2.18	0.09	0.01

Notes

(i) t-ratios in parentheses.

(ii) F tests the restriction that the planned and unplanned components of the CBI survey responses contribute equally to the explanation of the CSO measure of the corresponding variable. The critical values are 4.20 at the 0.05 level and 7.64 at the 0.01 level of significance.

duced by differencing successive surveys. The overall fits are far from impressive. If the official statistics could be regarded as definitive, the low coefficients of determination might be interpreted as indicating the limitations of qualitative survey data; but this interpretation is clouded by the fact that the official statistics, especially of stockbuilding, are themselves subject to a substantial margin of error.

It is not surprising that the worst fit of all is for changes in work in progress, where the CBI respondents are unlikely to make the adjustment which in the national accounts allocates progress payments, particularly important for aerospace and shipbuilding, to the fixed investment of the purchasing industries (CSO, 1985), It is far from obvious, however, that this adjustment can account for the poor performance of unplanned changes, which as measured make absolutely no contribution to the explanation of changes in work in progress. The differences between intentions and reported outcomes appear to be pure noise, despite their comparability with the discrepancies in the other survey categories. Investment in stocks of materials and fuel, which involves no imputation problems and has the highest correlation with the survey responses, exhibits similar though less extreme characteristics: the measure of unplanned change is statistically significant but attracts a coefficient only about half as large as that on planned changes.

The qualitative differences shown in the table suggest that there are serious costs of aggregating across the three categories of manufacturers' inventory investment. Stocks of finished goods are the classic buffer, reflecting planned and unexpected changes equally. If there are any involuntary changes in work in progress, the survey information does not enable them to be identified. In terms of statistical results changes in materials and fuel occupy an intermediate position, reflecting in almost equal proportions the changes planned at the beginning of the quarter and those reported at the end. One interpretation of this result is that the interval between surveys exceeds the planning horizon: plans are always realised but are revised at frequent intervals. Doubtless other interpretations are possible; but as the *F*-test reported in the last row of the table indicates, the standard identity which breaks down *ex post* change into planned and unplanned components cannot plausibly be regarded as one of them.

The implication of these results, that over a period as short as a calendar quarter unplanned changes can be clearly identified only in stocks of finished goods, is consistent with the stockbuilding equations in the current vintage of large-scale models (Wallis *et al.*, 1987). In both the London Business School's equation for finished goods and the Bank of England's equation for finished goods plus work in progress the coefficient on current business activity is negatively signed,[4] whereas its effect is positive in their other equations for manufacturing. The other public models are less informative: the National Institute combines all three categories, and the Treasury does not include a measure of current output among the regressors; though in their developmental work on the latter model Kelly and Owen (1985) reported, with evident satisfaction, a negative effect of current activity on stocks of final goods.

There is an obvious parallel between these results and the analysis of retail stockbuilding by Blinder (1981). His argument applies immediately to materials and fuel: in a period when supply constraints were conspicuously absent, discrepancies between desired and actual stocks that were too large to be explained in terms of indivisibilities would indicate an implausible degree of inertia. It is even more difficult to envisage involuntary changes in work in progress, which involves no possibility of external interference.

Production-smoothing implies that unanticipated changes in demand will be reflected in unplanned changes in stocks of finished goods; but it does not generate any incentive to smooth suppliers' production by tolerating departures from planned stocks of materials, and it positively discourages short-term changes in work in progress. Investment in finished goods is a large and volatile component of the total but it does not dominate the other constituents of manufacturers' stockbuilding.

Determinants of planned stockbuilding

The credibility of the survey responses is strengthened by the relative success of the attempt to account for planned inventory investment reported in Table 9.5. There is a substantial measure of consistency in the answers to the individual questions, with the result that in all cases the dominant influences on plans are planned developments at subsequent stages of the production process. Indeed, for work in progress these are the only influences, as Hicks's (1950, p. 48) sausage-machine analogy suggests.

Apart from planned changes downstream, the other major influence on planned stocks of materials and fuel is 'large' changes in the price of these inputs. Modest experimentation indicated that the relationship is contemporaneous and non-linear. As the surveys are conducted at the beginning of the quarter, the absence of a lag suggests that plans are based on accurate

Table 9.5 Determinants of planned inventory investment

	Materials and fuel	Work in progress	Finished goods
Intercept	−3.74	−4.90	−13.83
	(1.45)	(3.62)	(16.70)
Forecast output change	0.31	0.37	0.49
	(2.24)	(7.50)	(13.43)
Planned change in work in progress	0.65	—	—
	(3.40)		
Planned change in finished goods	—	0.61	—
		(6.21)	
Rate of change of input prices (≥ 2% per quarter)	−1.03	—	—
	(2.53)		
Dummy 1978:4−1981:1	—	—	5.20
			(4.33)
Trend	−0.18	—	—
	(2.04)		
Error correction ($t-4$)	—	—	−0.24
			(2.89)
$\bar{R}^2$	0.94	0.97	0.88
D-W	2.20	2.43	2.00

anticipation. The evidence for non-linearity came from the successive improvements in overall fit and in the significance of price change itself when a threshold was imposed at successively higher values in the range from 0 to 2% per quarter; thereafter the fit began to deteriorate. The existence of a threshold effect is, of course, entirely consistent with the assumption of a 'just noticeable difference' in the probabilistic interpretation of the survey information.

A one-zero dummy variable to represent the temporary stock relief scheme made no contribution in the materials equation, possibly because 'large' price increases were concentrated in its operative period; but it exerts a highly significant effect in the finished goods equation. The abolition of the temporary relief in 1981 increased the balance of planned disinvestment by 50% of its sample average value. The abolition of the 'permanent' stock relief scheme in 1984 raised the costs of stock-holding in a smaller proportion (Sumner, 1984), and this second change in the tax system did not show up significantly in estimation.

The CBI responses exhibit the same declining trend in the ratio of material and fuel stocks to manufacturing production which appears in the national accounts. The significance of the trend, and of the intercepts in the other two equations, means that the fit statistics should be interpreted with caution.

Finally, the results confirm the interpretation suggested earlier of the difference between the planned and actual changes recorded in successive surveys. No role was found in the first two equations for lagged 'unplanned' changes in stocks. These negative results are consistent with changes of plan during the survey period and with scheduling errors respectively. Planned changes in stocks of finished goods, however, do respond to previous discrepancies, suggesting that unplanned changes in this sector are indeed involuntary. The only surprising feature is the length of time taken to correct errors. It was not worth trying to estimate a distributed lag on such a short data set; instead, some experimentation was carried out with alternative lengths of a discrete lag: a one-year delay, the maximum allowed, produced the best test statistics. This tentative result suggests that the replacement of involuntary stock changes is a much slower and smoother process than is assumed in simple models of the pure inventory cycle.

Surprises

As seen already, errors in the planning of production and stock levels are large and systematic. The characteristics of these errors are briefly described in the remaining tables.

Table 9.6 *Correlations among surprises*

	Materials and fuel	Work in progress	Finished goods
Work in progress	0.80		
Finished goods	0.52	0.42	
Output	0.15	0.21	−0.19

The most striking feature of Table 9.6 is that the only negative correlation is between involuntary changes in stocks of finished goods and unexpected changes in output. This result is again consistent with the inference that only finished goods inventories serve any buffering purpose: the magnitude of this effect is artificially reduced by using output surprises, rather than the more appropriate but unobtainable sales surprises. The positive entries elsewhere indicate that errors are reinforcing rather than offsetting.

The generally significant intercepts of the autoregressions reported in Table 9.7 confirm the biases suggested by Table 9.3. The new information is the high degree of persistence exhibited by the inventory surprises, which seems too strong to be explained by the timing inconsistency in the surveys. For one or both of these reasons the process of production planning conspicuously fails to satisfy the requirements of rationality at all its stages.

Table 9.7 *Serial dependence of surprises*

	Surprise in			
	Materials and fuels	Work in progress	Finished goods	Output
Intercept	1.53	2.64	2.27	−5.67
	(1.20)	(2.07)	(2.01)	(2.91)
Lagged dependent variable	0.63	0.41	0.64	0.14
	(4.34)	(2.36)	(4.65)	(0.76)
$\bar{R}^2$	0.37	0.13	0.41	< 0
Durbin h	−0.53	−2.06	0.32	—
D-W	—	—	—	1.94

Conclusions

The main result of this enquiry is to limit the scope and severity of the pure inventory cycle. Only stocks of finished goods appear to be subject to involuntary changes, and the restoration of stocks to their planned levels is a protracted process. The length of this adjustment reduces the probability of overshooting in response to random disturbances. While the restriction of involuntary changes to finished goods is implicit in the concept of production smoothing itself, the limited scope of the pure cycle does not appear to have been generally recognised; and there is no previous evidence on the adjustment to involuntary changes.

A second and more general result is the degree to which manufacturing industry makes forecasting errors. Mistakes do not average out to zero, at least in this sample; and inventory surprises, though not unexpected changes in output, show a marked tendency to persist in successive periods. The rational expectations hypothesis would make little contribution to the analysis of this behaviour.

It is probably unnecessary to emphasise the provisional status of these conclusions. The brevity of the sample and the unusual character of the period both make generalisation hazardous. The results, including the negative findings and interpretative puzzles, do seem sufficiently interesting, however, to justify the obligatory plea for further research.

Notes

1 I am grateful to the Confederation of British Industry for providing the data.
2 The source of all national accounts data is *Economic Trends Annual Supplement*, 1987.
3 The survey questions invite the respondents to abstract from seasonal variations; accordingly the CSO's seasonally adjusted series are used as dependent variables. Dummy variables were initially included as a check on respondents' ability to adjust for seasonality, but they proved to be unnecessary.
4 Wallis *et al.* (1987, p. 107) are therefore incorrect in stating that 'unanticipated stock-building is treated as purely random' in all the models under review.

References

Blinder, A. S. (1981). 'Retail inventory behaviour and business fluctuations', *Brookings Papers on Economic Activity* 2, pp. 443–520.
Blinder, A. S. and Holtz-Eakin, D. (1986). 'Inventory fluctuations in the US since 1929', in R. J. Gordon (ed.), *The American Business Cycle: Continuity and Change*, NBER Studies in Business Cycles, vol. 25, University of Chicago Press, Chicago.
Carlson, J. A. and Parkin, M. (1975). 'Inflation expectations', *Economica*, vol. 42, pp. 123–38.
Central Statistical Office (1985). *The National Income Accounts: Sources and Methods*, 3rd edition (London: HMSO).

Coppock, D. J. (1959). 'The periodicity and stability of inventory cycles in the USA', *The Manchester School*, vol. 59, pp. 140–74, 261–99.

Coppock, D. J. (1965). 'The post-war short cycle in the USA', *The Manchester School*, vol. 33, pp. 17–44.

Hall, S. G., Henry, S. G. B. and Wren-Lewis, S. (1986). 'Manufacturing stocks and forward-looking expectations in the UK', *Economica*, vol. 53, pp. 447–65.

Hicks, J. R. (1950). *A Contribution to the Theory of the Trade Cycle* (Oxford: Oxford University Press).

Kelly, C. and Owen, D. (1985). 'Factor prices in the Treasury model', *Government Economic Service Working Paper no. 37*.

Metzler, L. A. (1941). 'The nature and stability of inventory cycles', *Review of Economic Statistics*, vol. 23, pp. 113–29.

Pesaran, M. H. (1984). 'Expectations formation and macroeconomic modelling', in P. Malgrange and P. Muet (eds), *Contemporary Macroeconomic Modelling* (Oxford: Basil Blackwell).

Sumner, M. T. (1984). 'The impact of stock relief', *Oxford Bulletin of Economics and Statistics*, vol. 46, pp. 169–79.

Wallis, K. F., Fisher, P. G., Longbottom, J. A., Turner, D. S. and Whitley, J. D. (1987). *Models of the UK Economy: A Fourth Review by the ESRC Macroeconomic Modelling Bureau* (Oxford: Oxford University Press).

Wren-Lewis, S. (1985). 'The quantification of survey data on expectations', *National Institute Economic Review*, vol. 113, pp. 39–49.

10

Privatisation in historical perspective: the UK water industry

Robert Millward

Introduction

The privatisation of the public utilities in fuel, transport, and related infrastructure has been a striking feature of the Conservative government's period of office in the 1980s. Initially rather tentative and small scale, it has now been extended to the big nationalised British Gas, British Telecom and the electricity boards, and the water industry is next in line. The virtues of private ownership and competitive regimes have been expounded with many an allusion to nineteenth-century Victorian thrift, initiative and entrepreneurship. I propose here to take a critical look at what evidence has accumulated on the advantages of private ownership, especially for large natural monopolies. The proposals for the water industry will be assessed in that context, and in the light of the experience of Victorian Britain when private water companies flourished.

I cannot expect that Dennis Coppock, to whom this volume is dedicated, will agree with the broad thrust of my critique. In the 1960s at Manchester he was one of the few privatisers around, and he must be pleased with the programme of the current government. However, I hope he will get some enjoyment from this essay at the least because of its historical dimensions. As an undergraduate at Hull University I was exposed by John Saville, then Senior Lecturer in Economic History, to the debate on the Victorian climacteric. Dennis maintained economic history as one of his interests in the 1950s and 1960s when, to a degree, the relevance of history was rarely expounded to newcomers to economics. He will be pleased that the links between economics and history are now being re-forged both here and in the USA.

The public–private mix, competition and the evidence on performance

The government's broad stance has been that privatisation and an active competition policy should go hand in hand. The shift to private ownership in the production of goods and services was to be accompanied by a reduction in the element of regulation and subsidy and by the promotion of competition. The underlying motives have included a desire for wider share ownership and for a smaller PSBR. But efficiency has, on the face of it, been central and this will be the main concern of this paper. It is useful to distinguish two aspects. The first relates to allocative efficiency in the range of goods and services produced. Notwithstanding all the difficulties with the concept, allocative efficiency here may be gauged by the relationship of prices to marginal social cost. For an enterprise operating in the utility sector, this raises the question of the extent to which prices are related to the enterprise's costs and, on the other hand, to any input and output spill-overs which create a wedge between social and private cost. The second aspect of efficiency is cost-effectiveness, that is, the degree to which the cost of producing a given quality and quantity of goods and services varies with ownership and/or the regulatory environment. It would be appropriate in this context also to distinguish between technical efficiency and input price efficiency, and to assess the extent to which the input prices facing an enterprise reflect social costs.

There are now some eight years of experience with the government's privatisation programme. Some indications of the effect of deregulation and the ownership change are emerging, but they are as yet on a small scale. However, economists have also been prompted to look at the evidence on public versus private and the role of deregulation in other countries and other periods. In the area of fuel, transport, water and related infrastructure, there are four main conclusions we can make so far.

First is that ownership by itself has little impact on cost-effectiveness. The point is clear from the utility sectors of countries like the United States where large numbers of both public and private undertakings coexist in the same industry, and where cost and production functions have been estimated. In the UK for much of the postwar period such studies have not been possible because any given sector has been either public or private. There has been some assessment of activities marginal to the main nationalised industries like the sale of gas and electric appliances and Sealink where Pryke (1982) found private operators had a better record. He had to work with rather thin data (on turnover per employee, for example – as also in his study of airlines), made no estimate of returns to scale, and was not able to make any formal allowance for differences in factor prices or in networks and routes. Detailed case studies of railways and airlines in Canada and Australia, where public and private have coexisted in the postwar period, suggest no difference in technical efficiency. Much the same can be said, as we shall see, for water supplies in the USA. The costs of producing and supplying electric power appear consistently lower in the

publicly owned electric utilities of the USA during the 1960s and 1970s
than in the privately owned firms (Millward and Parker, 1983). In Britain
in the pre-1945 period, when both species coexisted, the private firms had
slightly lower costs (Foreman-Peck and Waterman, 1985). Cost function
estimates for the gas industry in Britain, again for an earlier period, suggest
no difference between public and private (Millward and Ward, 1987).

Many economists have accepted this evidence and see improvements in
cost-effectiveness arising, not from ownership, but rather from more active
competition (Kay and Silbertson, 1984; Shackleton, 1984; Wright 1987;
Helm *et al.*, 1988). Publicly owned electricity utilities in the United States
have lower costs, *ceteris paribus*, when confronted with a competitor in
their area of supply. There is already evidence that deregulation of long-
distance coaches in the UK in the 1980s has encouraged real cost cutting in
National Express (Jaffer and Thompson, 1986, p. 62), quite apart from the
more aggressive marketing that has emerged from this publicly owned
company, as well as from British Rail. Even in the absence of competition,
emulation of enterprise in other geographical areas may be important.
Hard evidence of this is still rather thin but underlies the projected break-
up of large organisations like the Post Office into separately accountable
business centres; letters, parcels, counters, Girobank (Albon, 1988); it is
reflected also in the reservations which commentators have expressed over
the disinclination of the government to break up British Gas into generating
and distributing units.

The third point is that natural monopolies remain a problem. Competition *in the field* lowers the potential cost advantage of a single firm.
Competition *for the field* is undermined in the presence of sunk costs,
leaving regulation as the only alternative. The US experience of regulatory
capture and/or overinvestment is strong. Evidence on contestability in the
utility sector in Britain is still limited (but see the later part of this chapter
on nineteenth-century water supplies). In so far as National Express did
enjoy an element of natural cost advantage, its sunk costs allowed both
predatory prices and an aggressive policy with respect to its key 'unnatural'
monopoly advantage, that is, its ownership of passenger terminal facilities
(Davis, 1984; Jaffer and Thompson, 1986).

Fourthly, a shift to private ownership is likely to induce a closer align-
ment of prices with private costs; deregulation has also a similar effect.
There is clear evidence from the US electric power industry of the 1960s
and 1970s that private utilities, even when regulated, have tariffs more
closely reflective of costs than public firms, and offer a wider range of rate
schedules. The traditional element of cross-subsidy by regime or function
in British public enterprise is well known. British Telecom is already moving
away from the subsidy by business users of domestic users. Deregulation of

long-distance coach travel in the UK has in the 1980s led to a fall in the real level of fares on densely trafficked routes and a rise in the real level of prices on the more costly lightly trafficked routes where service levels have fallen (cf. Jaffer and Thompson, 1986). In summary, privatisation and active competition tend to cut out activities which are privately unprofitable.

Privatisation and the UK water industry in the 1980s

In the light of this experience and evidence, it is relevant to note the following features of the UK government's programme. Privatisation itself had a rather tentative start. From 1979 to the closing months of 1984 most of the privatised enterprises, other than BP, were small, with many like Ferranti, British Sugar, Amersham, BR Hotels, and Sealink, selling for less than £100 million. The active privatisers like Beesley and Littlechild (1983) expected the gains would be largest in coal and rail, but these were avoided. Nevertheless, useful experience of floatation problems was acquired. The council house sales proved popular, and the absence of opposition to the wider programme encouraged the government further. Now, some of the big nationalised industries are being floated and the Conservative government is viewed abroad as setting the pace for the USA and the Third World.

The second feature is that, notwithstanding the lack of evidence on the link between ownership and cost-effectiveness, transfer of ownership has remained a paramount feature of the government's drive for economic efficiency. In 1985 John Moore, then the primary Conservative spokesman in this area, emphasised that the government would 'continue to return state-controlled industries to the private sector. We will encourage competition where appropriate, but where it does not make business or economic sense, we will not hesitate to extend the benefits of privatisation to natural monopolies' (speech July 1985 – see Kay *et al.*, 1986, p. 96). The period 1985–7 saw the sale of the nationalised telecommunications and gas industries. British Telecom's licence left it with only a slender element of competition from Mercury. British Gas was left intact. All the area electricity boards are to become uncontested local private monopolies, each with a slice of a new monopoly transmission company, with the generating part of the CEGB left to a private duopoly.

Hence, as many have now observed, the government's priority – ownership – has been one with the smallest likely economic gains, and one which has put heavy requirements on the regulatory arrangements. The effectiveness of the arrangements for dealing with safety, environmental health and related spillovers has yet to be tested, but these issues are crucial to the case of water supply, which combines natural monopoly with widespread environmental issues.

It is expected that, during their third term, the Conservatives will privatise the water industry, the broad approach to which was set out for England and Wales in a White Paper (February 1986). Evidence of the performance of publicly owned water supply undertakings is similar to the evidence for other utilities. The White Paper affects the nine English regional water authorities and the Welsh Water Authority. It would be remarkable if, for such large organisations, there was no scope for improvement in technical efficiency or overall cost-effectiveness. Yet recent White Papers which set out the case for privatisation contain little evidence of significant performance deficiencies. In the 1988 White Paper, *Privatising Electricity* (Cmnd. 322), the performance of the CEGB in managing the national grid does not appear to be a source of concern. In the case of water, paragraphs 34 and 35 of the 1986 White Paper contain some partial information on labour productivity. The only other reference to performance arises where he government records its approval of the recent rise in the proportion of water resource investments financed from ploughed-back funds; for an industry with few user charges and where revenue from the non-metered domestic sector is tantamount to a local tax, the advantages of higher self-financing are not self-evident.

One country where public and private water supply undertakings have coexisted and where detailed productivity and cost studies have been performed is the USA. Here we find no advantage in private ownership in terms of cost-effectiveness. The American Water Works Association produces a large amount of data on water supply undertakings, and several economists have used cross-section samples for 1960 and 1970 to estimate cost functions of varying degrees of sophistication. Crain and Zardkoohi (1978, 1980) expressed costs as a function of the volume of water supplied and the level of wage rates and interest rates, and found private utilities had significantly lower costs than public firms. They excluded large public firms from their sample, even though all the studies show sizeable scale economies. Moreover, Bruggink (1982) has argued that they ignored environmental differences across the sample of undertakings; with that adjustment he found costs some 24% *higher* in the private firms. Cost studies which do not capture all the dimensions of output are always subject to the danger of attributing to ownership differences which should be treated as exogenous features of the water supplied. Feigenbaum and Teeples (1983; see also the critique by McGuire and Ohsfeldt, 1986 and the reply by Teeples *et al.*, 1986) included various measures of water quality as well as treating energy and water as explicit inputs, and they found no difference in costs between public and private.

The government proposes in the UK to maintain the present system of unified river basin managements. It accepts that such systems are natural monopolies and the plan is to convert them directly into Water Supply PLCs. The White Paper envisages increased opportunities for competition in services such as overseas consultancy and recreation, but these are clearly not central issues and are possible under current ownership arrangements. Also the 'regulatory system will enable comparisons of performance to be made between WSPLCs' (p. 16); such emulation is seen as a central tenet of the monitoring system, though, yet again, this is possible under current arrangements. The WSPLCs are to have uncontested markets underwritten by licences running for at least 25 years, albeit subject to review. The licences are not to be offered as franchises.

Thus the source of any improvement lies for the large part in the change of ownership *per se*. The demands on the regulatory system are, therefore, considerable. All industrial and many commercial customers pay direct user prices. Domestic users are not metered at present; in effect, residents acquire what is equivalent to a licence to tap into the system, not too dissimilar to the road fund licence except that in the case of water, the fee varies with rateable value. Glynn (1988) has recently shown the sizeable issues that have to be confronted in designing suitable price and rate of return formulae which, at the time of writing, have not yet been published. Moreover, the water industry plays a key role in public health and the environment. The water authorities have explicit responsibility for environmental conservation, fisheries, navigation, flood defence and land drainage.

In this light it is relevant to look at the one previous major UK privatisation experience – in the nineteenth century. The technology of both water supply and of government administration were of course then very different. Few are naive enough to view the nineteenth century as a period of unblemished private initiative and enterprise. But the strains which were imposed on arm's-length government regulation of an industry characterised by strong spillovers and elements of natural monopoly is striking. In the early part of the nineteenth century privately owned water undertakings flourished; by the mid-century there was increased regulation; by the First World War, 80 per cent of the industry was in public ownership.

The privatisation of UK water supply in the nineteenth century

Water has for many centuries in the UK often been supplied by some collectively owned organisation. During the early nineteenth century, however, the number of private joint-stock water companies grew considerably. There was often direct competition for customers, though this had largely given way by mid-century to a situation where each area had only one supplier. But it should be recognised from the start that such supplies by specialist water undertakers, whether publicly or privately owned, were greatly outnumbered by private proprietors of water. In a country like the UK there is ready access throughout much of the country to untreated water. Springs, lakes, reservoirs and rivers were all important sources, in addition to rain which could be collected in storage tanks. This must largely explain why by the end of the eighteenth century, the provision of water was still organised in a variety of ways. The rich institutional mixture of suppliers can be also partly attributed to English common law which recognised the right of a landowner to use water running through his land, but allowed sale only when the water was not in defined channels (Balfour Committee, 1928, pp. 324–5). Water was often begged or stolen, and private ownership of water rights was common. By 1915 there were an estimated 1055 private proprietors as compared to 200 statutory private joint-stock companies, and 84 other private water companies. Hence, private proprietors supplying largely their own needs outnumbered all other private undertakings even by the early twentieth century, though the quantity in question was only a small percentage of the total. In other cases, joint use of a common source was practised sometimes without any great distribution network. Thus, underground water was readily available in parts of Manchester where property owners owned pumps and rented them out to tenants (Chadwick Report, 1842, p. 136).

From the earliest time, however, it was found economic for a water source to supply a wide geographical area, necessitating the construction of mains pipes. In several towns the rights to ancient springs were owned and operated by the Corporation (as at Bath) or leased to private individuals (as in Norwich, Longton and Coventry), who operated a distribution system of mains pipes (Commissioners on the State of Large Towns, Second Report, 1845, pp. 47–50). In other cases waterworks would have to be constructed, and especially in the case of large towns this was done in the early nineteenth century by joint-stock companies or by Improvement Commissioners as in Huddersfield and Hull. Mains would take water to streets where it was then available at standpipes, public fountains and public wells or, for those who could afford it, piped to the houses where it would be stored in cisterns. Such supplies were often intermittent in the sense that the water undertaking would 'turn on' the supply at certain times of the day. Charges would be per volume at the standpipes or, in the case of piped supplies, a certain charge for a number of hours over a period, which again was effectively a per-volume charge. Thus, to a large extent, water was available for sale by publicly or privately owned undertakings in the early nineteenth century at prices which varied with quantity acquired.

The involvement of local and central government authorities in water supplies had a long history, but these powers had been allowed to lapse by the late eighteenth century. Industrialisation and urbanisation in the early nineteenth century created demands for water which were accompanied by the growth of private companies. Hassan has characterised this period and especially between 1831 and 1851 as *partial privatisation*. Of a sample of 81 large towns in Britain in 1801, joint-stock companies were involved in the water supply of 5 towns rising to 44 by 1851; the number of towns where the local authority ran the water supply rose from 7 to 16, leaving 21 towns still with unauthorised water undertakings in 1851 (Hassan, 1985, Table 3).

The evidence suggests that in the early nineteenth century the central governmental authorities, and Parliament in particular, regarded water supply as a normal commercial venture (Chadwick Report, 1842, p. 145; Commission, First Report, 1844, p. xi; Second Report, 1845, p. 46; Dakyns, 1931, p. 21). The securement of an adequate supply of water was not, in contrast to drainage and paving, for example, an obligation laid on local authorities, and there was not even a *general* Parliamentary Act (cf. the 1832 Lighting and Watching Act) enabling local authorities to supply water if they chose. In 1821 the Select Committee studying London's water supply remarked (p. 8) on the absence of official channels through which customer complaints could be made, and the position had hardly improved by the time of the public health reports of the 1840s. For the large part, then, investment in waterworks and in distribution systems was subject to normal commercial criteria. Water went to those who were prepared to pay for it, so that in the case of domestic supplies it was the streets of the wealthy rather than the poor which were laid with mains.

The companies had to deal with central government because the laying of water mains meant large capital requirements; limited liability status was therefore advantageous and this, at that time, could be obtained only through Parliament. In addition, Parliament granted permission for the opening up of streets only to incorporated companies. Finally, parliamentary approval would be needed in some cases for the commercial use of water already running in defined channels. The public interest was to be secured by checking the financial and engineering soundness of the companies, and by encouraging competition (Falkus, 1977, p. 142). Exclusive franchises were never given, and overlapping was encouraged; certainly, in some areas, competition did exist. In Nottingham there were two companies in active competition. In London at the turn of the century there were three companies – London Bridge, New River and Chelsea – but, as the 1821 Select Committee reported, in the following decade the 'East London, West Middlesex and Grand Junction Companies were formed under...several Acts of Parliament...they began to supply the towns about the year 1811. The principle of the acts under which these companies were instituted was to encourage competition' (p. 3; see also Chadwick Report, 1842, p. 144; Commissioners, Second Report, 1845 pp. 52–3; Dakyns, 1931, pp. 22–3; Finer, 1941, p. 42). And there is plenty of evidence of streets with two or three sets of mains, turncocks and pipe layers, and of plumbers switching tenants from one company to another. On the other hand, the cost advantage of being an exclusive supplier led in many cases to *de facto* monopolies with towns being districted by companies. This had happened early in Liverpool, and it became the pattern in London from 1815. In a survey by the Commissioners on the State of Large Towns and Populous Districts, only two towns by the 1840s had more than one company (Second Report, 1845, pp. 47–53). No doubt partly in general recognition of this, Parliament did impose certain obligations on the companies. They had to provide fire plugs on the mains and to supply at will in such an emergency; in addition they had to make supply available to everyone living on a street where a main was laid. Following the 1821 Select Committee's revelation (pp. 8–9) that the districting agreement in London had been followed by a 25% rise in water rates, and the 1828 Select Committee Report's finding (p. 5) that prices were still rising, all special Acts between 1822 and 1845 incorporating water companies included clauses relating to maximum prices, with charges linked to the value of the property.

Operation and distribution by *local* government were rare. Even by 1845 only 10 out of 190 municipal corporations had their own water supply, and although 70 of the then 212 bodies of Improvement Commissioners had obtained water powers by local Act, there is no evidence they had made much use of them (Dakyns, 1931, p. 21; Falkus, 1977, pp. 142–3). The already noted absence of enabling powers and obligations to supply cannot explain the absence of public provision. In earlier centuries the local authorities had, in fact, been active in the development of water supplies, with authority stemming from Royal Warrant, Charter and Statutes until Private Acts became common. But these powers had been allowed to lapse by the late eighteenth century so that even where the water source was owned by the local authority it had been leased out to contractors, as for example in Gloucester, Leicester, Leeds and Plymouth (Robson, 1935, pp. 311–12). Prior to the 1835 Municipal Corporation Act, much local administration was inefficient and capital raising powers were limited. The main ratepayers, owners of small freehold and leasehold house property, were opposed to such municipal initiatives. It is significant that the 1837 Act for Leeds transferred the waterworks from Water Commissioners to a limited company even though it simultaneously gave enabling powers to the Corporation to repurchase the works in 12 years time.

As Dakyns suggests, from 'the rate payers' point of view in these early days, joint stock finance under the protection of limited liability was an immeasurably better mode of providing local amenities than rateable value' (1931, p. 22).

Conditions of the water supply by the mid-nineteenth century

The problems arising in the economic organisation of water supply were complex. Public health matters were mixed with problems of market structure, producing a rather confusing set of issues. As we shall see there were many criticisms of the water supply and several writers, including Robson (1935, p. 319) and Falkus (1977, p. 14), have attributed these deficiencies to the private enterprise system and explained the emergence of municipal operations as the solution to the problem. Such an explanation is unsatisfactory. The basic economic problems were that water enjoyed some economies of scale and its social value exceeded its private value. Various institutional devices, apart from public ownership, were available in both theory and practice to deal with these problems. The question is why public ownership was chosen. This section sets out the problems that arose from scale economies, from spillovers, and from the contestability of the water markets. The next section discusses the problems that arose from the use of arm's-length regulation of the private companies.

The conditions of the water supply which gave rise to concern had three dimensions. First was that many supplies were polluted. One writer reflecting on the reports of the Registrar-General in mid nineteenth century linking cholera to the water supply suggested that some 'methods of collecting water indeed represented no more than a transfer of pollution from houses and streets to streams and rivers' (Stern, 1954, p. 999). To take one town, Leeds, as an example, a statement to Parliament in 1837 claimed the water was 'bad in *quality* and deficient in *quantity*, the water being taken from the River Aire which is greatly defiled by the refuse from the mills and dyehouses, and by the common sewers and drains of the town' (Frazer, 1970, p. 51). The conclusions of the 1850 General Board of Health Report on London water supplies is a catalogue of reported pollutions of the Thames such that 'even when taken above the reach of pollution from the sewers of the metropolis, it contains an excess, varying with the season, of animal and vegetable matter' (p. 312).

A second source of concern was the delay in the introduction of piped water to domestic households, and in particular the development of comprehensive integrated piped systems under continuous pressure. Of the 50 towns studied by the Commissioners on the State of Large Towns and Populous Districts, in only a half were water supplies provided under a local Act. Thus in Bristol, for example, only 5000 out of a total population of 130,000 had piped supplies. The Commissioners found that 31 of the 50 towns were deficient and a further 13 were indifferent, leaving only 6 which came up to the standard which they deemed relevant for public health purposes (First Report, 1844, pp. xi–xii; Second Report, 1845, pp. 48–51). The third problem was that many companies had low profitability with some not declaring a dividend. Suitable data on profit rates is available for 1870–6 when profit rates in the UK economy were quite high. The return on equity in water at 7.9% was well below the 11.2% earned in railways, manufacturing and commerce (Edelstein, 1982, chapters 5 and 6).

There were several basic reasons why these difficulties had arisen. The two which we first consider are well recognised in the literature, namely decreasing costs and spillovers. That the industry was subject to declining average costs over some ranges was well recognised at the time. The 1821 Select Committee Report on London Water (p. 3) had pointed out the importance of 'fixed machinery' to the costs and charging policy of the London water companies. The 1845 Second Report on the State of Large Towns (p. 53) quoted data for Nottingham waterworks suggesting the operating expenses increased at only one-third the rate of output as the quantity of water supplied was increased. Decreasing costs also arose to the extent that domestic consumers could share the use of a mains pipe and other parts of the distribution network, whereas street standpipes required a superintendent whose wage bill would be largely invariant to volume. Moreover, there were certain institutional overheads for large waterworks, like the cost of obtaining Parliamentary Acts and the establishment of a board of directors together with headquarters staff and Chadwick (Report, 1842, p. 144) went as far as believing that scale economies in headquarters staff were sufficiently large that even if within a town competition were eliminated by districting, the replication of central staff in each district would still constitute a waste. When competition did exist, the phenomenon of decreasing cost meant that average costs, other things being equal, would be higher than in the case of a single supplier. Thus the Chadwick Report (1842, p. 144) suggested that the duplication of facilities in London accounted for the lower dividend rates of 4–6% and a general inhibition to the extension of supplies. Chadwick also felt (1859, Section II) competition in such a context induced 'skimping', and others have attributed the state of pollution of London water supplies and the absence of filtration to competition in the overlapping areas. In Nottingham, where competition was strong, the companies were struggling to declare any dividend. The general point about competition and higher costs has been a commonplace from John Stuart Mill onwards (cf. Schwartz, 1966, p. 76; Falkus, 1977, pp. 144–5).

The second basic reason for the condition of the water supply relates to externalities. A more extensive and better quality supply would directly reduce disease and the associated financial demands on sick charges and Poor Law relief. Also a water supply piped under constant high pressure was required for fire fighting and would reduce the health hazards exacerbated by stagnant water in cisterns and wells under the current arrangements of intermittent supply. Then there was the recognition that water supply needed to be considered in conjunction with drainage and sewerage, and that integrated operations were therefore important. What Chadwick and others in the public health movement had stressed was that the link between health and the general conditions of urban life was not so much a matter of the quality and size of the buildings as the deficient services to them, drainage, sewerage and water supplies in particular. The exclusion of poor streets and poor residents from piped water supplies was significant precisely because on health grounds these were the areas in most need. Consumers would pay for, in terms of quantity and quality, no more than the private value of the water to themselves. Hence there would be consistent underprovision of supplies to the extent that there were genuine external effects. 'Joint-stock companies could not resist the temptation', states Stern (1954, p. 1002), 'to make the charges fit the efforts required to produce the supply by levying additional charges for "high service" (delivering the water above a certain height, usually measured from pavement level), water closets and sometimes even fixed baths in consumers' houses. From a public health point of view, such extras constituted an undeniable incentive for certain consumers to do without water supplies.' But the behaviour of the private companies is readily understandable. What was needed was an institutional setting in which there would be incentives for the private companies to perform the required standards.

The third reason why the condition of the water supply was critical has not always been given its due weight. Even when competition 'in the field' had largely disappeared by mid-century, companies continued to face the threat of competition. Although, as we have seen, districting was often encouraged, Parliament never granted exclusive franchises nor gave legal endorsement to exclusive suppliers, so that the threat of entry remained. Official investigations of the 1850s and 1860s claimed this threat had inhibiting effects on the incumbent companies (Commissioners, Second Report, 1845, p. 53; General Board of Health Report, 1850, p. 296). I have elsewhere (Millward, 1986) argued why this threat contributed significantly to the unsatisfactory nature of the water supplies and here only a summary is necessary. The production conditions had elements of natural monopoly but the markets were contested. This involved three problems. First, each company did not necessarily have a natural monopoly over all the area in which it was located and hence it could never be certain, as the single firm, that it would undercut entrants supplying only a part of the market. In Manchester and Salford the water company supplied only one-fifth of the industrial and commercial firms; in Bath in 1875 there were eight undertakings supplying different groups; everywhere there were springs, wells, even ditches for the desperate. Second, any natural monopoly position arose from the distribution network as much as from 'production', and hence it was vital to catch all the customers in any given area. But when this required an investment by customers in items like meters and sinks, the company could be far from certain that it would capture all the market, and hence enjoy all the economies of customer contiguity. That contiguity economies were important is manifest from the complaint of the 1840s reports of the absence of proper supplies in small towns, and the costs of connection pipes to small groups of customers (Commissioners, First Report, 1844, pp. xi, xii; Dickinson, 1956, p. 102). Customer costs were particularly important when the companies wanted to develop piped constant-pressure supplies since residents then faced the prospect of expenditures on drains and sinks. Thirdly, we should note that the water companies were trying to expand supplies in a context where average costs were rising. This was in part because of the need, as in Manchester, Liverpool and Glasgow, to look further afield for water sources (cf. Shaw, 1890; Smart, 1895). In addition, the development of constant-pressure systems involved increased monitoring of the company's service pipes for leakage and misuse. Matters became very complicated for supply to homes with landlords and tenants. Metering had to be weighed against the alternative of levying charges related to rateable value. A natural monopoly can still exist when average costs are rising but, as the recent contestable markets literature has emphasised, an entrant could meaningfully threaten to supply, say 60% of the market, thereby undercutting the incumbent whose natural monopoly position is unsustainable in a market environment (cf. Millward, 1986).

The attempts at regulation 1840–70

It has been argued up to this point that the problems of decreasing cost, externalities and contestability underlay the critical condition of the industry at mid-century. But their resolution did not necessarily imply public ownership. There were at least two ways in which the involvement of private companies could be continued. One was Chadwick's competition 'for the field'. Standards of service are established by the relevant local and central authorities and incorporated into franchises for which private contractors could bid. The alternative is arms length regulation of the companies under statute. The latter was the alternatie chosen, but it should be noted that franchising was contemplated. In the late 1840s Edwin Chadwick was considering '...whether Joint-Stock companies cannot be got to undertake improved supplies of water as renters or lessees for terms of years instead of as proprietors' (Finer, 1952, p. 241; cf. also Chadwick, 1959, section VII). The Towns Improvement Company was established to perform contracts in the areas of drainage, sewage, water supply, refuse disposal for local authorities. It was envisaged that such contracting for the performance of services would be financed from rates. The venture was not successful. Indeed the General Board of Health in 1850 felt that 'the principle of contract merely for *services* appeared to be a barrier to extensive support, and in the money market it was objected to the plan that it required too much skill in the management for a joint-stock Company and embraced more than one object'. More generally the Board had 'strong and unanimous testimony to the unsuitableness of the existing trading Companies to execute, or even aid in executing combined works for the metropolis' (pp. 298–9).

Regulation rather than franchising was therefore the route chosen. Prior to 1840 the regulation was half-hearted since competition was still at that stage seen as an important mechanism. Thus the maximum prices for water stipulated in the local Acts from the 1820s seem to have been set at such a level as to leave plenty of scope for the companies, quite apart from the fact that the maxima appeared to be more favourable to those water users with high-valued property. Dividend restrictions before 1840 have been noted only in the Acts for Chester and Leeds. Moreover, some of the specific obligations laid on the companies could be avoided. The requirement relating to the provision of fire plugs excluded any references to minimum distances between them and to continuity of water supply, and the fire hazard remained a serious problem. The obligation to make supply available to all residents of an area only applied to streets where mains were laid so that the streets with poorer residents never benefited from this provision and, in any case, the obligation on the company only held so long as this did not affect its own customers (Commissioners, Second Report, 1845, pp. 47–53; Dakysn, 1931, pp. 22–4; Robson, 1935, p. 314).

Over the thirty years from 1840 progress towards ameliorating the deficiencies highlighted by the reports of the 1840s was slow. In part, this reflected the very general difficulties involved in achieving rapid improvements in the public health area; although the reports had indicated clearly the importance of strong municipal involvement they were not always comprehensive and specific in their recommendations. Local authority control of water supply as it emerged in legislation was, as for other public health areas, permissive and the regulatory restrictions on water undertakings were not accompanied by strong monitoring agencies.

Whereas the 1840 Select Committee on the Health of Towns was conscious of the deficiencies in water supply, it did no more than propose the establishment of Boards of Health, envisaging that such boards would draw attention to the need to improve water supplies (p. xx). The Chadwick Report wanted local authorities to be charged with the responsibility of ensuring adequate water supplies and argued that a municipal agency would be the best mode of operation. But beyond this little was said (pp. 148–50 and conclusions pp. 422–5). The Commissioners put much stress on introducing piped water at constant pressure and of imposing a duty on local authorities to secure adequate water supplies. For attaining the latter, it would be necessary for management to be in the hands of an independent and disinterested body (which would also have control over sewerage and drainage), and for the distribution of water to be regular and available at a reasonable price. This meant legal powers to enable local authorities to require water companies to provide an adequate supply and if this was not forthcoming or if, as in small towns, no company existed, the local authority should have powers to obtain independent supplies or to set up their own works and, as in the case of Leeds, in all cases to have enabling powers to expropriate after twelve years any private company found wanting. The Commissioners wanted domestic water to be financed, like drainage, from the rates with the water undertakings, public or private, operating for a fee under a contract with the local authority (Second Report, 1845, pp. 50–5).

The subsequent legislation and government action was very much affected by some general difficulties in the way of rapid improvements in public health (cf. Lubenow, 1971, pp. 85–100; Frazer 1973, pp. 60–4). The administrative changes that were needed could not be dealt with on a piecemeal basis. The expected rise in public spending and local taxation raised objections from the beginning, quite apart from the doubts about placing increased powers in the hands of local authorities. But perhaps more than anything there was a fear of the central authority undermining local interests which, though themselves in some disagreement (Water Commissioners, Highway Surveyors, Poor Law Commissioners), were united in opposing strong central interference. The specific government measures on water supply which emerged were, therefore, permissive rather than mandatory in laying the responsibility for securing an adequate supply on local authorities. Competition was no longer to be encouraged but the sole undertakings were left largely in private hands. By way of a price for having a local monopoly and as a means of implementing the target of improved supplies, the obligations and restrictions relating to the companies were increased, but it would appear that this regulatory framework had insufficient enforcement powers for it to be effective.

Thus the 1848 Public Health Act authorised the establishment of local Boards of Health but only if this was recommended by the General Board of Health and if at least 10% of ratepayers petitioned for one. The local boards had enabling powers to secure adequate water supply, to erect free public cisterns and pumps, and to establish their own waterworks, but these were not mandatory duties and in the last case require the agreement of a local water company where one existed. Whereas the stress of the reports of Chadwick and the Commissioners on the strategy of central supervision plus local administration had largely been maintained, the legislation was weak and in the context of promoting municipal enterprise, in Robson's view, stultifying (1935, p. 315; cf. also Lubenow 1971, pp. 60–1, Frazer, 1973, p. 65; Falkus, 1977, p. 65). Parliament's discretion over the companies in the new regulatory framework might have been a useful support for the Public Health Act. Ceilings on profit rates and obligations with respect to supply had been imposed for Leeds in 1837, Sunderland in 1846, and Hartlepool in 1846. The 1847 Waterworks Clauses Act then imposed a general obligation to supply pure water if a demand existed and if an appropriate price were paid. It specified prices to be related to rateable values and that dividends were not to exceed 10%. But again this was only enabling legislation in that it specified clauses which should be inserted in any new bills for water supply, and even this was at the discretion of the Private Bills Committee (Dakyns, 1931, pp. 25–6; Finer, 1941, p. 44; Falkus, 1977, p. 146).

The number of water companies with statutory powers grew significantly in the period, from 67 in 1845, to 147 in 1865. There was no standardisation in accounts and the dividend levied was ineffective because the capital base could be 'watered' (see Millward, 1986), and 10% was a high figure. As late as 1880 a House of Commons Select Committee was noting the ease with which the limit could be evaded by the companies' being able to take one year with another. More generally, dissatisfaction with the water supplies of private companies was still being voiced by the end of the 1860s especially in London where progress towards an improved and integrated service was slow, and where the companies were explicitly criticised by the 1869 Royal Commission (paragraphs 238, 241, 243, 248) for their neglect in complying with the law with respect to water quality. In the same year the Medical Officer of the Privy Council had commented unfavourably on the quality of the metropolitan water supply and the need for stronger supervision of the companies. The 1871 Royal Sanitary Commission noted (p. 42) that promoters of water bills were still being allowed to escape the obligation to provide a constant water supply. In the early 1850s unsuccessful attempts had been made in Parliament to promote the amalgamation of the existing London companies and the regulation of their sources of supply. In addition the 1852 Waterworks Act compelled the companies to give constant service, but it was required that the pipes and fittings be in a proper condition to receive such a supply. There was a problem in monitoring domestic arrangements with respect to leakage and other waste, and a Select Committee of 1880 (p. v) suggested that progress in this area required the companies to link closely with a metropolitan public body. The problems remained when the Royal Commission on the Water Supply reported in 1869.

The move to public ownership

As Table 10.1 shows, the number of statutory water companies increased by about one-third in the latter part of the nineteenth century, and in this they were facilitated by the 1870 Gas and Water Facilities Act which short-circuited the Private Bill procedure by making the Board of Trade the empowering authority via Provisional Orders (Finer, 1941, p. 44). Local municipal undertakings grew however more rapidly, trebling over the 50 years from 1865. The number of municipal corporations (i.e. in municipal boroughs) who conducted their own water supply grew even faster, from 61 in 1865, to 326 in 1914, with the pace slackening only in the 1885–94 period. And certainly all the evidence suggests public opinion was increasingly favouring municipal operations. By the mid-1860s Sir John Simon, the Medical Officer of Health to the Privy Council, had come to the conclusion that in the public health field the permissive legislation needed to be replaced by obligatory powers, and this was echoed in the observations on water supply made by the 1871 Royal Sanitary Commission (p. 38). The 1869 Royal Commission on Water Supply stressed the 'expediency and advantage of consolidating the water supply under public control' and suggested that the ancient practice be resumed whereby water supply was a municipal function (paragraphs 246–8). By the turn of the century the Permanent Secretary to the (Local Government) Board which actually approved funds for compulsory acquisition of private works was declaring that the board's view was that water should be in the hands of the sanitary authority (Frazer, 1973, p. 69; Falkus, 1977, p. 146).

Why did municipalisation grow? The 1869 Royal Commission on Water Supply had pointed to the scale economies that would accrue from amalgamation of the London water companies, an improvement in quality, the purification of the Thames, and an improved supply for public purposes, especially fire fighting. In the same vein, though more generally, Falkus (1977) has argued that the main factor was probably dissatisfaction with existing supplies and the growing awareness of the importance of pure water. But such problems in theory could be dealt with by regulation and subsidy for the private companies, and it is clear that such problems had motivated the framework of restrictions and obligations from the 1840s.

Moreover, any general dissatisfaction with the water companies was not directed to questions of competence. In several instances between 1890 and 1911 (Eastbourne, Southampton, Hartlepool, Norwich, Glamorgan, Cambridge), local authority applications to compulsorily acquire the companies were refused by Parliament and though the 1887 Sheffield Bill was approved, the chairman of the respective House of Lords committee specifically said there was no question of mismanagement; rather, it was a matter of public policy.

The major determinants of the move to public ownership were:

(1) the standards of service required, when added to the need for control of prices and dividends, imposed a heavy burden on the regulatory mechanism;
(2) regulation was not effective in the 1840–70 period;
(3) hence the public authorities shifted away from the use of private companies as agents to a direct employment of resources.

In support of this hypothesis, it may seen from Table 10.1 that it was from the 1870s that a large expansion of public ownership occurred. The number of publicly owned water undertakings trebled from 250 to 786 in the period 1871 to 1915; in the same period the number of authorised private companies increased by only one-third and, of course, part of this constituted a transformation of unauthorised private undertakings or private proprietors into corporate entities.

It was also from the 1870s that the legislative basis for municipalisation

Table 10.1   Number of authorised water undertakings in the UK

	(Municipal) corporations	Other local authorities	Statutory companies
1845	10	n.a.	67
1865	61	n.a.	147
1871	250		n.a.
1875	127	n.a.	n.a.
1895	237	n.a.	n.a.
1914	326	n.a.	n.a.
1915	786		200

Sources: Dakyns, 1931, pp. 21–5; Robson, 1935, pp. 316–19; Finer, 1941, p. 41; Falkus, 1977, Table III.

was eased, although legal powers of expropriation were never provided by Parliament. The 1847 Waterworks Clauses Act had given enabling power to local authorities to set up their own waterworks but, as already noted, this was fenced in with safeguards for existing water companies. There never was in the nineteenth century any general water supply legislation enabling the local authorities to compulsorily purchase a company as in the case of tramways and electricity, but Parliament did move towards sanctioning municipalisation in appropriate circumstances. In 1858 the Local Government Act gave powers to directors of private water companies to sell to local authorities given the support of two-thirds of the shareholders. In 1871 the Local Government Board was established and the local counterpart to that in this area was the 1872 Public Health Act which, following the 1871 Royal Sanitary Commission's Report, divided all the country into sanitary districts under local authorities and consolidated the provisions of the 1847 and 1858 Acts. Finally, under the 1875 Public Health Act the sanitary authorities were obliged to secure an adequate water supply. They could establish, lease, or purchase waterworks, and the rights of any existing water companies were to be respected only where they were already providing an adequate water supply – with adequacy determined by arbitration. Purchase of works could be achieved by agreement or by arbitration or, and this was rarely used, by Parliamentary Bill (Balfour Committee, 1928, p. 35; Robson, 1935, pp. 315–18; Finer, 1941, pp. 44–5; Frazer, 1973, p. 70; Falkus, 1977, pp. 145–7). Municipalisation could proceed apace and came to dominate supplies much more than in gas. By the period 1912–15 approximately 80% of authorised water undertakings were municipal, accounting for an even larger proportion of net output. London was behind the rest of the country, essentially awaiting the emergence of a metropolitan local authority, but the Metropolitan Water Board was finally established in 1903.

Conclusions

This essay has provided a review of the UK government's 1986 proposals for privatising the water industry in the context of the available evidence on public and private performance, and in the light of the earlier historical experience of a private water supply. The evidence that has accumulated on water supply and other infrastructure utilities in energy and transport suggests that a mere change of ownership has little impact on cost-effectiveness, but could well change the range of goods and services provided. More important for cost-effectiveness is the element of competition, except of course where, as in the case of natural monopoly, there are other market considerations. The government, nevertheless, proposes to convert the existing river-basin systems into Water Supply PLCs with no change in the competitive regime. These will be licensed private natural monopolies with large external effects in health and the environment so that any economic gains will have to come from the regulatory regime which is developed.

The major legislative and institutional developments which underlie current arrangements for the UK water industry date from the later part of the nineteenth century with the 1875 Public Health Act, and the shift to 80% public ownership. Whereas the involvement of public authorities in water supplies has a long history, the extra demands of urbanisation and industrialisation in the early part of the nineteenth century were associated with the growth of joint-stock water companies. In this period the industry exhibited all the problems of a natural monopoly with strong spillover costs. Initially there were overlapping companies and duplicate facilities, but this had given way by mid-century to single suppliers in each area. The restrictions on quantity and quality were exacerbated by the fact that the companies were never granted legally exclusive franchises and a competitive threat remained. Moreover the market structure problems, making for limited water supplies, exacerbated the health and environmental issues which create a wedge between the private profitability and social value of supplies. By the 1840s water supplies in UK were in a terrible condition. The stream of official Commissions and Reports was followed by an attempt at arm's-length regulation of the industry in terms of prices, dividends, obligations to supply, and the development of constant-pressure systems. The level of service expected made heavy demands on the regulatory regime which proved ineffective. Hence, municipal corporations and local sanitary districts took over many waterworks in the latter part of the century, and this pattern of public ownership has dominated up to the 1980s. In this light, the current proposals for privatisation will show economic gains only if regulatory mechanisms can be established which surmount the problems experienced by regulatory regimes in other countries and in the UK in the past.

References

Albon, R. (1988). 'Liberalisation of the Post Office' in C. Johnson (ed.) *Privatisation and Ownership*, Lloyds Bank Annual Review, vol. I.

Balfour Committee on Industry and Trade (1928). *Further Factors in Industrial and Commercial Efficiency*.

Beesley, M. and Littlechild, S. (1983). 'Privatisation: principles, policies and priorities', *Lloyds Bank Review*, no. 149, July, pp. 1–20.

Bruggink, T. H. (1982). 'Public versus regulated private enterprise in the municipal water industry: a comparison of operating costs', *Quarterly Review of Economics and Business*, vol. 22, no. 1 spring, pp. 111–25.

Chadwick, E. (1842). *Report on the Sanitary Conditions of the Labouring Population of Great Britain: 1842*, M. W. Flinn (ed.), (Edinburgh: Edinburgh University Press), 1965.

Chadwick, E. (1859). 'Results of different principles of legislation and administration in Europe; of competition for the field, as compared with competition within the field, of service', *Journal of the Royal Statistical Society*, vol. XXII.

Commissioners on the State of Large Towns and Populous Districts, *First Report* (1844), *Second Report* (1845), London: HMSO.

Crain, W. M. and Zardkoohi, A. (1978). 'A test of the property-rights theory of the firm: water utilities in the United States', *Journal of Law and Economics*, vol. 21, no. 2, October, pp. 395–408.

Crain, W. M. and Zardkoohi, A. (1980). 'Public sector expansion: stagnant technology or attenuated property rights', *Southern Economic Journal*, vol. 46, no. 4, April, pp. 1069–82.

Dakyns, A. L. (1931). 'The water supply of English towns in 1846', *Manchester School*, vol. 2, no. 1, pp. 18–26.

Davis, E. (1984). 'Express coaching since 1980: liberalisation in practice', *Fiscal Studies*, vol. 5, no. 1.

Dickinson, H. W. (1956). *The Water Supply of Greater London*, Courier Press.

Edelstein, M. (1982). *Overseas Investment in the Age of High Imperialism: The United Kingdom 1850–1914* (London: Methuen).

Falkus, M. E. (1977). 'The development of municipal trading in the 19th century', *Business History*, vol. 19, no. 2, July, pp. 134–61.

Feigenbaum, S. and Teeples, R. (1983). 'Public versus private water delivery: a hedonic cost approach', *Review of Economics and Statistics*, vol. 65, pp. 672–8.

Finer, H. (1941). *Municipal Trading* (London: Allen & Unwin).

Finer, S. E. (1952). *The Life and Times of Sir Edwin Chadwick* (London: Methuen).

Foreman-Peck, J. and Waterson, M. (1985). 'The comparative efficiency of public and private enterprise in Britain: electricity generation between the World Wars', supplement to *Economic Journal*, vol. 95.

Frazer, D. (1970). 'The politics of Leeds water', *Proceedings of the Thorensby Society*, vol. 3, pp. 50–70.

Frazer, D. (1973). *The Evolution of the British Welfare State* (London: Macmillan).

General Board of Health (1850). *Report on the Supply of Water to the Metropolis*.

Glynn, D. (1988). 'Economic regulation of the privatised water industry' in C. Johnson (ed.) *Privatisation and Ownership*, Lloyds Bank Annual Economic Review, vol. I.

Hassan, J. A. (1985). 'The growth and impact of the British water industry in the 19th century', *Economic History Review*, vol. 38, no. 4, November, pp. 531–47.

Helm, D., Kay, J. and Thompson, D. (1988). 'Energy policy and the role of the state in the market for energy', *Fiscal Studies*, vol. 9, no. 4, February, pp. 41–61.

Howe, F. C. (1906). 'Municipal ownership in Great Britain', *Bulletin of the Bureau of Labour*, no. 62, January, pp. 1–123.

Jaffer, S. M. and Thompson, D. J. (1986). 'Deregulating express coaches: a reassessment', *Fiscal Studies*, vol. 7, no. 4, November, pp. 45–68.

Kay, J. A. and Silberston, Z. A. (1984). 'The new industrial policy – privatisation and competition', *Midland Bank Review*, Spring, pp. 8–16.

Kay, J. A., Mayer, C. and Thompson, D. J. (1986). *Privatisation and Regulation: The UK Experience* (Oxford: Clarendon Press).

Knoop, D. (1912). *Principles and Methods of Municipal Trading* (London: Macmillan).

Lubennow, W. C. (1971). *The Politics of Government Growth: Early Victorian Attitudes Toward State Intervention 1833–1848*, Archon Books.

McGuire, R. A. and Ohsfeldt, R. (1986). 'Private versus public water delivery: a critical analysis of a hedonic cost function', *Public Finance Quarterly*, vol. 14, no. 3, July, pp. 339–50.

Millward, R. (1986). 'The emergence of gas and water monopolies in 19th century Britain: contested markets and public control' in J. Foreman-Peck (ed.) *Reinterpreting the 19th Century British Economy*. An earlier version appeared as *Salford Papers in Economics* 86-4.

Millward, R. and Parker, D. (1983). 'Public and private enterprise: relative behaviour and efficiency' in R. Millward, L. Rosenthal, M. T. Sumner and N. Topham, *Public Sector Economics* (London: Longman).

Millward, R. and Ward, R. (1987). 'The costs of public and private gas enterprise in late 19th century Britain', *Oxford Economic Papers*, vol. 39, pp. 719–37.

Pryke, R. (1982). 'The comparative performance of public and private enterprise', *Fiscal Studies*, vol. 3, no. 2, pp. 68–81.

Robins, F. W. (1948). *The Story of Water Supply* (Oxford: Oxford University Press).

Robson, W. A. (1935). 'The public utility services', in H. J. Laski, W. I. Jennings and W. A. Robson (eds), *A Century of Municipal Progress: the Last Hundred Years* (London: Allen & Unwin).

Royal Commission on Water Supply (1869). *Report of the Commissioners* (London: HMSO).

Royal Sanitary Commission (1871). *Report*.

Schwartz, P. (1966). 'John Stuart Mill and laissez faire: London water', *Economica*, vol. 33, February, pp. 71–83.

Secretary of State for Energy (1988). *Privatising Electricity: the Government's Proposals for the Privatisation of the Electricity Supply Industry in England and Wales*, Command 322 (London: HMSO).

Secretary of State for the Environment, Secretary of State for Wales, Ministry of Agriculture, Fisheries and Food (1986). *Privatisation of the Water Authorities in England and Wales* (London: HMSO).

Select Committee on the Health of Towns (1840). *Report*.

Select Committee on London Water Supply (1880). *Report*.

Select Committee on the Supply of Water to the Metropolis (1821). *Report*.

Select Committee on the Supply of Water to the Metropolis (1828). *Report*.

Shackleton, J. R. (1984). 'Privatisation: the case examined', *National Westminster Bank Review*, May, pp. 59–73.

Shaw, A. (1890). 'Glasgow: a municipal study', *Century*, vol. XXXIX, pp. 721–36.

Smart, W. (1895). 'Glasgow and its municipal industries', *Quarterly Journal of Economics*, vol. IX, no. 2, January, pp. 188–94.

Stern, W. M. (1954), 'Water supply in Britain: development of a public service', *Royal Sanitary Institute Journal*, vol. 74.

Teeples, R., Feigenbaum, S. and Glyer, D. (1986). 'Public versus private water delivery: cost comparisons', *Public Finance Quarterly*, vol. 14, no. 3, July, pp. 351–66.

Wright, M. (1987). 'Government divestments and the regulation of natural monopolies in the UK: the case of British Gas', *Energy Policy*, vol. 15, no. 3, June, pp. 193–216.

11

Trade, technology and evolutionary change

J. Stanley Metcalfe

It is a commonplace observation that patterns of international trade are in a continual state of flux, driven primarily by different national patterns of technological change. Over the longer term, patterns of comparative advantage can change dramatically with formerly profitable industries being eliminated and new industries rising to maturity in entirely new locations. The history of the British cotton textile industry, the Swiss watch industry, and more recently, the American television and consumer electronics industries are three examples from many which bear ample witness to the influence of technological development on trade patterns.[1] In this essay I propose to explore the relationships between trade and technological change by drawing upon recent developments in the evolutionary theory of technological change.

Correspondingly, the focus of attention will not be on positions of long-run trading equilibrium but rather on the process which shapes the development of trade patterns over time. In so far as this process is ultimately driven by innovation and the subsequent diffusion of those innovations it can claim to be a Schumpeterian account of international trade. It will be apparent that international trade is a rich ground for the study of evolutionary processes; for evolutionary competition is driven by economic variety, and national differences in technologies and economic environment are a potent source of differences between countries in the competitive strengths of their respective industries. At this point it is vital to distinguish two aspects of technological change which in static theory cannot be distinguished, namely innovation and diffusion of innovation. Innovation is the act of injection, the first application, of a new product or process into a country's technology set. Diffusion is the subsequent spread of that innovation within the economy, and it is the diffusion process which is crucial in determining the effects of that innovation on patterns of foreign trade. For if an innovation does not acquire economic weight or significance relative to other technologies then it can have no lasting effect on the economic system. It may survive, it may be of interest to antiquarian students of technology, it may even be a stepping stone to the future development of more significant innovations but it cannot be of interest to the particular concerns of the international economist. Diffusion, not innovation *per se*, is the key to the shaping and reshaping of trade patterns and so this essay will discuss the effects of a simple, multi-technology, evolutionary process of diffusion upon patterns of international trade. It should also be made clear that by an evolutionary process is meant a process of competition or economic selection, a process driven by economic variety between rival technologies. Such a view of competition, of course, is far removed from the economic view of competition as an equilibrium state.[2]

I hasten to add that the direct effects on foreign trade are only one dimension of international technological competition: a full treatment should include the effects on direct foreign investment, international joint ventures, technology transfers and international subcontracting arrangements for production and marketing. Such a comprehensive treatment is beyond my present purpose, which is solely to treat some rather traditional questions from an evolutionary perspective. We shall conclude that while the traditional concern of trade theorists with efficiency is an important part of the explanation of trade patterns, this needs to be supported by a treatment of the ability of national industries to translate efficiency into the growth of capacity and their creative ability to enhance their respective technology sets. Consideration of these matters leads us to support the view that traditional notions of long-run comparative advantage may bear little relation to actual trade flows. The long-run positions to which they relate are at best reference points towards which short-run patterns of trade may eventually gravitate in appropriate conditions.

We begin the essay with a brief review of some of the principal contributions to dynamic trade theory, follow this with an outline of evolutionary theory, and then proceed to develop the analysis of trade in a single industry. From this we formulate the evolutionary equivalent of the law of comparative advantage and apply this to the analysis of a two-country, two-commodity evolutionary model of trade. The essay ends with a very brief discussion of the rate of innovation in an evolutionary context.

I Equilibrium and technology in a trading world

There can be no doubt that one of the great achievements of economic analysis has been the formulation of rigorous and coherent theories of international trade and investment. In terms of essentials these are theories of general market equilibrium extended to explain trade in goods and exchanges of productive agents between countries. For present purposes the critical insight they contain is that the direction of trade in different commodities or the movement of productive agents is to be explained by the existence of differences in autarky commodity and factor price structures, differences which free trade or free mobility of productive agents eliminates. In turn, different autarky price structures are to be explained by appropriate combinations of inter-country differences in consumer preferences (including the willingness to save), in process technology and in stocks of productive agents, land, labour, capital goods, and so on.

The two major trade theories differ only in their emphasis as to the origin of price differences.[3] The Ricardian theory stresses international differences in technology in conjunction with international differences in real wage levels, while the Heckscher–Ohlin theory (essentially current orthodoxy) assumes the international identity of tastes and technology, tracing the origins of trade to *given* differences in endowments of the primary productive agencies. In either case, illuminating propositions may then be derived concerning the determinants of the terms of trade (i.e. the price structure in a trading world), the distribution of the gain from trade, and the costs and benefits of policies to restrict trade. Moreover, the long-run effects of hypothetical changes in tastes, technology and resources on these dimensions of an equilibrium trading world are readily deduced.

These theories are extremely powerful and of considerable practical significance but for our purpose a critical deficiency of both is their treatment of technological data as exogenous to the economic system, and consequently their failure to offer any understanding that changes in technology (or tastes) are properly to be viewed in terms of an economic process – a failure which is closely linked to a dependence upon the long-period equilibrium method of analysis.

In the long-period method it is taken that all agents are fully informed so that there are no unexploited production opportunities. Of course, this assumption does not cohere with the world as we know it. Individuals may well be rational but their deliberations are necessarily constrained by bounded knowledge sets, limited with respect to contemporaneous and future information. Individuals have different information sets because information is costly to acquire and interpret, and they have different abilities to turn data into knowledge, differences premised in part upon the knowledge they have acquired in the past. In a world of changing knowledge there is not the slightest reason to expect the emergence of a long-run position, with technological information diffused equally to all economic agents. Two consequences follow from this. First there is scope for expectation and imagination in decision making. Secondly there is scope for innovative, entrepreneurial activity, which can find no place in the long-period equilibrium framework. Indeed by innovation we normally mean the application of privileged information to economic activity.

This problem with the treatment of information and technology is reflected also in the concept of competition which underpins the Ricardian and HOS (Heckscher–Ohlin–Samuelson) trade theories. Competition is a state of equilibrium with atomistic agents treating prices as exogenous data, and freedom of movement of free capital equalising the rate of return on capital invested in different production activities. This contrasts sharply with the process view of competition in which it is the differences between firms which drive the competitive process, differences which are continually generated and regenerated by innovative and imitative activity. Competition here entails rivalry and a struggle for market share; it is a perpetual condition of disequilibrium and change, not a state of balance between forces of equal marginal significance. This concept of competition as a process owes a great deal to Austrian theoretical perspectives, not only to Hayek but, in particular, to Schumpeter with his emphasis on change from within the capitalist system and the competition which is fostered by acts of innovation. Of all the different sources of competitive advantage it is undoubtedly those based on superior product and process technology which are of dominant long-run importance since they underpin superior profitability and thus the resource base to enhance further competitive advantage.

In terms of the theory of international trade and investment in manufactured products the implications are far-reaching. There is no reason to expect agents in different countries to have the same technological information sets and indeed every reason to expect the opposite. Differences in language, history, culture and resource endowments mean that countries cannot be expected to produce identical sets of commodities, or to produce a common commodity by the same production methods, or to have common preferences at comparable income levels. Imperfect diffusion of knowledge is clearly a fundamental determinant of patterns of international trade. Moreover, knowledge is not static and we must expect patterns of trade to change over time in a way which reflects different national capabilities in the production of new knowledge. In the modern world, trading opportunities are continually being generated by the emergence and diffusion of new technology. In this sense Ricardian theory has a better claim for attention than its HOS rival but neither comes to terms with the evolutionary nature of competition driven by economic variety.

II Technology and international trade

An understanding of knowledge creation and dissemination as economic processes has only gradually been brought to bear upon the theory of international trade and investment, and we introduce here three of the more significant contributions to this issue.

A useful starting point is the concept of 'technological gap' trade, first presented systematically by Posner (1961), although the initial insight can certainly be traced to previous writers. The essence of Posner's approach is to consider a world in which there are no comparative advantages of the traditional kind and thus no trading opportunities, since production sets and demand conditions are initially assumed to be the same everywhere. Into this situation an innovation, creating a new commodity, occurs in one country and is followed by the emergence of a demand for that new commodity in foreign markets. A basis of trade has been created, the foundation of which is differential access to technological knowledge in a world of identical demand patterns. After a further lapse of time it is assumed that foreign countries imitate and restore the initial position of technical parity, so eliminating the basis for trade. Trade persists only for so long as there is a net time lapse, or lag, between the transfer of preferences and the transfer of production technology. Of course, a continual stream of innovations can sustain a permanent flow of technology-gap trade.

One may then interpret patterns of trade in terms of differential national capacities to innovate and imitate, or technical dynamism as Posner terms it. The insights of this theory are considerable and do not depend on his initial assumption that comparative advantages are non-existent or on his simplified dynamics of demand and capacity growth. Indeed, in general terms, Posner's formulation has since received quite impressive empirical confirmation. In a paper published contemporaneously with Posner's, Devons (1961) saw quite clearly that considerations specific to individual firms and countries, as distinct from generally available factors of production, greatly influence trade in manufactures. Nor are these considerations to be interpreted as specific factors of production in the accepted sense, rather they depend on the 'energies, capacities, initiative and enterprise of individual business'. He might have added that these are precisely the Schumpeterian dimensions of the competitive process encompassed by the entrepreneurial function.

A second major contribution to a process perspective on international trade is Vernon's (1968) theory of the product life cycle. The central insight of this approach is its focus upon distinct stages in the evolution of a technology. In the initial stages of development, technological and market uncertainty is considerable with various rival designs competing for a market niche. Survival at this stage requires close attention to user needs and frequent contact with suppliers of produced inputs. Hence production horizons are limited to the domestic market alone. With time a dominant design emerges in terms of accepted product characteristics and this more stable situation permits rapid development in process technology, frequently directed at large-scale production methods to service growing markets at home and abroad. Finally, the technology evolves into its mature stage with standardised products and processes for which competitive advantage is determined by conventional comparative cost conditions. To connect the various stages of technical change with trade and investment patterns it is argued that different countries will provide different innovation-inducing environments and will be differentially endowed with the inputs needed to exploit a technology at each different stage. The progressive maturing of a technology results in a shifting world pattern of the most profitable locations for production. In general terms, Vernon argues that the innovation advantage lies with advanced nations, particularly the USA, while the advantage with the mature technologies lies with the less developed nations. Trade patterns are thus the outcome of a repeated process of technological divergence and convergence.

As a final contribution to this literature we may consider the paper by Krugman (1979) which places the Posner and Vernon theories within a simple but formal general equilibrium framework.[4] The world is divided into two regions, North and South, and in the absence of innovations knowledge would be equally diffused, no comparative advantages would exist, and *per capita* incomes would be everywhere the same. The North, however, develops new product innovations at an exponential rate, creating technology-gap trade advantages and raising real incomes above the level of the South. What prevents this income disparity rising indefinitely is the assumption that, after a time lapse, new technologies are transferred by imitation to the South, which has a comparative advantage based solely upon its lower wages – just as the product cycle theory requires. Exports of 'new' goods from the North are balanced by exports of 'old' goods from the South. The model of technical progress which Krugman employs is extremely crude, with rates of technical innovation and transfer assumed to be exogenous constants. Nevertheless, it captures with stark simplicity the idea of trading patterns and income levels based on the temporary exploitation of monopoly rights in new technology. Trade is simply a reflection of the dynamics of knowledge creation and dissemination.

At the heart of the Krugman model is the idea that individual countries or groups of countries have quite different technology or product sets, and this has been explored further in a paper by Feenstra (1982). Basing the analysis on a Chamberlinian model of imperfect competition, it is shown how national differences in demand structures and the cost of research result in different but possibly overlapping sets of commodities being produced in different countries. When the same goods are produced in both countries then traditional comparative advantage determines the pattern of trade, but otherwise the countries exploit their absolute advantages in monopolistic fashion.

One might be tempted at this stage to follow Johnson's persuasive suggestion (1968), and take a broad Fisherian view of the nature of capital and absorb the above insights with a factor proportions explanation, including skills and intellectual capital within the compass of a nation's capital endowment. However, this proposal would seem to encounter a number of serious obstacles, partly because stocks of intangible capital, like their tangible counterparts, cannot be treated in long-run equilibrium as exogenous and independent of production patterns, partly because of their industry-specific nature and related valuation problems but more significantly because they are agents of change, not constraints on equilibrium. If anything is to be emphasised in this respect it is that national differences in education, training and research activities and institutions will be a key determinant of national differences in innovation and imitative capability. To subsume this dimension within a static factor-endowment approach would be to seriously misread the connections between knowledge creation and its dissemination and the consequences for international trade (Soete & Dosi 1988).

III   Elements of an evolutionary approach

The principal feature of the evolutionary approach which we shall employ can be summarised in the statement that evolution is a process of selection driven by economic variety.[5] As such it emphasises three features of an industry, each of which has accumulated a considerable degree of empirical support: that within a national industry there are wide variations in the productivity levels of competing firms; that internationally there are corresponding differences in the distributions of efficiency, as measured say, by average productivity levels; and that new technologies diffuse but slowly into the prevailing industrial structure, coexisting with prior technologies for long periods of calendar time.

To take account of these empirical features we shall replace the traditional emphasis on representative, ideal economic types with an explicit recognition of the coexistence of economic variety in an industry. The entities which are subject to evolution in this paper will be populations of competing technologies. It is the distribution of variety in which we are interested and economic change is to be measured by changes in the statistical moments of the respective distributions.

The mechanisms of evolutionary change of the kind employed here depend upon the operation of three principles: the principle of variation, that members of a population vary with respect to at least one characteristic with selective significance; the principle of heredity, that there are copying mechanisms to ensure the replication of the elements in the population; and the principle of selection, that some varieties are better suited to environmental pressure and thus increase in relative significance compared to inferior forms.

Our population will consist of a set of technologies for producing a homogeneous product, each technology being identified by a particular unit-cost level defined to include a normal rate of return on the capital invested. Each technology is operated by one or more distinct firms and the source of the difference in unit costs may be a difference in the technological knowledge base of the firm or a difference in the organisational knowledge base through which it translates technology as knowledge into technology as artefact.[6] Indeed it appears to be impossible to treat the technology of a firm independently from its organisational structure. This is one major reason why technologies contain substantial elements of tacit knowledge which it is difficult to transfer to other firms.[7] The evolutionary approach makes a sharp distinction between the objects of selection and the environment in which selection takes place. In our case the direct objects of selection are process technologies although the matter is complicated by the fact that they are articulated by firms which become the indirect focus of the selection process. Thus, to simplify, we identify each firm with a particular process technology and distinguish the population of firms by three attributes. First, there is the efficiency of the firm as measured by its unit-cost level and implied factor-productivity level. Secondly, there is the propensity of the firm to expand its productive capacity, as measured by the ratio of its growth rate to its unit profit margin. Growth depends upon access to internal and external finance, upon the investment requirements to expand productive capacity, on the ability to manage expansion without loss of efficiency, as argued by Penrose (1981), and on the simple willingness to grow, which can never be taken for granted. Finally, there is the creativity of the firm, its ability to enhance its process technology, through learning activity, through investing resources in R&D, and through its design capabilities at turning knowledge into artefact. We expect firms to differ substantially in their creativity, particularly when the possibilities for technical advance are extensive, and such differences in creativity may cumulate into substantial differences in efficiency levels between firms and between countries. Thus the evolution of the pattern of international trade is to be found in national differences in efficiency, national differences in propensities to grow, and most fundamental of all, national differences in creativity.

The selection environment, or the 'market' as we shall call it, also has a number of distinguishing attributes. It generates a price structure for products and factor inputs, the latter enabling differences in technical efficiency to be translated into differences in unit costs. The market has a growth rate and it imposes a degree of selective pressure on firms such that if they deviate from average behaviour they lose or gain sales at a faster or lower rate. In what follows we explore a simple, and in some respects, traditional, specification of the market environment. Selection operates continuously through time and selection pressure is at a maximum in that all firms, from whatever country, are forced to sell their output at the ruling world market price for the commodity. National market environments for the product are completely integrated and are growing at the same compound rate over time, g_d, so that each country accounts for a constant share of world consumption. On the factor market side, imperfect international mobility of productive agents allows international differences in relative factor prices which may or may not survive in the trade context.

There are two final aspects of the evolutionary framework which need emphasis. The first is its concern with process rather than state. Our focus is upon how the trading world changes and the attention naturally shifts from the levels of national output and consumption of different commodities to the rates at which these levels change over time. The second is the need to introduce inertia into the behaviour of firms, for if adaptation was always uniform and instantaneous then variety could not exist and selective mechanisms could not operate.[8] Evolutionary models are precisely needed to cope with imperfect adaptability and the inertia which holds variety sufficiently constant relative to the speed of selective forces. The sources of inertia are many, 'X-efficiency' (Leibenstein, 1978), technological interrelatedness (Frankel, 1955), organisational (Morgan, 1986) and conceptual (Loasby, 1976), but they each play a crucial part in explaining the persistence of economic variety.

IV   The evolution of foreign trade

We now consider the evolution of foreign trade in a single industry. There are two countries, home (A) and foreign (B) and all prices and cost levels are expressed in terms of the national currencies and converted from foreign currency values at the exchange rate, r. Each national industry is described by a given technology set, a distribution of coexisting and competing ways to produce the same product. Each technology has its own level of unit cost, h_i, which is independent of the scale of output from that technology. Unit costs range from best practice to worst practice and the technology distributions in the two countries are assumed to be different. Thus production and trade take place in the context of economic variety both within and between the two countries. In this sense our framework is an extension of the selection frameworks pioneered by Downie (1955), Steindl (1952), Alchian (1951) and Nelson and Winter (1984). The analysis is dynamic in that it is concerned with a process of change, although for purposes of exposition we begin by imposing limitations on the kinds of change which can take place. In particular, the technology set in each country is given, and we permit neither innovation nor imitation, nor any elements of technology transfer. Nor do we permit direct foreign investment or international capital mobility.

Measures of international competitive performance
The traditional measure of international competitive performance is, of course, comparative advantage defined in terms of the pre-trade or autarky relative cost levels in the trading countries. This static measure yields a prediction of which commodities will be exported by each country in a trading equilibrium but tells us nothing about how the volume of trade will change over time. In an evolutionary context we need measures which are concerned with changes in actual production and trade patterns and two such measures are immediate candidates. Our first measure is the share of the home economy in the world production of the commodity, and we shall denote this share by e. The rate at which this market share changes over time is given by

$$\frac{de}{dt} = e[g_A - g] = e(1 - e)[g_A - g_B] \tag{11.1}$$

where g_A and g_B are the national capacity growth rates and $g = eg_A + (1 - e)g_B$ is the world capacity growth rate. It follows that e is rising or falling as the growth rate of production at home exceeds or falls short of the foreign growth rate of production. Holding the growth rates constant, the share in world production follows a logistic path towards zero or unity depending on whether g_A is less than or greater than g_B. If there are persistent and uniquely ordered differences in growth rates then one country must come to *relative* dominance in the long run as the economic weight of the other drops into insignificance.

For the second measure of trade performance we take a measure of openness to trade, namely the ratio of the trade volume to the national production volume in the home country, denoted by b, which depends on a comparison of the world distribution of production with the world distribution of consumption. If the share of the home country in world consumption is c, then

$$b = 1 - \frac{c}{e}. \tag{11.2}$$

Clearly, the home country is an exporter or an importer according to whether e exceeds or is less than c. The relation between the trade-balance ratio and the share in world production, for any given value of c, is shown in Figure 11.1. The maximum possible value for the trade balance ratio is $1 - c$, corresponding to situations in which the home country accounts for the entire world production. Holding e constant, a higher value of c implies a lower value of b. Hence, any deterioration in the home country's trade balance in this commodity can be explained by some appropriate combination of loss of share in world production or rise in share of world consumption.[9] The rate of change in the trade balance ratio is equal to

$$\frac{db}{dt} = (1 - b) \left[\frac{1}{e} \frac{de}{dt} - \frac{1}{c} \frac{dc}{dt} \right]$$

Since we wish to focus the evolutionary argument on the accumulation of productive capacity we shall assume throughout that demand for this commodity grows at the same rate in each country, c is constant, and so

$$\frac{db}{dt} = (1 - b)(1 - e)[g_A - g_B]. \tag{11.3}$$

Figure 11.1 Relation between trade-balance ratio and share in world production

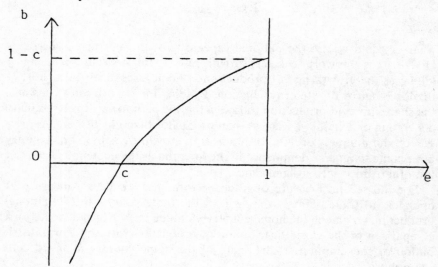

A growth rate advantage in favour of the home country implies a rising share of world production and an improving trade-balance ratio. In this case, statements about the dynamic path of *e* can always be translated into equivalent statements about the dynamic path of *b*. No doubt the evidence is tenuous but casual empiricism would seem to suggest that between the industrialised countries, at least, shares in world production change far more rapidly than do shares in world consumption. In any event, we maintain this hypothesis as a guide to exposition.

Short-run trade equilibrium

We may now describe the world trading equilibrium consistent with the given national technology sets and patterns of installed productive capacity, see Figure 11.2. Here S_A is the supply curve in the home country, the height of each step reflecting the unit-cost level of a technology and the length of each step representing installed capacity. There is a similar supply curve in B. Converting the foreign cost levels into home currency at the ruling exchange rate and adding this supply schedule to S_A gives the world supply schedule, S_w. Given that the market selection environment is such as to impose the law of one price on the competing firms ($P_A = rP_B$) we can also draw the world demand curve D_w, which is the horizontal sum of the respective domestic demand curves. The equilibrium price is P_o and world output is OX with the home country's share in production being

Figure 11.2 Short-run world trading equilibrium

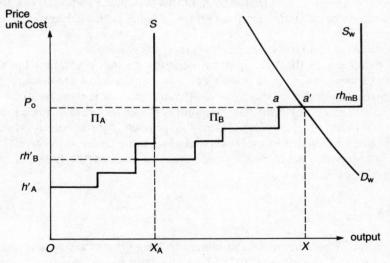

measured by OX_A/OX. As drawn there are three different technologies coexisting in A and four coexisting in B. Best practice in A (h'_A) is superior to best practice in B (h'_B), A has no marginal technology although B does, namely the technology which just breaks even with $p = rh_{mB}$. Apart from this marginal technology all the remaining ones earn positive profits or quasi rents, the aggregate national profits being given by the areas Π_A and Π_B respectively. Notice that all the technologies are being used to full capacity except the marginal one for which there is surplus capacity measured by the distance aa'. Since we adopt the strong bankruptcy rule, negative profits entail the immediate withdrawal from production of a particular technology, the world market price determines the upper end of the range of technologies from which there is positive production in both countries.

Within each country we can now derive the average-practice unit-cost levels. Let wi_A and wi_B be the respective shares of a technology in national production, then the average practice cost levels are defined by

$$\bar{h}_A = \Sigma w_{iA} h_{iA}, \qquad h'_A \leq h_{iA} \leq p,$$
$$\text{and} \quad r\bar{h}_B = r\Sigma w_{iB} . h_{iB}, \qquad rh'_B \leq rh_{iB} \leq p.$$

respectively. Notice that average practice is defined with respect to the set of profitable technologies. As indicated in Figure 11.2, average practice in A is inferior to that in B at this particular point in the evolutionary process. The situation shown is a snapshot of the evolutionary process at work. Over time growth in the market will displace the world demand curve to the right and the process of accumulation in each country will displace the respective supply schedules to the right in a systematic fashion. How these dynamic processes influence the pattern of trade is treated next.

Trade and accumulation: national differences in efficiency
The evolution of the trade pattern depends on the interaction between three national differences, in efficiency, in propensity to accumulate, and in creativity. In this chapter we shall concentrate solely on national differences in efficiency. Our starting point is the growth rate of the capacity invested in the ith technology. If v_i is the 'physical' capital output ratio, p_m is the price index of capital goods and Π_i is the propensity to invest (the ratio of growth rate to profit rate), then for each of the home country technologies we can write

$$g_{iA} = \left(\frac{\Pi_i}{p_m v_i}\right)_A (P - h_{iA}). \tag{11.4}$$

We shall choose units to set the home currency price of machines equal to unity and call the ratio $(\Pi_i/v_i)_A$ the propensity to accumulate of the ith technology and denote it by f_{iA}. In order to focus solely on the effects of differences in efficiency let $f_{iA} = f_A$ for all the technologies in A, so the aggregate growth rate of home capacity is given by

$$g_A = \Sigma w_{iA} g_{iA} = f_A(p - \bar{h}_A). \tag{11.5}$$

The higher the average profit margin, the higher is the national capacity growth rate. Exactly similar factors govern the accumulation of capacity in B, and providing the law of one price applies to capital goods we have

$$g_B = \Sigma w_{iB} g_{iB} = f_B[p - r\bar{h}_B]. \tag{11.6}$$

Using this information we can determine the evolution of the ratios e and b. From (11.1), (11.5) and (11.6) we have

$$\frac{de}{dt} = e(1 - e)[(f_A - f_B)p + [f_B r\bar{h}_B - f_A \bar{h}_A]]$$

which on setting $f_A = f_B = f$, to isolate the effect of efficiency differences, yields

$$\frac{de}{dt} = e[\bar{h} - \bar{h}_A) = e(1 - e)f[r\bar{h}_B - \bar{h}_A] \tag{11.7}$$

$$= e(1 - e)f . \Delta$$

where $\bar{h} = e\bar{h}_A + (1 - e)r\bar{h}_B$, is the world average-practice cost level, and Δ is defined as the selective advantage enjoyed by country A. Thus, in so far as differences in efficiency can be isolated, the home country increases its share of world production and its trade-balance ratio whenever it is more efficient than the world average or, in this two-country case, more efficient on average than its foreign rival. In an evolutionary framework it is the selective advantage which measures the appropriate technology gap between the two countries. Notice that this gap is not measured, as is often the case, by the difference between national best practice or, even less appropriately, by the difference between foreign best practice and average domestic practice. It is the difference between national average levels of performance which governs the evolution of the trade pattern.

Aggregating across the two countries to derive the growth rate of world capacity we find $g = eg_A + (1 - e)g_B = f[p - \bar{h}]$ so that the average world profit margin determines the world growth rate of capacity. It is easy to see that the dynamics of this selection mechanism tend to drive g into equality with g_d, and p into equality with what we shall term the reference price p_r, namely that price at which world demand and world capacity grow at the same rate. This reference price is related to the world growth rate by $p_r = g_d/f + \bar{h}$. For, if $p > p_r$, world capacity grows more quickly than world demand, and so p tends to fall towards p_r, and conversely when $g < g_d$.

This is not to suggest that $p = p_r$ at all stages of the selection process, of course. Shocks to the demand and supply curves will prevent this, as will situations in which there exists a marginal technology in one or both of the countries. In this last situation the world price is equal to unit costs with the marginal technology and any discrepancy between g and g_d on a world scale is absorbed in variations in the degree of capacity utilisation of this particular technology.

Because of the close connection between profits and capacity growth in each country there is a correspondingly close connection between national growth rates and the share of a country in total world profits. Defining country A's profit share by ϱ_A, it follows that

$$\varrho_A = \frac{g_A}{g} \cdot e. \tag{11.8}$$

The share of country A in world profits exceeds its share in world production by exactly the same proportion as the national capacity growth rate exceeds the world capacity growth rate. Thus, a country which is losing its share of world production necessarily has a share in world profits which is less than its share in world production, and conversely.

A currency devaluation
Consider now the consequences of a devaluation of the home currency assuming for the sake of argument that $\bar{h}_A < r\bar{h}_B$. The impact effect of the devaluation is to lower the foreign currency price of the commodity at the ruling home currency price or, equivalently, to raise foreign unit costs measured in home currency. Either way the result is to reduce the rate of accumulation of capacity in the foreign country. However, the devaluation also results in an excess world demand for the commodity and a corresponding increase in the home currency price p, depending on the magnitude of the supply and demand elasticities at home and abroad. This secondary effect stimulates accumulation in A and has a similar effect on B; indeed it may be strong enough to counter the initial adverse effect on the foreign industry's growth rate. However, whether the foreign growth rate is increased or not, the growth rate difference, $g_A - g_B$, is certainly greater after the devaluation and so the home country's share in world production and its trade-balance ratio will rise more rapidly than previously. In short a devaluation gives the home country a greater dynamic competitive advantage in the selection process.

A protective tariff
By similar reasoning we can demonstrate that an import tariff levied by the foreign country will raise the foreign price relative to the home country

price, lower the home country price, in absolute terms, according to the relevant elasticities, and increase the foreign growth rate at the expense of the domestic growth rate. Consequently, the international selection process is biased in favour of the tariff-imposing country.

Selection and changes in average efficiency
So far we have examined the selection process as it operates at the international level. Equally the process of selection is operating at the domestic level in a way which reacts back upon the evolution of our indicators, *e* and *b*. Within the home country, the market share of each technology evolves according to a multi-technology diffusion process, with the shares in domestic production changing according to the relations

$$\frac{dw_{iA}}{dt} = w_{iA} f(\bar{h}_A - \bar{h}_{iA})$$

The relative importance of the different technologies is changing over time in favour of the more efficient technologies, and this steadily reduces the average unit-cost level even though there is no technical progress in the proper sense. In the home country this yields

$$\frac{d\bar{h}_A}{dt} = \Sigma\left(\frac{dw_{iA}}{dt}\right)h_{iA} = -fV(h_A) \tag{11.9}$$

where $V(h_A)$ is the variance in unit costs across the profitable portion of the technology set ($h_{iA} < p$). Selection necessarily implies progress. Similar arguments for country B lead to

$$r\frac{d\bar{h}_B}{dt} = -fr^2V(h_B)$$

where $V(h_B)$ is the variance of unit costs in B measured in foreign currency.

In each country the process of internal selection progressively reduces average-practice unit costs and focuses the selective effort on the best-practice technologies which ultimately come to dominate the respective domestic markets. As a consequence of the internal processes of selection the balance of selective advantage held by country A is changing over time, with

$$\frac{d\Delta}{dt} = f[V(h_A) - r^2V(h_B)]. \tag{11.10}$$

Country A's selective advantage increases or declines according as the variance of unit costs across the technology set in A is greater or less than the corresponding variance in country B, when both variances are measured in home currency. Hence, A's selective advantage can only remain constant if the exchange rate is set equal to the ratio of the standard deviations of unit costs in the two countries – a most unlikely constellation of circumstances. Notice also that an exogenous reduction in the world price of the commodity will typically eliminate some technologies in either or both of the countries, and reduce each country's variance of unit costs. How this shock will influence the rate of change of selective advantage it is not possible to determine on *a priori* grounds. However, it is clear that this selection process is quite compatible with reversal and re-reversal of the selective advantage of a country over time.

The internal selection process implies corresponding reductions in the world average unit-cost level, $\bar{h}$, with

$$
\begin{aligned}
\frac{d\bar{h}}{dt} &= e\frac{d\bar{h}_A}{dt} + (1 - e)\mathrm{r}\frac{d\bar{h}_B}{dt} + [r\bar{h}_B - \bar{h}_A]\frac{de}{dt} \\
&= -f[eV(h_A) + (1 - e)r^2V(h_B) + e(1 - e)[r\bar{h}_B - \bar{h}_A]^2 \\
&= -fV(h).
\end{aligned}
\tag{11.11}
$$

Thus the same selective principle applies at international as well as at national levels, with the rate of decline of world average unit costs being proportional to the variance in world unit-cost levels, $V(h)$.

Ultimately this international selection process will converge on best practice in the home country since, by assumption, $h'_A < rh'_B$. The variances of unit costs are driven to zero in both countries as competition consumes the given variety in the national technology sets. Hence $\bar{h}$ converges on $\bar{h}_A$ as e tends to 1. Although the home country ultimately dominates world production in relative terms this need not entail the elimination of foreign production. In a long-run selection equilibrium, the market price settles down to the value $g_d/f + h'_A$ and if this exceeds rh'_B then production can survive and grow in absolute scale in B even though it will continue to decline in relative terms. Notice, though, that production in B can only survive if the world market for this commodity continues to grow at a sufficient rate. The point to be clear is that the survival of a technology and its long-run international economic weight are quite different matters.

V   The principle of dynamic comparative advantage

At least since the publication of Haberler's (1936) famous treatise on international trade, the multi-commodity version of the theory of comparative advantage has been expressed in terms of a chain of relative cost ratios, with demand conditions, via the exchange rate or relative money costs, determining where this chain is cut in order to separate exports from imports. The question now arises as to what it is that these relative cost levels refer to. Is it average practice, worst practice, best practice, or some other cost concept? Provided we consider static long-period equilibrium conditions, as in Haberler's exposition, the answer is clear. The appropriate cost levels are the best-practice ones operated, under conditions of normal profitability. Indeed in static long-period conditions the only techniques to survive are the best-practice ones. However, it should scarcely need saying that actual trade flows do not take place under conditions of long-period equilibrium. In any short-run situation technologies and firms with different cost levels typically coexist, in which case best-practice technology ceases to be a guide to the immediate pattern of comparative advantage. Indeed in any short-run capacity-constrained situation, it is the worst-practice technology in each country which is the candidate to define comparative advantage. Consider two possible situations or autarky equilibrium. In the first, the respective worst-practice technologies are also marginal in economic terms with autarky prices equal to worst-practice unit costs in both countries. Suppose that $p_A < rp_B$ holds in terms of autarky prices. Clearly A exports this commodity once trade is opened and, since $h_{mA}/h_{mB} < r$, the chain rule holds good when defined in terms of worst-practice technology. Now take the second situation in which in either or both countries the autarky price exceeds unit costs with the worst-practice technology. Then $p_A < rp_B$ need not entail $h_{mA}/h_{mB} < r$ and the chain rule breaks down. The point is simple, the autarky prices at any time are dependent on the entire past history of demand growth and capacity accumulation in the two countries and at any given moment those prices may bear no systematic relation to either best-practice or worst-practice unit costs. Needless to add, the ranking of commodities by relative best-practice costs may be quite different from their ranking by relative worst-practice costs.

However, the evolutionary framework allows us to reformulate the chain argument in a different way, as a statement of dynamic competitive performance. At any point in time all the commodities produced, both at home and abroad, can be ranked in terms of relative average-practice costs $\bar{h}_A/\bar{h}_B$, as shown in Figure 11.3. Introducing the exchange rate to cut the chain indicates that for the first n commodities, country A is at a selective disadvantage and will be losing world market share in the production of these commodities. For the remaining $n + 1$ to s commodities, A has a selective advantage and its world market share in these commodities will be improving. Of course, this is only a snapshot picture, over time the ranking of average cost ratios will change under the pressures of internal selection, and in the close proximity of the exchange rate there could be a

Figure 11.3 Ranking of commodities produced in terms of average-practice costs

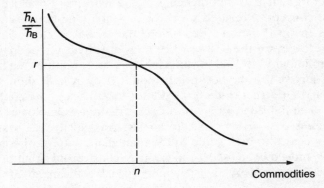

continual flux as commodities pass from having a positive to a negative selective advantage. Indeed, the same commodity may experience several reversals of trade direction over time. Now this particular formulation of the chain rule is clearly relevant to those tests of the doctrine of static comparative advantage which are expressed in terms of average-practice unit costs or related productivity measures.[10] However, from an evolutionary perspective any attempt to relate average-practice costs to the direction and volume of trade is misspecified. Rather, the relation to investigate is that between changes in trade patterns and comparative average costs. As formulated here, the conventional tests are an investigation of the theory of dynamic comparative advantage not an investigation of the traditional doctrine of long-run comparative advantage.

VI   Trade and evolution: a two-country model

To illustrate further this principle of dynamic comparative advantage, we may consider how evolution according to selective advantage works in the familiar setting of a two-country world in which two goods are produced subject to constant returns to scale and under conditions of constant cost. For the moment, let the exchange rate and the levels of money unit costs in each country be given. The two countries are A and B, and e_1^A denotes A's share in the world production of commodity 1, while e_2^B denotes B's share in the world production of commodity 2. Figure 11.4 depicts the possible situations which can arise in this simple world economy. The market shares are shown on the axes and any point in the unit square is a possible world output pattern, reflecting the past history of accumulation in the currently profitable techniques for producing each commodity. Point C is the cor-

Figure 11.4 A two-country model of the world economy

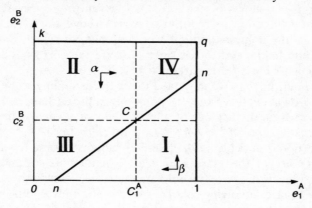

responding pattern of world consumption. Given our central concern with the evolution of production, we shall continue to assume that the structure of world consumption is constant over time and that the world demand for both commodities grows at the common rate, g_d. Taking the world consumption point as origin, we can divide the pattern of world specialisation into four categories, I–IV in the diagram. In regions I and II trade equilibrium is not possible. In region I, country A is exporting both commodities and so has a trade surplus, while in II, the converse is true with B having the trade surplus. Clearly any point in these two regions must entail offsetting capital or monetary flows between the two countries or some adjustment of the exchange rate between their currencies. By contrast, regions III and IV are regions of possible trade equilibrium. In region III country A is exporting commodity 1 and country B is exporting commodity 2, while the converse trade pattern holds in region IV. Note that while it is plausible to argue that any longer-run evolutionary equilibrium will lie in either of these latter two regions it should be stressed that at any historical moment the world economy could be anywhere within the unit square. The trade pattern then corresponds exactly to differences in the international pattern of production relative to the international pattern of consumption. However, given that trade is two-way, the terms of trade consistent with balance of trade equilibrium can be expressed as follows:

$$\left(\frac{P_2}{P_1}\right)^* = P^* = \left(\frac{e_1^A - c_1^A}{e_2^B - c_2^B}\right) S \tag{11.12}$$

where S is the ratio of the world outputs of commodity 1 to commodity 2, a constant ratio given our assumptions about world demand. This condition (11.12) enables us to define all the combinations of e_1^A, e_2^B which, at the given terms of trade, P^*, are consistent with balanced trade. These combinations are shown by the locus $n-n$ which passes through point C, and partitions the unit square into two parts. Above and to the left of this locus are all the combinations of world output for which B is in trade surplus, while below and to the right of it are the corresponding output patterns which yield a trade surplus for A.

At any point in time we may take the world economy to be at a point such as α. How it evolves from this point, given the exchange rate and cost levels, depends on the balance of selective advantage across the two commodities, that is, upon $\Delta_1^A = [r\bar{h}_1^B - \bar{h}_1^A]$ and $\Delta_2^B = [\bar{h}_2^A - r\bar{h}_2^B]$. Movement in any direction is possible, with e_1^A and e_2^B falling or rising together only if Δ_1^A and Δ_2^B are of the same sign. Clearly under assumptions of given average cost levels the system would gravitate to any one of the boundaries of the unit square, involving relative specialisation for one or both of the countries. However, we also know that the process of internal selection drives average cost levels in each country to the prevailing best-practice values and this must make the selection process alight in the long run on one of the four corner points. For example, should best-practice levels in B be less than those in A for both commodities then the world system evolves to point k at which $e_2^B = 1$ and $e_1^A = 0$. Naturally, since this point involves a trade surplus for B it can only be sustained if A can be granted unlimited credit or if A has unlimited stocks of foreign exchange reserves. It is appropriate, therefore, to introduce the requirements for international monetary equilibrium into the picture and show how they result in selection equilibria which satisfy the dynamic law of comparative advantage.

Let the exchange rate be given and consider point α again, at which B exports both commodities. We can imagine that 'gold' will flow from A to B to balance the international accounts, setting in motion an inflation in cost levels in B and a deflation of cost levels in A. This change in relative cost levels will continue as long as the world economy remains in sector II and must sooner or later establish the inequalities

$$\frac{\bar{h}_1^A}{\bar{h}_1^B} < r; \quad \frac{\bar{h}_2^A}{\bar{h}_2^B} < r,$$

irrespective of how relative cost levels stood initially. But this means that A will now have a selective advantage in both lines of production with $\Delta_1^A > 0$ and $\Delta_2^B < 0$. Hence the balance of payments adjustment mechanism creates a situation in which country A is gaining world market share in both lines of production. Consequently, point α will move in the direction indicated by the arrows out of region II. This same reasoning applies to any point to the left of the locus $n-n$. Similarly, at point β, where country A has the trade surplus, the inflation occurs in A and the deflation occurs in

B, so the point β evolves according to the arrows and moves out of region I, with

$$r > \frac{\bar{h}_1^A}{\bar{h}_1^B}; \ r > \frac{\bar{h}_2^A}{\bar{h}_2^B} \text{ and } \Delta_1^A < 0, \ \Delta_2^B > 0.$$

This argument also applies in turn to any point to the right of $n-n$, at which country A has a surplus. It follows immediately that stable monetary conditions at given terms of trade require the world economy to be on a terms-of-trade locus such as $n-n$. This in turn requires that e_1^A and e_2^B either increase together or decrease together at the given terms of trade. For this to be possible, the average cost levels and the exchange rate must satisfy

$$\frac{\bar{h}_1^A}{\bar{h}_1^B} < r < \frac{\bar{h}_2^A}{\bar{h}_2^B},$$

which is precisely the dynamic law of comparative advantage as enumerated in the previous section. Each country must have a selective advantage in a different commodity if international equilibrium is to be possible, let alone maintained over time.

We have established that all patterns of selection consistent with payments equilibrium must lie in region III or IV. It follows immediately that the only possible terminal selection equilibria are given by the points O and q respectively. Point q will dominate if A has a comparative best-practice advantage in commodity 1 and point 0 will dominate if the pattern of comparative advantage is reversed. At point q the equilibrium terms of trade are given by

$$P^* = \left(\frac{1 - c_2^B}{1 - c_1^A}\right) \cdot S$$

and at the origin they are given by

$$P^* = \frac{c_2^B}{c_1^A} \cdot S.$$

It is not surprising to find that, in each case, the long-run terms of trade take values which depend only upon demand conditions in the two countries. Constant returns to scale and constant relative costs ensure that this is so.

To sum up, all evolutionary patterns consistent with continuous trade equilibrium must lie in sectors III and IV with the pattern of production lying in a locus such as $n-n$. Of course, the slope of this locus will change over time as the equilibrium terms of trade change with the evolution of e_1^A and e_2^B but all of these loci will pass through point C. Conversely, any disturbance to payments equilibrium, for example, a capital transfer, will change the pattern of evolution of world production, perhaps taking it for 'temporary' periods into region I or II.

While the dynamics of these adjustment processes are complex the general principles of evolutionary change are clear. The requirement for payments equilibrium drives the world economy in to region III or IV and ensures that dynamic comparative advantages are respected at each point in time.

VII Concluding comments

The argument so far has emphasised the link between trade patterns and the process of selection across and between different national technology sets. It is appropriate that we conclude with a brief comment on the role of innovation in creating international differences in technology sets, the raw material on which selection processes operate. This is a highly complex question to which there are no ready answers, although over the longer term it is clear that national differences in technological and organisational creativity have a dominant effect on trade patterns. The point to be emphasised here is that while process innovations create the technology set, these innovations only influence the flow of trade to the extent that they are diffused within the economy of their introduction and in this way influence the national level of average-practice unit costs. Thus the impact effect of any individual innovation is likely to be negligible and its cumulative effect depends on where it stands in economic terms relative to the existing technology set. Only if it is superior to existing national average practice is it likely to have an effect on the trade balance. Many process innovations, therefore, will have impermanent consequences for the pattern of trade, although these consequences may be spread over many years. The case of product innovations is naturally more complicated and cannot be treated satisfactorily without investigating the characteristics of the products and the valuations placed on those characteristics by users. But this would take us way beyond the intendedly limited purpose of these notes.

By way of a summary, our purpose in this chapter has been to explore some consequences of an evolutionary picture of international trade, a picture which emphasises the forces making for changes in the flow and direction of trade and which allowed us to formulate a dynamic analogue to the traditional concept of comparative advantage. Within this picture, national differences in efficiency, propensities to accumulate, and technological and organisational creativity interact to create economic variety and select between competing economic varieties of technology and organisation. The simplicity of our approach will be obvious and implicitly defines an agenda for future research. Questions of product variety and differing national propensities to accumulate will be high on this list but such developments must await another occasion.

This paper is an extension of work carried out with my colleagues in PREST over several years. I am grateful to the ESRC for financial support and, in particular, to Professor M. Gibbons, with whom much of my thinking on economic evolution has been shaped. The final draft of this paper was written during a visit to Nankai University, Tianjin, China. I am obliged to Professor Gu, his colleagues and students, for their generous hospitality and the provision of a stimulating academic environment. Sections I and II of the paper elaborate on a previous analysis of international diffusion processes – written jointly with Luc Soete. I am grateful for his permission to draw on this work in this paper.

Notes

1 See, for example, Rosenbloom and Abernathy, 1982; Zysman and Tyson, 1983; and Landes, 1983.
2 On the process view of competition consult Hayek, 1948; and McNulty, 1968.
3 Bhagwati and Srinivasan, 1983, provide an excellent account of the nature of current trade theory.
4 For a detailed analysis and development of the Krugman argument see Cimoli, 1987.
5 This view is amplified in detail in Metcalfe and Gibbons, 1988.
6 This important distinction between technology as knowledge and technology as artefact is explored in Layton, 1974.
7 On the role of tacit knowledge see Pavitt, 1984. and the interesting essay by Mathias, 1975.
8 This is the thrust of Alchian's controversial article, 1951. See also the authoritative extension by Winter, 1963.
9 The recent NEDO, 1984, study of the UK electronics industry provides ample evidence on the rapidity with which a trade balance ratio can change.
10 See Bhagwati, 1969, for a detailed discussion.

References

Alchian, A. (1951). 'Uncertainty, evolution and economic theory', *Journal of Political Economy*, vol. 68.
Bhagwati, J. (1969). 'The pure theory of international trade: a survey', reprinted in J. Bhagwati, 1987, *Essays in International Economic Theory*, vol. 2 (Cambridge, Mass.: MIT Press).
Bhagwati, J. and Srinivasan, T. (1983). *Lectures on International Trade* (Cambridge, Mass.: MIT Press).
Cimoli, M. (1987). 'Technological gaps and institutional assymetries in a North–South model with a continuum of goods', University of Venice, mimeo.
Devons, E. (1961). 'Understanding international trade', *Economica*, vol. 28.
Downie, J. (1955). *The Competitive Process* (London: Duckworth).
Feenstra, R. C. (1982). 'Product creation and trade patterns: a theoretical note on the "bio-

logical" model of trade in similar products', in J. Bhagwati (ed.), *Import Competition and Response* (Chicago: University of Chicago Press).

Frankel, M. (1955). 'Obsolescence and technological change', *American Economic Review*, vol. 65.

Haberler, G. (1936). *The Theory of International Trade* (London: W. Hodge).

Hayek, F. (1948). *Individualism and Economic Order* (Chicago: Chicago University Press).

Johnson, H. (1968). *Comparative Cost Theory and Commercial Policy in a Developing World Economy* (Stockholm: Alunquist & Wicksell).

Krugman, P. (1979). 'A model of innovation, technology transfer and the world distribution of income', *Journal of Political Economy*, vol. 87.

Landes, D. (1983). *Revolution in Time* (Cambridge, Mass.: Harvard University Press).

Layton, C. (1974). 'Technology as knowledge', *Technology and Culture*, vol. 15, no. 7, pp. 31–41.

Leibenstein, H. (1978). *General X-Efficiency Theory and Economic Development* (Oxford: Oxford University Press).

Loasby, B. (1976). *Complexity, Choice and Ignorance* (Cambridge: Cambridge University Press).

McNulty, P. (1968). 'Economic theory and the meaning of competition', *Quarterly Journal of Economics*, vol. 80.

Mathias, P. (1975). 'Skills and the diffusion of innovations from Britain in the eighteenth century', *Transactions, Royal Historical Society*, vol. 25.

Metcalfe, J. S. and Gibbons, M. (1988). 'Technology, variety and organisation: a systematic perspective on the competitive process', in R. S. Rosenbloom and R. Burgelman (eds), *Research on Technological Innovation, Management and Policy* (Greenwich, Conn.: JAI Press).

Morgan, G. (1986). *Images of Organisation* (London: Sage).

National Economic Development Organisation (1984). 'Crisis facing UK information technology', *Report on Information Technology*, August.

Nelson, R. and Winter, S. (1984). *An Evolutionary Theory of Economic Change* (Cambridge, Mass.: Harvard University Press).

Pavitt, K. (1984). 'Sectoral patterns of technical change: towards a taxonomy and a theory', *Research Policy*, vol. 13.

Penrose, E. (1981). *The Theory of the Growth at the Firm* (Oxford: Basil Blackwell).

Posner, M. (1961). 'International trade and technological change', *Oxford Economic Papers*, vol. 13.

Rosenbloom, R. S. and Abernathy, W. (1982). 'The climate for innovation in industry', *Research Policy*, vol. 11.

Soete, L. and Dosi, G. (1988). 'Technical Change and International trade', in G. Dosi, *et al.* (eds) (1988), *Technical change & Economic Theory* (London: Frances Pinter).

Steindl, J. (1952). *Maturity and Stagnation in American Capitalism* (New York: Monthly Review Press).

Vernon, R. (1968). 'International investment and international trade in the product cycle', *Quarterly Journal of Economics*, vol. 80.

Winter, S. (1963). 'Economic "natural selection" and the theory of the firm', *Yale Economic Essays*, Yale University, New Haven, Conn.

Zysman, J. and Tyson, L. (eds) (1983). *American Industry in International Competition* (Ithaca, NY: Cornell University Press).

12

International transport costs with produced means of transportation: a Sraffian approach

Ian Steedman

In his recent and useful survey of the theoretical literature on transport costs in international trade, Casas (1983) notes, as others have noted, that that literature is surprisingly small. Indeed Casas's survey considers, in effect, only three previous analyses, those due to Samuelson (1954) and Mundell (1957), to Herberg (1970) and to Falvey (1976). As Casas makes clear, the Samuelson–Mundell model, in which transport costs are depicted as wastage rates in the quantities of commodities exported, implies that the conditions of production are just the same as they would have been in the absence of transport costs, so that transport costs have their effect only via changes in domestic relative prices; simple as it is, however, the model does serve to bring out the role of the supply of and demand for commodities in determining the division of the transport cost burden (Casas, 1983, section 2 and p. 107). The Herberg model introduces a distinct transport service, so that the activity of transportation involves a direct use of resources and changes the conditions of production of the other commodities; although it is assumed arbitrarily that each country transports its own imports, the model does indicate that the technical conditions in transportation influence relative prices and who 'pays' for transport (Casas, 1983, section 3 and p. 107). Falvey's analysis takes a further step beyond Herberg's by providing an endogenous, market determination of who provides the transportation, even if, as Casas points out (p. 104), that is possible *only* because Falvey assumes that the 'capital-intensity' of the transport industry does not lie between that of the other two industries. The analysis shows that technical conditions in transportation affect the origin of the resources used up in transport activity (Casas, 1983, section 4 and p. 107; see also Casas and Kwan Choi, 1985, for further analysis based on the Falvey model).

In seeking to make a small, further step in the direction of an adequate theory of international transport costs, one must immediately face three issues thrown up by the analyses referred to above. The first is that it is not good enough to proceed as if only *consumption* commodities are traded and transported. Means of production account for a large part of international trade and, as Mainwaring (1986, p. 112) has pointed out, 'The literature on effective protection should alert us to the dangers' of supposing that the effects of transport costs for produced inputs will be identical to those of transport costs for final consumption commodities. The second issue is that even Falvey's analysis (the most polished one) works with a 'capital and labour' version of the standard HOS (Heckscher–Ohlin–Samuelson) model, though treating 'capital' just like a non-produced, primary input (land). No reference is made to any sector or industry in which capital goods are produced; and Falvey even refers to the shipping costs of capital (p. 542 and n. 1) as, apparently, something quite distinct from the shipping costs of the produced commodities. Since Falvey is, then, not referring here to the shipping costs of *capital goods* – and obviously is not referring to the shipping costs of *money capital* – it would seem that, as so often in the HOS literature, 'capital' here is used simply as a misnomer for 'land' (some forms of which may perhaps be transportable) (cf., Steedman, 1979a, Chapter 1; 1979b, Introductory Essay). A necessary feature of an adequate theory of international transport costs is that it must allow explicitly for the production of and trade in produced inputs.

The third issue which arises clearly from the existing literature concerns the joint or non-joint nature of costs in transport activities. No doubt there are 'carriers' of an essentially one-directional nature – for example, pipelines (Casas, 1983, p. 104), refrigerator ships for meat, or oil tankers (Mainwaring, 1986, p. 119) – but so many 'carriers' can and do carry different cargoes in different directions, not to mention many products in a given direction, that it would seem appropriate in a basic analysis to allow for joint costs in transportation, leaving the 'one-directional carriers' for later treatment. (In their paper proving 'the existence and Pareto-optimality of a competitive world equilibrium in which the carriage of commodities from one country to another is not costless', Hadley and Kemp, 1966, p. 125, suggested in their opening paragraph that a major reason for the lack of success in integrating transport costs into general equilibrium trade theory had been 'the analytical difficulties posed by elements of jointness, both in the supply of and in the demand for carriage'.) It may be noted here that the paper by Casas includes a brief section entitled 'Transport as a jointly produced service' (1983, section 5). In this section Casas is not in fact arguing that transport costs are (or are not) typically joint costs but is suggesting, rather, that the question 'which country supplies the transport services?' may well be a misleading and unhelpful question. International shipping, for example, will require port facilities and dockers in *both* countries; international air traffic will require airports and their workers in *both* countries and so on. 'The relevant question therefore is not which country supplies transportation but how much of each country's resources will be absorbed in supplying it' (p. 106). This suggestion seems eminently reasonable and will be accepted in what follows.

A very simple analysis

Consider a competitive trading world consisting of two countries A and B; there is no government expenditure or taxation. Under autarky each country would have two single-product industries, operating under constant returns to scale and using the two commodities and a homogeneous primary input, labour, to produce the gross output of the industry in question. There is no choice of technique in either A or B and the technical conditions of production differ between the two countries. Under autarky the relative price of commodity 1 would be lower in A than in B, so we consider first a world of free trade, with no transport costs, in which A is completely specialised in producing commodity 1 and B is completely specialised in producing commodity 2. In an obvious notation, we shall have:

$$a_{11}p_0 + a_{21} + a_1 w_0^A = p_0, \tag{12.1}$$

$$a_{12}p_0 + a_{22} + a_2 w_0^B = 1, \tag{12.2}$$

where, in each country, commodity 2 is used as the standard of value. If x_1 denotes the (positive) quantity of 1 imported by B and x_2 the (positive) quantity of 2 imported by A, balanced trade requires that

$$p_0 = (x_2/x_1) \tag{12.3}$$

From (12.1), (12.2) and (12.3),

$$w_0^A = \left[\frac{(1 - a_{11})(x_2/x_1) - a_{21}}{a_1} \right], \tag{12.4}$$

$$w_0^B = \left[\frac{(1 - a_{22}) - a_{12}(x_2/x_1)}{a_2} \right]. \tag{12.5}$$

It will be clear from (12.4) and (12.5) both that w_0^A and w_0^B are inversely related and that a necessary condition for $w_0^A > 0 < w_0^B$ is that

$$(1 - a_{11})(1 - a_{22}) > a_{12}a_{21}, \tag{12.6}$$

the Hawkins–Simon condition applied to the trading world as a whole.

We now introduce transport costs, continuing to suppose that, if there is trade at all, it involves the production specialisation assumed above. (See further consideration of this question below.) Consider a joint-cost, two-way transportation activity which, in order to deliver x_1 to B and x_2 to A, uses up X_1 of commodity 1 and quantity L^A of labour from A and X_2 of commodity 2 and quantity L^B of labour from B. (Note that X_i is gross of x_i, $i = 1, 2$.) Let p^A be the relative price of 1 in A and p^B that in B. With wage rates w^A and w^B, in terms of commodity 2, (12.1) and (12.2) must be replaced by

$$a_{11}p^A + a_{21} + a_1w^A = p^A, \tag{12.7}$$

$$a_{12}p^B + a_{22} + a_2w^B = 1. \tag{12.8}$$

The transport activity will have total costs equal to its total revenue if

$$(p^AX_1 + w^AL^A) + \pi(X_2 + w^BL^B) = x_2 + \pi p^Bx_1 \tag{12.9}$$

where π is the price of 2 in B relative to that of 2 in A when both are expressed in a common currency. In (12.9), no attempt is made to separate the transport costs of delivering x_1 to B from those of delivering x_2 to A, and account is taken of the suggestion, due to Casas, that resources will be required from both A and B. The existence of positive transport costs is expressed in (12.9) by the assumption that at least one of the inequalities

$$X_1 \geq x_1,$$
$$X_2 \geq x_2,$$
$$L^A \geq 0,$$
$$L^B \geq 0.$$

holds strictly.

If all the activities accounted for in (12.9) were organised by entrepreneurs operating from A, that country would have balanced trade when

$$X_2 + w^BL^B = p^Bx_1. \tag{12.10}$$

(The trade balance, for each country, now includes payments made in connection with trade-related transportation activities, of course. Note that, from a formal point of view, (12.9) and (12.10) allow for the possibility that some of those activities take place *within* A and B – and not merely between them – but since no such activities are allowed for in (12.1) and (12.2) this is not a great advantage!) From (12.9) and (12.10),

$$p^AX_1 + w^AL^A = x_2. \tag{12.11}$$

Similarly, if all the activities accounted for in (12.9) were organised by entrepreneurs operating from B, that country would have balanced trade when (12.11) obtained and this, with (12.9), would imply (12.10). While there are slightly less extreme assumptions under which (12.10) and (12.11) would continue to be the balanced-trade conditions, they would not so continue under the most general assumptions about the location of sources of finance for the various aspects of the overall transportation activity. For simplicity, however, we shall suppose (12.10) and (12.11) from this point on – which makes (12.9) redundant, of course. It will be seen that (12.7) and (12.11) provide two equations involving only two 'price' variables, p^A and w^A, just as (12.8) and (12.10) provide two equations in p^B and w^B. The *jointness* of transport costs will only emerge below, in equations (12.18–21).

From (12.10) and (12.11) we see that

$$p^A = \left(\frac{x_2 - w^A L^A}{X_1}\right) < \left(\frac{x_2}{x_1}\right) < \left(\frac{X_2 + w^B L^B}{x_1}\right) = p^B. \qquad (12.12)$$

Hence,

$$p^A < \left(\frac{x_2}{x_1}\right) < p^B \qquad (12.12')$$

by contrast with (12.3) for the 'no-transport-cost' case. With transport costs, each commodity is relatively cheaper in the country from which it is exported – a familiar result. From (12.7), (12.8), (12.10) and (12.11) it follows at once that:

$$w^A = \left[\frac{(1 - a_{11})x_2 - a_{21}X_1}{(1 - a_{11})L^A + a_1 X_1}\right], \qquad (12.13)$$

$$p^A = \left[\frac{a_{21}L^A + a_1 x_2}{(1 - a_{11})L^A + a_1 X_1}\right], \qquad (12.14)$$

$$w^B = \left[\frac{(1 - a_{22})x_1 - a_{12}X_2}{a_{12}L^B + a_2 x_1}\right], \qquad (12.15)$$

$$p^B = \left[\frac{(1 - a_{22})L^B + a_2 X_2}{a_{12}L^B + a_2 x_1}\right]. \qquad (12.16)$$

For any given (x_1, x_2) it will be clear from (12.4) and (12.13) that if $L^A > 0$ or $X_1 > x_1$, then

$$w^A < w_0^A;$$

while from (12.5) and (12.15) if $L^B > 0$ or $X_2 > x_2$, then

$$w^B < w_0^B.$$

More generally, if (x_1, x_2) are held constant and $w^A > 0 < w^B$, it follows from (12.13–16) that w^A, w^B and p^A are non-increasing and p^B is non-decreasing with respect to each of $(X_1 - x_1)$, $(X_2 - x_2)$, L^A and L^B. More loosely, increases in transport costs lower real wages and force the two domestic price ratios further apart. (Conversely, of course, technical progress in transportation activity will raise real wages and narrow the 'wedge' between domestic price ratios.)

When will w^A and w^B both be positive? Only, from (12.13) and (12.15), when

$$(1 - a_{11})x_1 > a_{21}X_2$$

and

$$(1 - a_{22})x_2 > a_{12}X_1.$$

A necessary condition for $w^A > 0 < w^B$ is thus:

$$(1 - a_{11})(1 - a_{22})x_1x_2 > a_{12}a_{21}X_1X_2. \tag{12.17}$$

If $x_1 < X_1$ or $x_2 < X_2$, it is clear that (12.17) places a more demanding condition on the a_{ij} than does the corresponding 'no-transport-cost' condition (12.6). Alternatively, given that (12.6) obtains, we may regard (12.17) as placing a restriction on the extent to which transport costs may raise the X_i above x_i without destroying the possibility of positive with-trade wage rates in both countries. From either point of view (12.17), which will be considered further below, can be seen as an extension of the familiar Hawkins–Simon condition (12.6).

The requirement that $w^A > 0 < w^B$ is, of course, a very weak one: each wage rate will in fact need to exceed the corresponding autarky wage rate if transport costs are not to destroy trade. Let w_a^A, w_a^B, p_a^A and p_a^B denote the autarky wage rates and prices ratios in A and B. Then from (12.13), (12.15) and the autarky equivalents of (12.1) and (12.2), we may readily deduce that $w^A > w_a^A$ if and only if

$$x_2 > w_a^A L^A + p_a^A X_1. \tag{12.13'}$$

and that $w^B > w_a^B$ if and only if

$$p_a^B x_1 > w_a^B L^B + X_2. \tag{12.15'}$$

Relation (12.13') shows that $w^a > w_a^A$ if and only if the imports of 2 into A are greater than the (gross) transport costs incurred by $A - L^A$ and $X_1 -$ when these latter are valued, in terms of 2, at *autarky* wages and prices in A. Similarly (12.15') shows that $w^B > w_a^B$ if and only if the imports of 1 into B exceed the (gross) transport costs incurred by $B - L^B$ and $X_2 -$ when these latter, like x_1, are valued in terms of 2, at *autarky* wages and prices in B.

Joint costs in transportation

To proceed further, we must specify how the resources used up in the transport activity, namely $(X_1 - x_1)$, L^A, $(X_2 - x_2)$ and L^B, are related to the quantities delivered, namely x_1 and x_2. Any 'realistic' answer to (the multi-dimensional version of) this question would, no doubt, be highly complex. Here we shall simply try to capture the joint-costs aspect of transportation by specifying that:

$$(X_1 - x_1) = \max[t_{11}x_1, t_{12}x_2], \tag{12.18}$$

$$(X_2 - x_2) = \max[t_{21}x_1, t_{22}x_2], \tag{12.19}$$

$$L^A = \max[\ell_{11}x_1, \ell_{12}x_2], \tag{12.20}$$

$$L^B = \max[\ell_{21}x_1, \ell_{22}x_2], \tag{12.21}$$

where the t_{ij} and ℓ_{ij} are non-negative constants, at least one of them being positive. Relations (12.18–21) stipulate, of course, that each of the four resource quantities used in transportation must be adequate to meet the demands of transport activities in *both* directions, no matter which demand might be the greater for any given resource. We naturally make no claim that (12.18–21) suffice to capture all aspects of transportation costs. For example, if all the t_{ij} and the ℓ_{ij} were positive it would follow that (x_2/x_1) could be sufficiently high (low) that transport costs were independent of x_1 (of x_2) and this might well be thought too extreme. We shall suppose, however, that the t_{ij} and ℓ_{ij} are such that a wide range of (x_2/x_1) ratios is compatible with transport costs' depending on both x_1 and x_2 and that, moreover, any 'solution' (x_2/x_1) ratios considered do in fact fall within that range. (More formally, we could add $(\theta_{11}x_1 + \theta_{12}x_2)$, $(\theta_{21}x_1 + \theta_{22}x_2)$, $(\lambda_{11}x_1 + \lambda_{12}x_2)$ and $(\lambda_{21}x_1 + \lambda_{22}x_2)$ to the right-hand sides of (12.18–21) respectively. With θ_{12}, θ_{21} and all the λ_{ij} positive, each of X_1, X_2, L^A and L^B would now always depend on both x_1 and x_2, whatever the ratio (x_2/x_1). In the interest of simplicity, however, we shall work with (12.18–21) as they are given above.) Relations (12.20) and (12.21) suppose fixed proportions in the use of transport workers from the two countries, A and B. This is the less unreasonable (1) the higher the proportion of transport labour done in ports, airports, warehouses, and so on, and (2) the more that nationally based airlines, railways, and so on, employ only 'nationals'.

Using (12.18–21) we may now eliminate X_1, X_2, L^A and L^B from any earlier relationship in which they appeared. For example, (12.17), our extended Hawkins–Simon condition, may now be written as

$$(1-a_{11})(1-a_{22}) \geq a_{12}a_{21}\max\left[1+t_{11}, 1+t_{12}\left(\frac{x_2}{x_1}\right)\right]\max\left[1+t_{21}\left(\frac{x_1}{x_2}\right), 1+t_{22}\right],$$

$$(12.17')$$

which, for any *given* (x_2/x_1), defines a frontier below which the four a_{ij} and the four t_{ij} must lie if specialisation and trade is to be capable of allowing a positive wage rate in both countries. Condition (12.17') is not, however, the most informative condition that may be derived. From (12.13) and (12.18), $w^A > 0$ requires

$$(1 - a_{11})x_2 \geq a_{21} \max [(1 + t_{11})x_1, x_1 + t_{12}x_2], \tag{12.22}$$

while from (12.15) and (12.19), $w^B > 0$ requires

$$(1 - a_{22})x_1 \geq a_{12}\max [x_2 + t_{21}x_1, (1 + t_{22})x_2]. \tag{12.23}$$

It follows from (12.22) and (12.23) that $w^A > 0 < w^B$ requires

$$\max\left[\frac{a_{21}(1 + t_{11})}{1 - a_{11}}, \frac{a_{21}}{1 - a_{11} - a_{21}t_{12}}\right] \leq \frac{(x_2)}{(x_1)} \leq$$

$$\min\left[\frac{1 - a_{22}}{a_{12}(1 + t_{22})}, \frac{1 - a_{22} - a_{12}t_{21}}{a_{22}}\right] \tag{12.24}$$

where $(1 - a_{11}) > a_{21}t_{12}$. Only if the a_{ij} and the t_{ij} satisfy (12.24) is there an import ratio (x_2/x_1) such that the real wage rate is positive in both countries.

We now consider the stronger requirement that the real wage rate in each country should exceed the corresponding autarky level. It can be shown, by using (12.18–21) to eliminate X_1, X_2, L^A and L^B from (12.13') and (12.15'), that this requirement will be met if and only if

$$w_a^A \ell_{12} + p_a^A t_{12} < 1,$$
$$w_a^B \ell_{21} + t_{21} < p_a^B,$$

$$\max\left[w_a^A \ell_{11} + p_a^A(1 + t_{11}), \frac{w_a^A \ell_{11}}{1 - p_a^A t_{12}}, \frac{p_a^A(1 + t_{11})}{1 - w_a^A \ell_{12}}\right] \leq \left(\frac{x_2}{x_1}\right) \leq$$

$$\min\left[\frac{p_a^B - w_a^B \ell_{22}}{1 + t_{22}}, \frac{p_a^B - t_{21}}{w_a^B \ell_{22}}, \frac{p_a^B - w_a^B \ell_{21}}{1 + t_{22}}\right].$$

It will be obvious enough that these conditions collapse to $p_a^A \leq (x_2/x_1) \leq p_a^B$ when all the ℓ_{ij} and t_{ij} become zero and that they constitute, in effect, a frontier restricting the ℓ_{ij} and t_{ij} which are compatible with gainful trade.

While it would be perfectly possible to use (12.18–21) to eliminate the X_i and L^j from (12.13–16), thus expressing each of w^A, p^A, w^B, p^B as a function of (x_2/x_1), it may be illuminating to proceed less directly. Using (12.18) and (12.20), let us rewrite (12.11) as

$$p^A\max[(1 + t_{11})x_1,\, x_1 + t_{12}x_2] + w^A\max[\ell_{11}x_1,\ell_{12}x_2] = x_2 \qquad (12.11')$$

and rewrite (12.7), for convenience:

$$a_{11}p^A + a_{21} + a_1w^A = p^A. \qquad (12.7')$$

In Figure 12.1, the upward-sloping straight line is the graph of (12.7'). The horizontal dashed line is the graph of (12.11'), *when* $t_{11} = t_{12} = \ell_{11} = \ell_{12} = 0$. When any one of the t_{11}, t_{12}, ℓ_{11} or ℓ_{12} is positive, however, p^A must be less than (x_2/x_1) and, indeed, if ℓ_{11} or ℓ_{12} is positive the graph of (12.11') is a downward-sloping straight line, for given (x_2/x_1) as shown in Figure 12.1. It is easily seen from the figure that increases in $(t_{11}, t_{12}, \ell_{11}, \ell_{12})$ lower both p^A and w^A for any given (x_2/x_1). Moreover, if we hold (x_2/x_1) 'constant' as between the actual case and the 'no-transport-cost' case, we see that $p^A < p_0 = (x_2/x_1)$ and $w^A < w_0^A$. If the transport costs are held constant while (x_2/x_1) is notionally increased, the upward-sloping line in Figure 12.1 is unchanged (see (12.7')) but the downward-sloping line shifts bodily upward (see (12.11')); hence p^A and w^A both rise as (x_2/x_1) increases.

The position in country B can naturally be analysed in just the same way. Using (12.19) and (12.21) we may rewrite (12.10) as

Figure 12.1

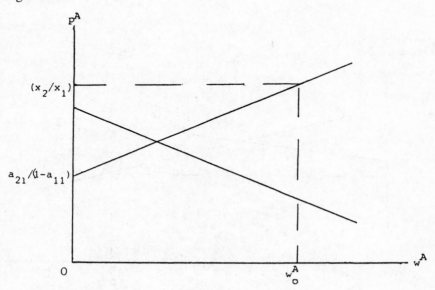

244 *Ian Steedman*

$$\max[t_{21}x_1 + x_2, (1 + t_{22})x_2] + w^B\max[\ell_{21}x_2, \ell_{22}x_2] = p^Bx_1, \quad (12.10')$$

and, for convenience, rewrite (12.8):

$$a_{12}p^B + a_{22} + a_2w^B = 1. \tag{12.8'}$$

In Figure 12.2, the downward-sloping straight line is the graph of (12.8′). The horizontal dashed line is the graph of (12.10′), *when $t_{21} = t_{22} = \ell_{21} = \ell_{22} = 0$*. When any one of the t_{21}, t_{22}, ℓ_{21}, or ℓ_{22} is positive, however, p^B must be greater than (x_2/x_1) and, indeed, if ℓ_{21} or ℓ_{22} is positive the graph of (12.10′) is an upward-sloping straight line, for given (x_2/x_1), as shown in Figure 12.2. Increases in $(t_{21}, t_{22}, \ell_{21}, \ell_{22})$ raise p^B and lower w^B for any given (x_2/x_1). Keeping (x_2/x_1) 'constant' as between the actual case and the 'no-transport-cost' case, we see the $p^B > p_0 = (x_2/x_1)$ and $w^B < w_o^B$. If the transport costs are held constant while (x_2/x_1) is notionally increased, the downward-sloping line in Figure 12.2 is unchanged (see (12.8′)) but the upward-sloping line shifts bodily upward (see (12.10′)); hence p^B rises and w^B falls as (x_2/x_1) increases.

Since $w^A(w^B)$ is positively (negatively) related to (x_2/x_1), we see that with transport costs, as without them, there is a downward-sloping frontier relating w^A and w^B. This frontier naturally lies nearer to the origin than does the 'no-transport-cost' frontier between w^A and w^B; we have already noted above that, for each given (x_2/x_1), $w^A < w_o^A$ and $w^B < w_o^B$.

Figure 12.2

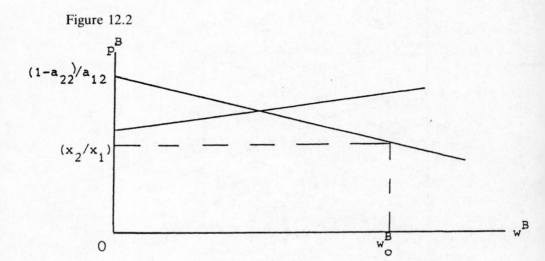

Quantities and closure

Thus far we have treated the import ratio (x_2/x_1) as a parameter and have, indeed, said little about physical quantities, having concentrated our attention upon wage rates and prices. Suppose now, however, that only commodity 2 is used in consumption and that neither economy is growing. Let q_1 and ℓ^A be the gross output of 1 and the total employment in A and let q_2 and ℓ^B be the gross output of 2 and total employment in B. Then:

$$q_1 = a_{11}q_1 + X_1, \tag{12.25}$$

$$x_1 = a_{12}q_2, \tag{12.26}$$

$$\ell^A = L^A + a_1q_1, \tag{12.27}$$

$$q_2 = a_{22}q_2 + X_2 + w^B\ell^B, \tag{12.28}$$

$$x_2 = a_{21}q_1 + w^A\ell^A, \tag{12.29}$$

$$\ell^B = L^B + a_2q_2. \tag{12.30}$$

From (12.25), (12.27) and (12.29),

$$q_1 = \left(\frac{X_1}{1 - a_{11}}\right) = \left(\frac{\ell^A - L^A}{a_1}\right) = \left(\frac{x_2 - w^A\ell^A}{a_{21}}\right), \tag{12.31}$$

while from (12.26), (12.28) and (12.30),

$$q_2 = \left(\frac{x_1}{a_{12}}\right) = \left(\frac{X_2 + w^B\ell^B}{1 - a_{22}}\right) = \left(\frac{\ell^B - L^B}{a_2}\right). \tag{12.32}$$

Result (12.13) above ensures that if the second equality in (12.31) is satisfied then so is the third equality in (12.31). Similarly (12.15) above ensures that if the second and third terms in (12.32) are equal then the second and third equalities necessary hold also. Taking account of (12.18–21) then, we may deduce from (12.31) that

$$\ell^A = \max[\ell_{11}x_1, \ell_{12}x_2] + \left(\frac{a_1}{1 - a_{11}}\right)\max[(1 + t_{11})x_1, x_1 + t_{12}x_2] \tag{12.33}$$

and from (12.32) that

$$\ell^B = \max[\ell_{21}x_1, \ell_{22}x_2] + \left(\frac{a_2}{a_{12}}\right)x_1. \tag{12.34}$$

Let us now treat ℓ^A and ℓ^B parametrically to *determine* x_1 and x_2 from (12.33) and (12.34).

We begin with (12.34) since it is the simpler of the two and, in order not to have to discuss too many cases, we suppose – reasonably enough – that all $\ell_{ij} > 0$. For any given ℓ^B, (12.34) determines a relation between x_1 and x_2 of the kind shown in Figure 12.3. Both parts of the frontier will shift out in proportion to any increase in ℓ^B. As for (12.33), suppose for the sake of illustration that $(\ell_{11}/\ell_{12}) < (t_{11}/t_{12})$; then for any given ℓ^A, (12.33) determines a relation between x_1 and x_2 of the kind shown in Figure 12.4. All three parts of the frontier will shift out in proportion to any increase in ℓ^A.

Suppose that Figures 12.3 and 12.4 are now superposed. For arbitrary values of ℓ^A and ℓ^B, the two frontiers may have no intersection in the positive quadrant. Or they may have one intersection; or two; or even three, as shown in Figure 12.5, if the values of ℓ^A, ℓ^B and the various production and transport cost coefficients so determine. Of course, any given (x_1, x_2) solution may or may not be consistent with the requirement that both w^A and w^B exceed their respective autarky values; or indeed with the weaker requirement of (12.24) above. The fact remains, however, that, for given coefficients, ℓ^A and ℓ^B *might* be able to take (relative) values such that there are up to three alternative (x_1, x_2) values consistent with transport-cost-ridden trade which generates a wage rate above the autarky level in each country. Of course, w^A, w^B, p^A, p^B, X_1, X_2, L^A, L^B, q_1 and q_2 are all determined once x_1 and x_2 are determined. Hence we can say that given values of ℓ^A and ℓ^B, in conjunction with the conditions of production and transportation and with the facts about consumption and accumulation behaviour, may suffice to determine completely (but perhaps not uniquely) our simple little model of trade with transport costs.

Some comparative statics

As a simple exercise, consider how the three alternative solutions shown in Figure 12.5 would have differed if, *ceteris paribus*, ℓ^B had been slightly greater. (It is not, of course, suggested that the case shown in Figure 12.5 is of greater significance than single- or double-solution cases.) It is immediately clear that at each of the 'outer' two solutions x_1 would have been greater and x_2 smaller; hence (x_2/x_1) would have been smaller. It then follows from our previous findings that w^A, p^A and p^B would all have been smaller and w^B greater. At the 'inner' solution, by contrast, (x_2/x_1) would have been greater, so that w^A, p^A and p^B would all have been greater and w^B smaller. We may use the 'inner' solution to illustrate the reasoning with respect to physical quantities. At this solution, $L^A = \ell_{12}x_2$, $L^B = \ell_{22}x_{22}$ and $X_1 = t_{11}x_1$; hence L^A and L^B would both have been greater and X_1 smaller. It follows readily from (12.31) and (12.32) that, with x_1 and X_1

Figure 12.3

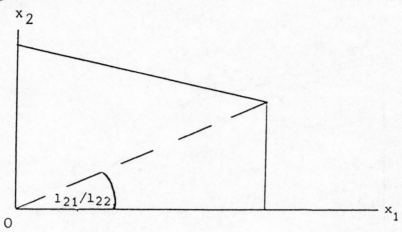

both smaller, both q_1 and q_2 would have been smaller. It appears not to be possible to determine the sign of the difference in X_2; this asymmetry between X_1 and X_2 will seem less surprising when (12.25) and (12.26) are compared with (12.28) and (12.29): our assumptions about consumption mean that the relationships between A and B are not symmetrical.

Figure 12.4

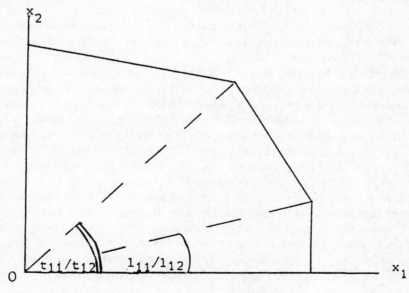

Figure 12.5

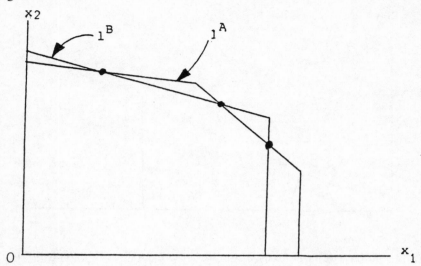

It will be clear from (12.33) and (12.34) that a lower transport-cost coefficient (whether a lower ℓ_{ij} or a lower t_{ij}) would, with respect to each part of the frontiers in Figures 12.3–5, be associated either with an unchanged frontier or with a frontier further from the origin. Since *no* difference in an ℓ_{ij} or a t_{ij} will affect *both* Figure 12.3 and Figure 12.4, it is straightforward to deduce what difference in (x_1, x_2), if any, will be associated with a given transport-cost difference. All the other differences, if any, will then follow as above.

Returning now to the case of a slightly greater ℓ^B, we may note that perhaps not all of our findings are immediately intuitive. At the 'inner' solution, for example, a *greater* ℓ^B was found to be associated with a *smaller* q_2 and hence, given the fixed coefficients in production, with a *smaller* level of employment in production (as opposed to transportation). At each of the 'outer' solutions, on the other hand, the *greater* ℓ^B was found to be associated with a *higher* real wage rate in B, which might not perhaps have been expected by a reader interpreting ℓ^B as an exogenously fixed labour supply. Nor should one be too quick to think of the three solutions in Figure 12.5 as being completely analogous to three alternative equilibria in an Edgeworth exchange-box, where the middle equilibrium is unstable and the other two are stable. For one thing, in Figure 12.5 it is, as just noted, the *two* '*outer*' solutions which exhibit a positive ℓ^B/w^B association and, for another, small changes to Figure 12.5 could produce a figure in which one of the 'outer' solutions remains as the *unique* solution. It may have to be accepted that trade models with joint costs in transportation do not always yield 'expected' results.

Who bears the cost?

We have already seen which resources each country has to devote to transportation activity: $(X_1 - x_1)$ and L^A in country A and $(X_2 - x_2)$ and L^B in country B. We now consider the question, 'Who bears the cost?', interpreting this question in terms of a comparison between the with-transport-cost wage rates, w^A and w^B, and the corresponding no-transport-cost wage rates, w_o^A and w_o^B. If one treats (x_2/x_1) parametrically the question is easily answered. Our (12.4), (12.5), (12.13) and (12.15) already give w_o^A, w_o^B, w^A and w^B as functions of (x_2/x_1). It is thus a purely mechanical operation to show, for example, that $(w^A/w_o^A) \gtrless (w^B/w_o^B)$ according as

$$a_1[(1 - a_{11})x_2 - a_{21}X_1][(1 - a_{22})x_1 - a_{12}x_2](a_{12}L^B + a_2x_1) \gtrless$$
$$a_2[(1 - a_{11})x_2 - a_{21}x_1][1 - a_{22})x_1 - a_{12}X_2][(1 - a_{11})L^A + a_1X_1].$$

This is (in principle) a simple inequality in (x_2/x_1), which shows how (x_2/x_1) interacts with the conditions of production and of transportation to determine whether transport costs weigh more heavily on the wage rate in A or on that in B.

If one were not satisfied by taking (x_2/x_1) as given in answering the present question but wished rather, for example, to take (ℓ^A/ℓ^B) as given, then two cases would have to be considered. It appears at once from (12.31) and (12.32) that, without transport costs, the kind of trading world being considered here is possible *only* when $[a_2(1 - a_{11})\ell^A = a_1a_{12}\ell^B]$. If given values of ℓ^A and ℓ^B did not satisfy this condition (as is likely) then a no-transport-cost solution would involve incomplete specialisation in one country (the 'large' country) and that country's no-transport-cost with-trade wage would equal its autarky wage rate. If, then, a with-transport-cost solution exists, it is immediate that the 'large' country bears *no* transport cost, in the sense that its with-transport-cost wage rate cannot fall short of its no-transport-cost wage rate. But if, as is much less likely, ℓ^A and ℓ^B did satisfy the condition for no-transport-cost complete specialisation, it would still remain to be examined whether they were consistent with a gainful with-transport-cost solution. Needless to say, if they were not, our question about bearing the cost would not arise.

Trade-pattern-reversal impossible

It has been supposed above that, if transport costs are not so high as to prevent trade altogether, then the with-transport-cost *direction* of trade will be the same as the no-transport-cost direction; in other words, that transport costs will not reverse the pattern of specialisation and trade. We should check that this assumption is justified. Let p_a^A and p_a^B be the autarky price ratios in A and B with, as above, $p_a^A < p_a^B$. If A were to specialise in producing commodity 2 and B in producing 1, trade could support real wage rates higher than the corresponding autarky wage rates only if

$$p^A < p_a^A < p_a^B < p^B. \tag{12.35}$$

But with the trade flows reversed, our balanced trade conditions (12.10) and (12.11) would have to be revised, with the result that (12.12') would be replaced by:

$$p^B < (x_2/x_1) < p^A. \tag{12.12''}$$

Since (12.12″) and (12.35) are evidently incompatible, transport costs cannot reverse the pattern of trade *in this model*. This (unsurprising) result is not inconsistent with the (more exciting) numerical example due to Mainwaring (1986, section V), since that example involves trade-pattern-reversal due to transport costs in a model with two countries and *three* produced commodities (in addition to transportation).

Concluding remarks

If our very simple analysis has taken account of both production and trade in produced inputs and the fact of jointness in the costs of transportation, as any analysis of international transport costs should do, it is no less true, of course, that we have ignored many other relevant issues. At a minimum, a choice of technique in production and in transportation should be introduced, as should the use of land and the presence of positive rates of profit. Then the analysis should be generalised to allow for arbitrary (and unequal) numbers of countries and commodities. Much remains to be done, therefore, but it is hoped, nevertheless, that the arguments presented above may point a way forward.

Note

I should like to thank the Department of Economics, Carleton University, Ottawa for their kind hospitality during Fall Term, 1987, when the first version of this chapter was written. I am grateful to F. R. Casas and L. Mainwaring for very helpful comments on an earlier draft.

References

Casas, F. R. (1983). 'International trade with produced transport services', *Oxford Economic Papers*, vol. 35, pp. 89–109.

Casas, F. R. and Kwan Choi, E. (1985). 'Some paradoxes of transport costs in international trade', *Southern Economic Journal*, vol. 51, pp. 983–97.

Falvey, R. E. (1976). 'Transport costs in the pure theory of international trade', *Economic Journal*, vol. 86, pp. 536–50.

Hadley, G. and Kemp, M. C. (1966). 'Equilibrium and efficiency in international trade', *Metroeconomica*, vol. 18, pp. 125–41.

Herberg, H. (1970). 'Economic growth and international trade with transport costs', *Zeitschrift fur die Gesamte Staatswissenschaft*, vol. 126, pp. 557–600.

Mainwaring, L. (1986). 'The theory of international transport costs with tradeable intermediate goods', *Scottish Journal of Political Economy*, vol. 33, pp. 111–23.

Mundell, R. A. (1957). 'Transport costs in international trade theory', *Canadian Journal of Economics and Political Science*, vol. 23, pp. 331–48.

Samuelson, P. A. (1954). 'The transfer problem and transport costs: analysis of the effects of trade impediments', *Economic Journal*, vol. 64, pp. 264–89.

Steedman, I. (1979a). *Trade Amongst Growing Economies* (Cambridge: Cambridge University Press).

Steedman, I. (ed.) (1976b). *Fundamental Issues in Trade Theory* (London: Macmillan).

Publications of D. J. Coppock

(a) Contributions to books

(i) *The UK Economy: a Manual of Applied Economics*
Author of Chapter 3, 'Foreign trade and the balance of payments' in 1st Edition (1966), 2nd Edition (1968), 3rd Edition (1970), 4th Edition (1972).
Co-author with J. S. Metcalfe of Chapter 3 in 5th Edition, (1974).
Co-editor (with A. R. Prest) *The UK Economy*, 4th–10th Editions (1972, 1974, 1976, 1978, 1982, 1984).

(ii) Parts of the 'Climacteric of the 1890s: a critical note' were published in 1963 in B. Supple (ed.) *The Experience of Economic Growth.*

(iii) (with N. J. Gibson). 'The volume of deposits and the cash and liquid assets ratio'. Reprinted from *The Manchester School*, September 1963, in H. G. Johnson and associates (eds), *Readings in British Monetary Economics*, Chapter 12. Clarendon Press, Oxford, 1972.

(iv) 'The causes of business fluctuations'. From *Transactions of the Manchester Statistical Society*, 1959, reprinted with minor amendments in D. H. Aldcroft and P. Fearon (eds), *British Economic Fluctuations 1790–1939*, Chapter 5. Macmillan, 1972.

(v) Comment on 'The international transmission of inflation', by J. Pattison, Chapter 11, *Inflation in the World Economy* (eds, J. M. Parkin and G. Zis), Manchester University Press, 1976.

(b) Articles

'A reconsideration of Hobson's theory of unemployment', *The Manchester School*, January 1953, pp. 1–21.

'The theory of effective demand in the 1920s', *The Manchester School*, January 1954, pp. 62–89.

'The climacteric of the 1890s: a critical note', *The Manchester School*, January 1956, pp. 1–31.

'Rising output and inflation', *The Banker*, December 1956, pp. 786–7.

'The periodicity and stability of inventory cycles in the USA (Part I)', *The Manchester School*, May 1959, pp. 140–74.

'The periodicity and stability of inventory cycles in the USA (Part II)', *The Manchester School*, September 1959.

'The causes of business fluctuations', *Transactions of the Manchester Statistical Society*, 1959/60.

'The causes of the great depression', *The Manchester School*, September 1961, pp. 205–32.

'Business cycles – endogenous or stochastic? A comment', *The Economic Journal*, June 1962, pp. 458–68.

'Income originating in the models of Harrod and Domar: a comment', (Co-author, A. Bajt), *The Economic Journal*, December 1962, pp. 982–8.

'Mr Saville on the great depression: a reply', *The Manchester School*, May 1963, pp. 171–84.

'The volume of deposits and the cash and liquid assets ratios', (Co-author, N. J. Gibson), *The Manchester School*, September 1963, pp. 203–22.

'British industrial growth during the "great depression" (1873–96): a pessimist's view', *The Economic History Review*, vol. 17, no. 2, 1964, pp. 389–96.

'The post-war short cycle in the USA', *The Manchester School*, January 1965, pp. 17–44.

'The alleged case against devaluation', *The Manchester School*, September 1965, pp. 285–312.

'Devaluation when exports have an import content', *The Manchester School*, December 1971, pp. 247–60.

'Some further notes on the classical transfer problem', *The Manchester School*, vol. 44, no. 3, September 1976, pp. 220–31.

'Some thoughts on the monetary approach to the balance of payments theory', *The Manchester School*, vol. 46, no. 3, September 1978, pp. 186–208.

'Further thoughts on the monetary approach to the balance of payments theory', *The Manchester School*, vol. 47, no. 1, March 1979, pp. 1–23.

'The impact effects of devaluation in a three sector monetary model', *British Review of Economic Issues*, no. 16, Spring 1985, pp. 1–46.